BUSINESS/SCIENCE/TECHNOLOGY DIVISION
CHICAGO PUBLIC LIBRARY
400 SOUTH STATE STREET
CHICAGO, IL 60605

D0148580

**CHICAGO PUBLIC LIBRARY**

FORM 19                                    · DEMCO

# Foreign Direct Investment in Central Eastern Europe

# THE MICROECONOMICS
# OF TRANSITION ECONOMIES

Series Editor: Josef C. Brada
Arizona State University

The hallmark of this series is its focus not on macroeconomic theory or ideological questions but on financial issues and the behavior of firms and enterprises in economies undergoing transition from socialist to capitalist forms of organization.

## FIRMS AFLOAT AND FIRMS ADRIFT
Hungarian Industry and Economic Transition

*Josef C. Brada, Inderjit Singh, and Adam Török*

## RESTRUCTURING AND PRIVATIZATION
## IN CENTRAL EASTERN EUROPE
Case Studies of Firms in Transition

*Edited by*
*Saul Estrin, Josef C. Brada, Alan Gelb,*
*and Inderjit Singh*

## CORPORATE GOVERNANCE IN
## CENTRAL EASTERN EUROPE
Case Studies of Firms in Transition

*Edited by Josef C. Brada and Inderjit Singh*

## FOREIGN DIRECT INVESTMENT
## IN CENTRAL EASTERN EUROPE
Case Studies of Firms in Transition

*Edited by*
*Saul Estrin, Xavier Richet, and Josef C. Brada*

# FOREIGN DIRECT INVESTMENT IN CENTRAL EASTERN EUROPE

## Case Studies of Firms in Transition

**Saul Estrin**
**Xavier Richet**
**Josef C. Brada**

*M.E. Sharpe*
Armonk, New York
London, England

HG
5687
.A3
F67
2000

Copyright © 2000 by M.E. Sharpe, Inc.

All rights reserved. No part of this book may be reproduced in any form
without written permission from the publisher, M.E. Sharpe, Inc.,
80 Business Park Drive, Armonk, New York 10504.

Selections previously published in *Eastern European Economics*, vol. 36, Nos. 4, 5, 6.

**Library of Congress Cataloging-in-Publication Data**

Foreign direct investment in central eastern Europe: case studies of firms in transition /
edited by Saul Estrin, Xavier Richet, and Josef C. Brada.
    p.cm.—(Microeconomics of transition economies)
    Includes bibliographical references (p.  ) and index.
    ISBN 0-7656-0255-5 (alk. paper)
    1. Investments, Foreign—Slovenia—Case studies. 2. International business
enterprises—Slovenia—Case studies. 3. Investments, Foreign—Czech Republic—
Case studies. 4. International business enterprises—Czech Republic—Case studies.
5. Investments, Foreign—Bulgaria—Case studies. 6. International business
enterprises—Bulgaria—Case studies. I. Estrin, Saul. II. Richet, Xavier. III.
Brada, Josef C., 1942– . IV. Series.

HG5687.A3 F67 2000
332.67′3′0947—dc21                                     99-086077
CIP

Printed in the United States of America

The paper used in this publication meets the minimum requirements of
American National Standard for Information Sciences
Permanence of Paper for Printed Library Materials,
ANSI Z 39.48-1984.

BM (c)  10   9   8   7   6   5   4   3   2   1

BST

RO1627 67075

BUSINESS/SCIENCE/TECHNOLOGY DIVISION
CHICAGO PUBLIC LIBRARY
400 SOUTH STATE STREET
CHICAGO, IL 60605

# Contents

# A Comparison of Foreign Direct Investments in Bulgaria, the Czech Republic, and Slovenia

Saul Estrin, Xavier Richet, and Josef C. Brada

## INTRODUCTION

In this chapter, we summarize the findings from twelve case studies of western firms' direct investments into state-owned enterprises in transition economies. The cases were carried out on the basis of a common methodology that led to the use of the same questionnaire by all investigators and to a similar framework for all the case analyses. Four case studies were undertaken in Bulgaria, in the Czech Republic, and in Slovenia respectively. The aim of the study was to throw light on the determinants of foreign direct investment into the region and upon its impact on the host economies. The effects of such investments fall into two categories—those upon the firm acquired by the foreign investor and those on the broader economy. The former includes the infusion of resources and technology, changes in business strategy and organization, and a new set of owners. The latter includes not only the aggregate investment and balance of payments effects, but also, in the context of the transition economies, an impact on the process of transition from plan to market.

In the remainder of this chapter, we provide a comparative overview to the twelve cases, eleven of which are published in this volume. In the following section we briefly consider the country sample and the differences in preconditions to reform and transition policies followed in Bulgaria, the Czech Republic, and Slovenia. The third section analyzes foreign direct investment into the transition economies, indicating the scale of the flows as well as the rationale and possible impact. The lessons from the cases are summarized in the fourth section, which includes case summaries and an analysis by host country, donor country, and sector. Policy conclusions are drawn in the fifth section. In the remainder of this first section, we briefly review the methodology of the study.

The project made use of a common analytical framework that was reflected in a questionnaire that became the basis for the information-gathering phase for all the case studies as well as for the analyses of the information obtained. Our research objectives were to study the determinants of each investment and to gauge its impact both on the firms themselves and, through spillover effects, on the host economy more generally. The questionnaire therefore sought to distinguish between cost, market, and strategic motives for investments and to highlight the main "pull" and "deterrent" factors in each investment project, including the economic, political, and institutional environment in each host country. The main effects on the firms being acquired by foreign investors were hypothesized to come from the transfer of technology and management know-how and from the development of labor skills in their workforce. Key mechanisms for this transfer of knowledge and resources were expected to be investment, training, reorganization, and the increased use of information technology. We also expected that important determinants of foreigners' interest in the these firms would be the quality and soundness of their production processes and their technological levels, the market structures in donor and host countries, and the nature of supply relationships up and down stream.

Sectors were chosen for the study so as to ensure adequate variation in firm size and industry and to reflect both the industrial status of each country and its technological skills. It was hoped that we would be able to keep two common sectors across the three countries—engineering, vehicles, or pharmaceuticals—and to allow for some country-specific differences (e.g., food processing in Bulgaria, chemicals in the Czech Republic). Finally, at least one of the cases in each country was to examine the experience of a small firm to allow some consideration of size effects. Lists of the major foreign investments into each country were developed, and firms were chosen approximately in size rank order according to the industry criteria. The refusal rate was quite high, no doubt reflecting exhaustion in many companies in the region with requests for access to managers by academic researchers. However, by intelligent replacement of refusals, the desired sectoral spread was nevertheless achieved.

The three countries were chosen to allow some comparison across the region in terms of economic preconditions and progress in reform.[1] The Czech Republic is widely regarded as having made a relatively successful and rapid early transition from plan to market and as being able to exploit its pivotal location at the heart of Europe. However, aggregate growth has been disappointing, corporate governance has not emerged as strongly as had been expected in the wake of privatization (Desai 1996), and there remain serious difficulties in capital markets (see, e.g., Begg 1998, Mejstrik 1997). Slovenia's high level of development and sustained sound money policies have acted to offset many of the problems associated with the disintegration of the Yugoslav federation, although, as in the Czech Republic, there may have been an over-reliance on tight monetary policy at the expense of economic growth. Slovenia is a small country to serve as a host for major Western investors (see Bohn 1992, 1993, 1994), especially given the instability in the former Yugoslavia, which has prevented Slovene firms from exploiting their traditional market ties to that region. Finally, among the ten European Union Association Agreement countries of Central Europe (see Estrin and Holmes 1998), Bulgaria was regarded as one making slower progress toward a liberal market economy (see Dimitrov 1997). It was hoped that this spread of country characteristics would highlight important variations in the nature and effects of foreign investments. We take up the question of country differences in more detail in the following section.

## TRANSITION SHOCK AND MACRO-STABILIZATION PROGRAMS

The three countries in our project are small in both geographic size and population and two of them share a similar experience of being a new political entity emerging from the disintegration of a larger state. However, there are also many differences among them in terms of historical background, the comparative advantages of their industries, macro-stabilization policy outcomes, privatization and transformation strategies, and these all influence the speed of industrial restructuring, the reorientation of their trade, and their attractiveness to foreign investors.

Two countries, Slovenia and the Czech Republic, were formerly parts (specifically republics) of federal states that were created at the end of World War I. Previously, they had both been part of the western, industrialized, Austrian-ruled part of the Austro-Hungarian Empire. In 1939, Czechoslovakia was ranked as the tenth most developed economy in the world (see Begg 1991), and the new Czech Republic was seen as one of the more promising economies in Central Europe after its separation form the Slovak Republic in 1993. Slovenia had been the most developed region of the Yugoslav Federal Republic, and its GDP per capita is by far the highest among transition countries. Its industries supplied the domestic Yugoslav market with many of its most sophisticated products and exported toward western economies a non-negligible part of their production. In quite different ways, both the Czech

Republic and Slovenia have been affected by the disintegration of their former political and economic entity, losing important commercial and industrial ties. Breaking the links with their former compatriots, on the other hand, has helped them to stabilize their economies and to reorient their trade, if not to restructure their industries. Bulgaria, which developed its industry mainly under the socialist system, was strongly integrated into the Council for Mutual Economic Assistance (CMEA) and particularly into the Soviet economy. Consequently, its economy has suffered much more from the political disintegration and economic problems of its former trading partners.

The three countries had different experiences in reforming their economic system before the final collapse of the former socialist system. Slovenia, as part of Yugoslavia, experienced self-management early on, gaining experience with both the negative and positive aspects of the exercise of insider power by workers and managers over the operation of their firms (see Estrin 1984). Thus, from 1965 on, Slovenian self-managed firms experienced market mechanisms both on the domestic market and in foreign trade; this has been a strong stimulant to enterprise adjustment, even if insiders have been able to maintain their stakes in terms of welfare provision and other collective consumption. Slovenia was also much more open than were the CMEA countries. Bulgaria and the former Czechoslovakia had much less experience with market-based mechanisms and with economic reform. Up to the end of the socialist period, they still remained strongly centralized and oriented toward the CMEA, relying on extensive exports of manufactures to the Soviet Union. Their price structures were also heavily distorted, and high barriers protected their industries from western competition.

Industries relied on different sources of comparative advantage in the three countries (see Jeffries 1992). Slovenian industry developed a measure of international comparative advantage vis-à-vis West European markets thanks both to its strategic location and to its level of development. Many Slovenian firms had developed industrial cooperation programs with foreign firms in the 1960s and the early 1970s. These efforts at cooperation gave them access to sophisticated technologies and paved the way to the creation of joint ventures. Structural deficits in Slovenian trade with the West were offset by surpluses in trade with the other parts of Yugoslavia. This allowed Slovenian industry to create niches in some sectors and to develop substantial exports of more sophisticated goods to advanced market economies. After the breakup of Yugoslavia, many Western investors saw Slovenia as a springboard for penetrating the surrounding markets. However, regional instability in the Balkans has prevented much of this potential from being realized even as the Slovenian government has sought to shed the country's Balkan image.

Even if limited industrial cooperation with Western firms did take place in

Czechoslovakia and Bulgaria in the 1960s and 1970s, it was severely constrained by the bureaucratic organization of the economy, leaving limited opportunity for enterprises to experience autonomy in managing their affairs and in developing their own strategies. Under the socialist system, Czech industry lived on its heritage, favoring conventional technologies that exploited the tradition of craftsmanship and the quality of the labor force and that sought to maintain the strong engineering industry that had been established in the pre-communist period. As has been highlighted in a variety of studies (see, e.g., Gomulka 1986, Jeffries 1992), the level of innovation remained low and concentrated on processes instead of on final products. However, the development strategy that Czech policy makers pursued under planning, with a heavy priority given to heavy industry, did not destroy its industrial potential, and, in many sectors, Czech industry had been able to keep up and even to upgrade to some extent its technology or its products. For instance, Škoda developed its models of cars virtually by itself while Polish and Russian carmakers relied heavily on technologies and designs provided by their Western partner, Fiat.

Bulgaria started its socialist industrialization from a far more backward situation. Its quasi-integration into the Soviet economy facilitated rapid industrial development on the basis of large industrial complexes in basic and processing sectors as well as in manufacturing. These plants were all oversized relative to the Bulgarian domestic market and thus had to rely on trade agreements with other CMEA countries to be able to export their production. Despite heavy investments directed toward these industries, the level of qualification of the workforce and the quality of the output remained behind the standards reached by the other socialist economies of Central Europe. The huge Soviet market, less sensitive to the quality of products, was able to absorb much of Bulgaria's production.

For the Czech Republic and Slovenia, the disintegration of their domestic market and, for all three countries, the disappearance of the former CMEA market hurt domestic production more than was the case in the more open and more Western-oriented economies such as Hungary and Poland. In this respect, Bulgaria has been more affected by the collapse of the CMEA than have Slovenia and the Czech Republic by the splitting up of their federal links.

Macro-stabilization policies and institutional reforms implemented after the systemic changes in the early 1990s have produced divergent outcomes. The three countries implemented stabilization policies in the context of harsh changes in their circumstances that strongly affected their economic performance. As can be seen in Table 1, the 1990s began with a steep recession in which GDP and industrial production fell by at least 20 percent and much more severely in Bulgaria. Slovenia and the Czech Republic were able to

Table 1

**Macro–Economic Conditions**

| | Bulgaria | Czech Republic | Slovenia |
|---|---|---|---|
| Real GDP Growth Rate (%) | | | |
| 1990 | −9.1 | −0.4[a] | −4.7 |
| 1991 | −11.7 | −14.2 | −8.1 |
| 1992 | −7.3 | −6.4 | −5.4 |
| 1993 | −2.4 | −0.9 | 1.3 |
| 1994 | 1.8 | 2.6 | 5.3 |
| 1995 | 2.6 | 4.8 | 3.5 |
| 1996 | −4.0 | 3.5 | 3.0 |
| 1997 | −6.9 | 1.0 | 3.8 |
| 1998 | 4.0 | −2.6 | 4.0 |
| | | | |
| Change in Retail Prices (%) | | | |
| 1990 | 26.3 | 10.8[a] | 550.0 |
| 1991 | 333.5 | 56.7 | 117.7 |
| 1992 | 82.0 | 11.1 | 201.3 |
| 1993 | 73.0 | 20.8 | 32.3 |
| 1994 | 96.3 | 10.0 | 19.8 |
| 1995 | 62.1 | 9.1 | 12.6 |
| 1996 | 95.4 | 9.0 | 10.0 |
| 1997 | 1,082.3 | 8.5 | 8.4 |
| 1998 | 154.8 | 10.7 | 7.9 |
| | | | |
| Unemployment (% labor force) | | | |
| 1990 | 1.5 | 0.8[a] | 4.7 |
| 1991 | 11.5 | 4.1[a] | 8.2 |
| 1992 | 15.6 | 2.6[a] | 11.6 |
| 1993 | 16.4 | 3.5 | 14.4 |
| 1994 | 12.8 | 3.2 | 14.4 |
| 1995 | 10.5 | 2.9 | 13.9 |
| 1996 | 12.5 | 3.5 | 14.5 |
| 1997 | 13.7 | 5.2 | 14.8 |
| 1998 | 12.2 | 7.5 | 14.5 |

[a]Data for Czechoslovakia.
*Source:* EBRD, *Transition Report*, 1996 and Wiener Institut für Internationale Wirtschaftsvergleiche, *Transition Countries in 1998/99: Widespread Economic Slowdown with Escalating Structural Problems*. Research Report No. 253. Vienna, February 1999.

resume steady economic growth, although, in the case of the Czech Republic, this growth turned to recession at the end of the 1990s. In both countries, moderate inflation was contained by stringent monetary policy, so that by early 1999 inflation had fallen to single-digit levels. Bulgaria has had a much more checkered macroeconomic record. The fall in output was greater than in the other two countries, and the inability or unwillingness of the government to face the realities of the transition led to a burst of hyperinflation. In 1997 the banking sector collapsed under its bad debts, and a new stabilization program had to be mounted. A new and more reform-oriented regime has made some headway in resolving Bulgaria's macroeconomic imbalances and in restoring growth and price stability. Unemployment has increased enormously in Bulgaria and Slovenia, though it should be borne in mind that the level of unemployment is high only by historic standards for these countries; by West European standards these levels of unemployment are not remarkable. The Czech Republic avoided high unemployment, in part through active labor market policies and perhaps due to an unwillingness of Czech firms to restructure aggressively. At the end of the decade, Czech unemployment has increased, in part as a result of the decline in economic output.

The evidence suggests that firms did begin to adjust in the early years of the transition, passively in most cases due to the lack of financial resources and to the high degree of uncertainty. Some firms, especially those with a strong comparative advantage, took a more strategic and fundamental approach to restructuring by seeking to develop links or partnerships with western firms (see Estrin et al. 1995; World Bank, *Development Report*, 1996). Restructuring, either passive or active, took place while industrial production was falling sharply. In Slovenia and the Czech Republic, where GDP and industrial production growth resumed, macro-stabilization measures presumably had strong effects on the adjustment of firms and on the development of de novo enterprises. In Bulgaria, inflation has been unacceptably high and growth prospects remain precarious. As a result, financial indiscipline among firms remains a problem, and the weakness of financial institutions continues to slow down the financial restructuring of the non-financial sector (see World Bank, *Development Report*, 1996).

The Czech Republic and Slovenia achieved some important macroeconomic objectives after facing the transition shock; inflation has been curbed, growth has been restored, and the level of public debt brought under control. These two countries, indeed, are probably closer to the convergence criteria of the EMU than many members of the European Union. Bulgaria continues to face serious structural imbalances (e.g., a high rate of inflation, slow growth, and structural deficits).

In Table 2, we report a summary of progress in various macroeconomic and business environment indicators compiled at about the same time our case studies were undertaken. Institutional reforms clarified how foreign investors could participate in the privatization of state-owned enterprises, and bankruptcy laws were passed, although even now they are only partially or recently enforced. Privatization strategies were not specially oriented to favor inflows of foreign direct investment.[2] In the Czech Republic, one aim of the privatization program was to transfer ownership to the population, either directly through stock ownership or indirectly through investment funds, in order to create so-called people's capitalism. It is important to realize that, in the first instance, this approach excluded foreign ownership for understandable reasons including the cheap value of national assets, the problem of the former German minority, nationalist attitudes on the eve of the splitting of the federation. Some strategic businesses were allowed to look for foreign investors, but FDI was not initially used as a tool to boost restructuring (Estrin 1994). Adjustment of firms relied mainly on incumbent management teams. The Czech Republic has now mostly achieved its privatization program, but restructuring of firms started later. Corporate governance of the newly privatized firms, perhaps with the exception of the few firms controlled by foreign investors, is still relatively weak, as most of the new Privatization Investment Funds had no experience of controlling and monitoring complex organizations in a market environment. As reported in Estrin, Hughes, and Todd (1997), macroeconomic stability fueled the inflow of FDI into the Czech Republic, and Table 3 shows that, after Hungary, the Czech Republic has attracted the largest share of FDI in Central Europe.

In Slovenia many firms have restructured without government or foreign intervention, but the assets of some strategic businesses have been sold to foreign investors. Nevertheless, the Slovenian government has repeatedly delayed its privatization program. It has been reluctant to proceed along the Hungarian path of encouraging foreign investors for nationalist reasons, reinforced by the small size of the country and by the importance of workers' stakes in state-owned enterprises (SOEs), an inheritance from the Yugoslav self-management system. The privatization program, by selling shares to workers at discounted prices, favors insider-controlled firms.

In Bulgaria, the privatization program was postponed several times by the different governments, all of them reluctant to proceed with the sale of state assets because of the threat of the former communist apparatus regaining its power by bringing back some of the money that they had previously transferred abroad to purchase the firms put up for sale. The new post-socialist majority that came to power in 1995 has also been cautious to avoid a loss of control over so-called strategic assets. The extent of the economic crisis, however, with a sharp decrease in industrial production, the collapse of the CMEA, and a lack of financial resources, have finally pushed the Bulgarian government to adopt a mass privatization program based on the Czech model. The scale of the transition shock and the delay in the implementation of deep institutional reforms have severely limited the extent of restructuring.

In summary, in the early phase of transition none of our three sample countries used forms of privatization particularly conducive to foreign direct

Table 2

**Progress in Transition**

| Countries | Enterprises | | | Markets and Trade | | | Financial Institution | | Legal Reform |
|---|---|---|---|---|---|---|---|---|---|
| Private sector share of GDP in %, mid -95 (rough EB Restimates)[a] | Large-scale privatization | Small scale privatization | Enterprise restructuring | Price liberalization | Trade & foreign exchange system | Competition policy | Banking reform & interest rate liberalization | Securities markets & non-bank financial institutions | Extensiveness & effectiveness of legal rules on investment |
| Bulgaria | 45 | 2 | 3 | 2 | 2 | 4 | 2 | 2 | 4 |
| Czech Republic | 75 | 4 | 4* | 3 | 3 | 4* | 3 | 3 | 4 |
| Slovenia | 45 | 3 | 4* | 3 | 3 | 4* | 2 | 3 | 3 |

*Source: Transition Report*, European Bank for Reconstruction and Development, 1996.

*Note:* Most advanced industrial economies would qualify for the 4* rating for almost all the transition indictors. Table 2 assesses the status rather than the pace of change. For instance, Slovenia's score of 4* on small scale privatization, despite the absence of a comprehensive privatization program, reflects the fact that small-scale activity in Slovenia was largely private before transition began.

[a]The "private sector shares" of GDP represent rough EBRD estimates, based on available statistics from both official (government) sources and unofficial sources. The underlying concept of private sector value added includes income generated by the activity of private registered companies as well as by private entities engaged in informal activity. Here the term "private companies" refers to all enterprises in which a majority of the shares are owned by private individuals or entities. The roughness of the EBRD estimates reflects data limitations, particularly with respect to the scale of informal activity.

Table 3a

**FDI Inflows ($m)**

| Country | 1994 | 1995 | 1990–95 | 1996–2000 |
|---|---|---|---|---|
| Hungary | 1,146 | 4,000 | 10,737 | 12,968 |
| Poland | 1,875 | 2,500 | 7,148 | 21,969 |
| Czech Republic | 878 | 2,500 | 5,666 | 15,466 |
| Slovakia | 187 | 200 | 775 | 2,150 |
| Slovenia | 87 | 150 | 501 | 3,052 |
| Albania | 53 | 75 | 205 | 583 |
| Bulgaria | 105 | 150 | 412 | 1,428 |
| Romania | 340 | 400 | 933 | 4,017 |
| Other Balkans | 120 | 100 | 300 | 2,210 |
| Baltic States | 430 | 400 | 1,280 | 1,890 |
| Russia | 1,000 | 2,000 | 4,400 | 269,960 |
| Ukraine | 91 | 113 | 574 | 1,400 |
| Other CIS | 640 | 800 | 2,300 | 5,085 |
| Eastern Europe | 27,344 | 10,075 | 27,344 | 63,847 |
| Eastern Europe & FSU | 6,952 | 13,388 | 35,898 | 99,186 |

*Source:* Economist Intelligence Unit, 1st quarter, 1996.

Table 3b

**Inflows and Stock of FDI in CEE and the Former Soviet Union**

| | 1990 | 1991 | 1992 | 1993 | 1994 | 1995[a] | 1995[b] | FDI stock per capita 1995[b] | % of GDP 1995[b] |
|---|---|---|---|---|---|---|---|---|---|
| Bulgaria | 4 | 56 | 42 | 55 | 105 | 150 | 800 | 94.1 | 8.0 |
| Czech Republic | 120 | 511 | 947 | 1,094 | 749 | 2,500 | 5,500 | 533.9 | 12.3 |
| Slovenia | -2 | 41 | 113 | 112 | 87 | 150 | 1,000 | 500 | 5.7 |
| Hungary | 311 | 1,459 | 1,471 | 2,328 | 1,097 | 4,000 | 10,000 | 970.9 | 25.0 |
| Total CEE | | 2,203 | 3,270 | 5,652 | 3,670 | 10,075 | | | |

[a]*Economies in Transition*, EIU, 1st quarter, 1996.
[b]Business Central Europe, February 1996.
*Source:* ECE/UN, 1995, UNCTD, Division on Transnational Corporations and Investment, 1995.

investment. Now, however, the focus of official policy has shifted more to favor strategic foreign partners in both the Czech Republic and Slovenia, although rather less so in Bulgaria.

## FDI, SPEED OF ADJUSTMENT, AND RATIONALE FOR INVESTING

### Flow of Foreign Direct Investment (FDI)

As can be seen in Table 3, the three countries have not received large sums of foreign investments in total, and there is a strong asymmetry between countries. Per capita, the Czech Republic and Slovenia have received similar amounts, but Bulgaria has a stock that is five times smaller. The Czech Republic is second to Hungary, which has been the leading country as far as FDI inflows are concerned due both to its investor-friendly privatization strategy and to its deeper and longer contacts with foreign businesses. Aside from these differences in volumes, the three countries have had an irregular flow of investment from year to year, and these fluctuations have increased. A few large investments realized in one year may easily be much larger than the sum of numerous other investments in small projects. This has been the case with FDI in the automotive industry in the Czech Republic, Hungary, Poland, and Slovenia. Often, large FDI flows reflect individual privatization measures. For instance, in Hungary, the privatization of public utilities in December 1995 brought in more money in one month than during the past two years. The privatization of the Czech telecommunications company brought a major inflow of foreign capital that swamped all previous investments in magnitude. According to projections, the growth of FDI in the Czech Republic and Slovenia should continue; it will be much slower in Bulgaria so long as there remains serious uncertainty about the future of reform.

### Rationale for Investing in Central and Eastern Europe (CEE)

Numerous factors induce enterprises to move production and to locate their operations in other countries, and we attempt to summarize these in Table 4. Both "pull" factors and deterrent factors are at work in CEE, but some are more important than others. The more important ones are low production costs, labor skills appropriate for industrial activities, market access, and eventual vertical integration or integration into the world economy. Three approaches based on the investing firm's market position and strategy are evident from our case studies:

- penetration of local markets; this strategy is then repeated across the region, as in the cases of beverages, tobacco, and consumer goods;
- penetration of one domestic market with the aim of conquering neighboring; markets, as in electronics and finance;
- market penetration and integration of the acquisition into the global economy, as in the car industry.

In each of the above three approaches, the strategic move of the investing firm threatens competing firms in the host country as well as the investing firm's competitors in other countries because these competitors may now

Table 4

**Attractiveness and Non-attractiveness of Transition Economies to Foreign Direct Investment**

| Push Factors | Deterrent Factors |
| --- | --- |
| Factor costs | Political stability |
| Skills | Legal and institutional infrastructure |
| Economic environment | Property rights, corporate governance |
| Expansion/establishment of markets | Corruption |
| Market access | Supply networks |
| Strategic moves: | Nature of firms and labor force |
| • bargaining with government and/or labor | Narrow markets |
| • oligopolistic games, first mover advantage, | Low purchasing power |
| follow-my-leader, threats | Business environment |
| Vertical integration | |
| Access to technology and plant | |
| Export incentives and import barriers | |
| Policy incentives, host country, home | |
| country, international institutions | |

find that there is an inadequate market in the host country to support their own ambitions for expansion there through FDI. In addition to the threats that FDI poses to other firms, it also may pose a serious threat to at least some members of the internal coalition within the firm that is being taken over by the foreign investor. A failure to recognize these internal interests can lead to serious problems after the takeover is complete The strategy followed by Volkswagen in the Czech Republic highlights the need to anticipate such issues. Volkswagen negotiated directly with the Czech government as well as with the management and labor representatives of Škoda. Volkswagen committed itself to the purchase of Škoda with a high price combined with promises to invest in Škoda's operations to a much greater extent than proposed by rival car makers. This offer appealed to both the external and the internal constituencies, and thus it closed off the possibility for competitors such as Renault to enter the market at a low price.[3] The other objective of Volkswagen was to integrate Škoda into the global economy by restructuring the firm and its affiliates in order to meet world competition.[4]

Firms in consumer goods, beverages, and electronics, whose strategy is to penetrate domestic markets, seek to obtain a monopolistic or oligopolistic position. The takeover of domestic firms by Western investors facilitates and speeds up their restructuring and their return to profitability. Several case studies conducted in Hungary (Lakatos and Papanek 1994) have shown the existence of a strong correlation between the mode of control, flows of exports, and profitability. Generally, firms with foreign capital are more profit-

able than local firms without foreign participation or those oriented toward
the domestic market. Firms 100 percent controlled by foreign investors or
those with majority foreign participation are more profitable than enterprises
with minority foreign-owned stakes or oriented toward the domestic market.
In the first case, global integration and flows of exports are higher; in the
second case, and especially in the third one, profitability is linked to the level
of internal demand which is presently stagnating. We will return to these
issues for our sample countries in the fourth section.

FDI has a strong effect on the adjustment and the behavior of firms even
if, as several case studies have concluded, Western investors face serious
difficulties in implementing their program (see Estrin, Hughes, and Todd
1997). Genco et al. (1993) reviewed internal and external factors that hampered the adjustment of foreign-owned or -controlled firms' FDI in different
countries. Seven factors have been highlighted by this study, the importance
of which might differ according to countries and sectors:

- problems relating to the weakness of the infrastructure and production
  system,
- manpower problems,
- inadequate distribution networks,
- firms' organizational problems,
- financial problems,
- problems with local partners or due to "red tape,"
- problems relating to uncertainty in the legal-legislative framework or
  political instability.

Restructuring of firms starts with the reorganization of production, often
by reducing the product range in order to attain minimum efficient scale, the
development of marketing and accounting departments, and the development of new links with suppliers and distributors. It also has a financial di-
mension, the settling up of bad debts. Such debts are generally resolved during
the negotiation of the transaction with the government agency in charge of
selling off public property. Restructuring affects production both upstream
and downstream. In the automotive industry, local subcontractors are put
under pressure to adjust quickly in order to reduce the cost of the parts they
supply to firms such as Volkswagen in the Czech Republic, Renault in
Slovenia, and Ford in Hungary, and to improve the quality and timeliness of
their supplies. In the case of strategies promoting the extension of market
shares, the incoming firm may try to reinforce links with local suppliers to
avoid their falling under the control of foreign investors. The control of local
enterprises has allowed a reduction in the range of products that could com-

pete with products made by Western firms. For some multinationals, an investment in one country is the starting point for further investments in the region, by taking advantage of the local firm's past links to the region's markets as in consumer goods (Electrolux) or electronics (Bull and Siemens).

## NEW OWNERSHIP AND RESTRUCTURING OF FIRMS

### *Lessons from the Cases*

The cases are based on interviews and questionnaires completed in twelve industrial enterprises in the three countries. These allow us to make some interesting cross-sectoral and cross-country comparisons. The cases highlight important questions on how the acquisition occurred and how cooperation developed after the start of the foreign acquisition or involvement, notably with regard to technology and know-how transfer, the speed of restructuring, and the upgrading of such functions as marketing, accounting, strategy. It is clear, on the other hand, that the modest sample of firms does not allow us to draw general conclusions. Our discussion is centered around the summary of findings in Table 5.

The enterprises selected operate in eleven industries belonging to two broad sectors: seven enterprises in intermediate products and five in final goods. The breakdown by nationality of owners shows a preponderance of West Europeans: 2.5 German, 1.5 Dutch, 1 British, 1 French, 1 Swiss, 1 Italian, 1 Danish; 2.5 are U.S. owners. One international bank, the EBRD, is also involved in minority control of a firm.[5]

The twelve firms have several features in common. All had achieved a certain minimum level of technological competence, and one, a Slovenian firm, had even overtaken its foreign partner in terms of innovation. This made them appealing to foreign investors, because these firms had a competitive advantage and a capacity to export and to cooperate with western firms. Nevertheless, these transition-economy firms believed that they could not survive by themselves in the open, competitive, market environment and that they needed to have access to the factors that they lacked, such as technology, cash, managerial know-how, and marketing. Most of the enterprises in our sample are in a monopolistic or oligopolistic position on their domestic markets. All the enterprises lacked financial resources and were unable to obtain funds from domestic capital markets. The need to search for a foreign partner had been accepted in the early stage of the transformation policy, even if it did not fit with national privatization policy. One Slovenian firm already had cooperation links with their partners.

Workers in the sample firms were for the most part well paid when compared to the wage level in their industry or in the region where the business

Table 5

## Summary of Cases

| Firm/country | Industrial sector | Country of investment | Motives[a] C | St | Mkt | Technology[b] H | M | L | Foreign brought[c] T | KH | Cash | Mkt Acc | Performance H | M | L | Greatest problems faced in the process | Takeover performance H | M | L |
|---|---|---|---|---|---|---|---|---|---|---|---|---|---|---|---|---|---|---|---|
| Vildima (Bg) | Metal product, glass, china | USA | x | x | x | x | | | | x | | | x | | | | x | | |
| Zagorka (Bg) | Brewery | NL–USA | (x) | | x | x | | | x | | x | x | x | | | Plant, equipment | x | | |
| Biterm (Sl) | Thermos/elect. | DK | x | | x | x | | | x | x | (x) | (x) | | | x | Technology, product | | x | |
| Kolektor (Sl) | Commutator/electronic components | USA | x | | x | x | | | x¹ | x | x | x | (x) | | | | (x) | | |
| Sarrio (Sl) | Paper | I | | x | x | (x) | | | | | | | | x | | Debt | | | |
| Tobacco (EBRD-Sl) | Tobacco | FRG/F | x | x | | x | | x | x | | x | x | x | x | | Product | x | x | |
| Linde (Cz) | Industrial gas | FRG | x | | | x | | | x | | x | x | x | | | Technology | | x | |
| Pražske (Cz) | Brewery | UK | x | | | | x | | x | x | x | x | | x | | Sales, marketing | | x | |
| Škoda (Cz) | Automotive | FRG | | x | x | x | | | x | x | x | x | x | | | Product | x | | |
| Temac (Cz) | Sealing | NL | x | x | x | x | | | x | x | x | x | x | | | Technology | x | | |
| Berg (Bg) | Iron & steel | SW | x | x | x | | | x | x | x | x | x | | x | | Technology/debt | | x | |
| Danone (EBRD-Bg) | Final good | F/EBRD | x | x | x | x | | | x¹ | x | x | x | (x) | | | Working capital | | | (x) |

¹Brand.
[a]C = Cost; S = Strategy; M = Market.
[b]H = High; M = Medium; L = Low.
[c]T = Technology; KH = Know How; Mkt Acc = Market Access.

was located. With the exception of one or two of the enterprises, dealing with excess labor was not an issue, and the restructuring that followed the takeover handled this question smoothly. The work forces have been retrained, and there have been special efforts to retrain middle and higher managers.

Restructuring took place quickly in these cases through the speedy implementation of a variety of measures such as upgrading product quality, reducing the range of products, reorganizing the different functions inside the enterprises, training the workforce and developing sales departments. Productivity and profit objectives were attained without decreasing the level of wages. Generally, the control of firms by the foreign owners has been quite lax in terms of monitoring, the extent of centralized decision making, and the presence of expatriate managers. Major exceptions to this are Škoda in the Czech Republic and Sarrio in Slovenia. The parent firm's headquarters makes strategic decisions, but routine operations have remained relatively autonomous. New forms of accounting and financial reporting have been set up in most cases.

Once the rules under which enterprises could be acquired by foreign owners and the list of firms that could be sold were formulated, host governments in the former socialist countries have also been unintrusive. Where they have retained ownership stakes in the firms being sold to foreigners, they have behaved as minority shareholders and avoided interfering in the decisions of the majority owners. This is true for all three countries, and it holds even when problems have arisen as, for example, when Volkswagen did not entirely fulfill its investment commitments due to changing business conditions. In almost all cases, the negotiation about the selling price and the assets to be sold was conducted at the Ministry level or by the agencies directly in charge of promoting privatization. This had a positive effect on the work force and particularly on managers.

Based on the information gleaned from our questionnaires, some interesting conclusions can be drawn from the cases. Germany has realized the highest level of investments, mostly capital intensive ones, located principally in the Czech Republic and in Slovenia. As can be seen from Table 5, the cost motive for investing has been quite significant, notably in the automotive and processing industries; it is second to the motive of market penetration, however. In the automotive, paper, and tobacco industries, a strategic move by the foreign investor to dominate the host market was the primary motive. For final goods, the most recurrent motive for investing seems to be market access, which can be associated with strategic motives in some cases.

The twelve enterprises that we study can be distributed into medium- and low-technology sectors. High-technology industries are generally seen as strategic industries, and, with the exception of telecommunications firms, they are less likely to be sold to foreign companies. The cases suggest that foreign investors did bring to their new partners what the latter had been looking for: technology, know-how, and, to a lesser extent, cash and market access for their products.

After the change of ownership and the start of restructuring, however, firms have only performed moderately well in financial terms. Firms that displayed a good performance previously, such as Kolektor in Slovenia, seem to have been restructured more easily. The same appears to apply to smaller companies, where presumably the problems are less severe. Škoda is an exception; the firm has been shaken up and reorganized in such a way that productivity has risen quickly. Otherwise, two conclusions can be drawn concerning this point:

- restructuring is time consuming; the more specific is the asset, the longer it takes to adjust and to solve problems arising in the process.
- rapid return on investment and short-term profitability have not been the main concern for foreign investors in our cases. Nevertheless, the reorganization and the development of new functions such as marketing and quality control have contributed significantly to improvements in profitability.

### Asset Specificity and Adjustment of Firms

The speed and range of an enterprise's adjustment depends on several factors such as the control of owners and creditors, the relative power of insiders, market structure, the nature of the product and the level of competition in the market. The enterprises from our sample adjusted in different ways according to the relative importance of these factors.

### Intermediate Goods Sector

Biterm is a small Slovenian firm specialized in the production of thermostats for refrigerators, a low-medium technology product. It is a single-product firm operating on an oligopolistic market, and it has attained the minimum efficient scale of production, employing 64 people including white-collar workers. It is quasi-integrated into its parent firm, Gorenje. The joint venture was created in 1994 although the parent firms have cooperated since 1985. Currently 75 percent of its assets belong to Gorenje, and a minority stake of 25 percent belongs to a Danish company, Danfoss. The Danish firm provides inputs and finds buyers for the output of the joint venture, but it provides only in-kind contributions and a loan as guarantee capital. For Biterm, the joint venture was a prerequisite for access to technology and know-how. For the foreign partner, the venture helped it to reduce its costs and offered a springboard for increasing its market share in Eastern Europe and in the European Union. The primary motivation of the Danish firm was to export thermometer kits at specific transfer prices. Biterm and its parent obtained up-to-date technology, new products, higher capacity utilization, management know-how and training. Biterm has contractual agreements with Danfoss for the thermometer kits that it purchases and for the sale of the assembled thermometers back to the Danish firm.

Production has increased since the joint venture was set up; marketing is not an issue as all the output is sold to the parent companies. Routine operations are run autonomously, there is no formal R&D, and all financing is internal. Danfoss can obtain full ownership of the venture when the market in the former Yugoslavia opens up. Biterm achieved profitability within a few months of its founding, in part because of productivity improvements. Training of the workforce was successful, and wages have increased. Nevertheless, if there are major technological changes in its products, the firm could be in jeopardy because it produces only one product and has no access to R&D. The specificity of the business activities of the venture and of the product explains the successful results thus far.

Kolektor, a Slovenian firm producing commutators, a medium-technology product, is an atypical case. It developed a cooperative agreement with a German firm, K&B, in 1968. The German firm was later taken over by an American competitor, Kirkwood, when K&B ran into financial difficulties. In this partnership, Kolektor enjoys considerable autonomy due to its management skills and its relatively high level of technology. Several of its products have reached international standards, and, in 1995, the company was nominated as the best supplier by the French firm Valeo and by the American firm United Technologies. Kolektor has 20 percent of the European market and exports 85 percent of its production. For Kirkwood, the desire to maintain control over Kolektor came from the need for effective access to the European market and to the technology supplied by Kolektor. For Kolektor, the relationship with a foreign partner provided an opportunity to obtain western technology and markets as well as financial resources. The success of this joint venture can be explained by a variety of factors, in addition to the high skills of the management. Kolektor's competitive strength on its market and the ability of Kolektor's employees to master and improve the available technology enabled the firm to prosper in the highly competitive market for automobile parts.

Sarrio is a Slovenian company producing cardboard. The company was heavily in debt and unable to make needed investments. As a result, it was sold to an Italian competitor, Saffa. Sarrio is located near the Italian border, and the capital stock of the firm was such that the company could be restructured. When Sarrio was put up for sale, Saffa offered a higher price than did the other bidder. Saffa had four main objectives in this transaction: to reduce significantly the number of employees, to eliminate activities that were not directly connected to the main business of the company, to improve the quality of management and production, and to transfer its culture to Slovenian employees. To implement these goals, Sarrio has been centrally managed and integrated into the parent firm's corporate culture. Sarno is now a functional division of Saffa, and it has to produce monthly reports and annual plans for the head office. The workforce was reduced, and some activities were spun off by transferring assets to workers being released. The quality of the production processes and of the products has increased. Relations with suppliers had been poor because the company often failed to pay its bills on a timely basis, and repairing this poor reputation remains an important task. Investment in new machinery has helped to rationalize production.

The company exports 60–70 percent of its production, the same level as before. Restructuring has been long and costly, and the Italian company had to inject both equipment and cash into the venture, in part to reorganize production and the control of operations. Financial performance is still only moderate even if profits are up; sales have not increased though margins have improved. This case is more typical of the characteristics of Slovenian firms: weak performance, financial difficulties, an oligopolistic sector, and medium technology.

Linde, a German firm, acquired a Czech company producing industrial gas in two plants. The Czech company was first transformed from a state-owned enterprise to a joint-stock company owned by the National Property Fund, and then 51 percent of the shares were sold to Linde, which has since bought the remaining shares. Linde provided technology, know-how, and training. For the Czech company, the search for a foreign partner was motivated by the desire to obtain finance and know-how, mainly in marketing. Linde chose the Czech firm because of the quality of its workforce, its high market share, and the distribution network that was already in place. Linde was seen as a good investor because the Czech company had a similar corporate structure and because Linde was financially quite strong.

Linde created a sales center and expanded the distribution network in the Czech Republic. The subsidiary was responsible for most other activities, and decisions were made by mutual agreement. Linde also diversified the affiliate's activities in the Czech Republic away from gas to the food industry and to water treatment. It has improved quality, monitoring, labor selection and testing. The process of adaptation to the new market environment is going on; the workforce is more highly motivated and flexible. However, the rate of return remains low due to the time needed to bring maturity to the development of new activities.

Temac, a manufacturer of gaskets and seals, was one of the most modern companies in the Czech Republic. Two alternative ways of privatizing the company were considered by management. The first was to look for a foreign partner who would provide greater market opportunities and access to new technology that would eliminate the use of asbestos. The second was to rely on the personal resources of the employees and on domestic capital. The foreign investor, from the Netherlands, was motivated by the opportunity to increase market share, by cost advantages, and by the quality of the workforce.

In the end, the first alternative was chosen, and an asbestos-free production line was transferred to the subsidiary, as were some R&D activities. Additional production has since been transferred from the parent to the subsidiary. After the acquisition, production capacity remained the same, but quality improved and new products were introduced. The company is now ready to supply a growing market in Eastern Europe. The restructuring has been smooth, due to the quality of the Czech firm's product, organization, and workforce, and to the convergence between the enterprise's aims and those of the foreign investor.

Vidima Ideal and Berg, in Bulgaria, are two small enterprises that created joint ventures with Western firms, Vidima with an American, and Berg with a Swiss company. In both cases, the Western interest was in cost savings and, secondarily, access to the domestic Bulgarian market. Vidima Ideal produces final and intermediate products while Berg makes intermediate products. The foreign investors brought financial resources, managerial know-how, and training. Performance levels are quite good. This is due to the small size of the investment and the relatively modest level of technology involved.

### Final Goods Sector

Tobacco Ljubljana was the first foreign direct privatization in Slovenia. The Slovenian company needed a good product to survive. It also needed to develop new sales and marketing techniques. Reemstma, a German company, faced international competition from Phillip Morris, British-American Tobacco (BAT), and Rothmans. It chose to cooperate with SEITA in order to compete more effectively.[6] The investment was made to obtain greater market share; it was also a strategic move in order to block the entry of other competitors. Several factors explain the rapid drive of major transnational tobacco firms toward Eastern markets. Legal constraints on consumption of tobacco products are not so severe in the East as in the West. The quality of Eastern tobacco products is relatively low, and there is a huge demand in the region for higher quality. Reemstma, an independent cigarette manufacturer, had an orientation toward Eastern Europe. Its intention, when acquiring the Slovenian company, was to supply the whole Yugoslav market. The Slovenian firm anticipated such a change in objectives and developed its own light cigarettes, but the German partner had to transfer technology and know-how plus working capital.

The development of this cooperation was successful, although not without problems. First, the loss of the Yugoslav market had negative effects on the performance of the joint venture. The introduction to the local market of new German and French brands created a crowding out effect for Slovenian brands and hindered the development of a better Slovenian brand. The Slovenian government also imposed higher taxes on cigarettes and demands payment of taxes that had not been paid before the creation of the joint venture.

Pražské Pivovary in the Czech Republic is a long-established brewery located near Prague. Its beer had a good reputation, but the company lacked the financial resources to modernize and to expand exports. The British brewer Bass purchased minority stake in the company, both to get access to the domestic market and to export Czech beer to the West. Bass contributed access to markets, advertising skills, managerial know-how, and technology. There were no major technological changes, however, only managerial and organizational ones. Upgrading of quality, reducing costs and strategic planning for exports on the one hand, and the opening up of new markets on the other, have contributed to increased profits.

Zagorka, in Bulgaria, was a brewery plagued by losses that increased with economic transformation for lack of financial and managerial resources. The company was transformed into a joint venture with Heineken and Coca-Cola, both of whom have considerable experience in restructuring firms that they acquire by bringing in capital and equipment and through aggressive advertising. The pace of restructuring was generally quick and profitable because the cost of penetrating the market and reorganizing production is low in this industry.

Škoda, in the Czech Republic, is a well-known and extensively studied case. A big one-shot direct investment gave Volkswagen (VW) most of the automobile market in the Czech Republic. Using its monopoly power, VW has obtained higher tariffs from the Czech government in order to protect its market share, a strategy followed by all other car makers who have invested in the region (*Transition Report*, 1994). But the VW strategy was not limited to the Czech market. VW wanted to integrate Škoda into its globalization strategy, on both Western and Eastern markets. The restructuring of the company, which was successful, had three priorities: quality, price, and service. Cooperation with suppliers is important in this industry, and one of the effects of restructuring was to outsource many activities, forcing Škoda's suppliers to join into an integrated supplier system in order to reduce costs and inventories and to produce on a just-in-time basis. Upstream Czech companies supplying Škoda were obliged to join with Western suppliers of VW in order to reduce costs by attaining the minimum efficient scale required in their business. As a result, more than 33 joint ventures were created in the Czech Republic. Today, Škoda is a springboard for VW's development eastward. Quality and cost improvements were evident with the launching of a new model, the Felicia, which is produced to Western standards at similar or even lower cost level.[7] Škoda is considered to have become the most efficient unit of VW. Even if wages are 25 percent higher than the average for the Czech industry, they are still ten times lower than German wages.

Danone Serdika JSCo, the Bulgarian food-processing firm, was taken over by the French transnational corporation Danone. The Bulgarian firm produced dairy products and yogurt, for which Bulgaria has a strong reputation. It was a challenge for the French company, which was already present in other transition economies, to show that it would be possible to produce yogurt of Western quality. Danone obtained 53 percent ownership and the EBRD became a sleeping partner. Prior to the ownership change, the Bulgarian firm had no profit-maximizing strategy because it was supplied by state farms and sold its output at controlled prices. The French company wanted to increase market share and brought new machinery and cash to the venture. Capacity in the plant has increased, and employment grew from 100 to 200 people. Nevertheless, despite the profitability of the business, the company faces many problems including threats by the Bulgarian government to block the firm's expansion, ceiling prices on food products, and difficulties in obtaining an adequate supply of fresh milk. The company constructed a supply network and contracted with farmers to overcome the supply problem. Downstream distribution was also a problem.

## CONCLUSIONS

Although it is difficult to draw general conclusions from only twelve cases, this research allows us to highlight some interesting points concerning the motivation and expectations of foreign investors, the behavior of enterprises under new management, and the main difficulties in restructuring firms.

The most important conclusion is that the pace of restructuring relies on a variety of factors, notably the nature of the product, the relative power of insiders, and the structure of the market. We find that there is a clear relationship between the sector and industry under consideration and the motive for foreign investment. Cost factors are important in the case of intermediate products, while strategic and market share factors are crucial in final goods production. Unsurprisingly, strategic factors are of particular significance in sectors where the foreign firms operate in oligopolistic markets. However, there is no particular relationship between the country of origin of the investment and the motivation to invest. Moreover, the bulk of the firms in the study have low or middle technology. From the perspective of the firms being acquired, the Western investors' most frequent and useful contribution was technology and know-how.[8] Market access and cash were sometimes also important factors, especially in the case of the final products. There seems little host country variation in this finding.

Turning to performance and impact of foreign direct investment, there is again a sharp distinction between intermediate and final goods. The former sectors take longer to restructure because their assets are more specific and the return on capital is slow to increase to Western levels. In the case of final products, the costs of turnaround seemed to be lower and the attainment of profitability more rapid.

With regard to the three countries in our project, incentives to invest by Western firms were more explicitly strategic in the more developed and larger countries. In the less advanced countries, Western firms took fewer risks, committed fewer resources, and chose projects of a smaller size and lower asset-specificity.

The findings also point to some important externalities from FDI. First, foreign firms do appear to bring some of the elements in short supply in transitional economies, especially technology, financial resources, and managerial know-how, notably in areas such as sales, marketing, and accounting.

Acquisitions were followed relatively rapidly by an upgrading of product quality and of manufacturing methods in most cases. In some important examples, the acquiring firm also exercised pressures up and downstream to improve product quality and production methods.

However, the foreign direct investment process also entails some costs for the recipient country. The overall effect on the balance of trade in some cases may have been negative because foreign owners sometimes adopted a strategy of increasing their market share by relying on their traditional foreign-based suppliers for parts and components, thus increasing the import content of production in the host country.

From the perspective of the investing firms, investments in the region appear so far to have been only modestly rewarding. One reason is that earlier investments often sought to obtain markets across the region, for example throughout the former Yugoslavia. These objectives became infeasible for political reasons. The variance in performance however, does not appear to be well explained by sector or country of investment.

## NOTES

This research was produced as part of ACE project no. Z/9109/94–0622–R. The authors wish to acknowledge comments and advice from Kirsty Hughes, Sarah Todd, and especially Hugo Radice. Discussion among the project team—Marie Bohatá, Malinka Koparanova, Matija Rojec, and Marjan Svetličič—has also been invaluable.

1. Progress in the transition process is surveyed annually by the European Bank for Reconstruction and Development in their *Transition Report*, and was summarized over a six-year period by the World Bank in the 1996 Development Report, *From Plan to Market*. These reports provide a comparative evaluation of macro economic, institutional and enterprise developments. This background information is beyond the scope of, but of course relevant to this study. Hence interested readers are referred to these publications as a starting point.

2. As has been suggested in the case of Hungary. See Estrin, Hughes, and Todd 1997.

3. However, in the fall of 1995 Opel and Fiat started "a price war," i.e., selling their two models at a price lower than that of the Škoda Felicia. The interest of local customers has been very high. An agreement with the only other carmaker, Tatra, with a smaller and more focused market, would not have allowed other Western firms to gain significant market shares.

4. In this respect, Renault has followed a similar approach in Slovenia. Although the initial investment was intended to take market shares in the former Yugoslavia, the joint-venture has been able to switch its sales to Southern European markets (Italy, south of France); the subsidiary, like Škoda, has rapidly become one of the most efficient units in the group.

5. The use of decimals reflects the fact that one firm can be purchased by several owners (generally two) of different nationalities.

6. At the time of the acquisition, it was still a French state-owned enterprise. It was privatized in 1995.

7. Apparently, however, the import content is very much higher for this new model.

8. In the case of Kolektor, however, it was the Western firm that was interested in the Slovenian technology.

## REFERENCES

*Business Central Europe*. February 1996, December 1995.

Begg, D. "Economic Reform in Czechoslovakia: Should We Believe in Santa Klaus?" *Economic Policy*, no. 13, 1991.

———. "Pegging Out: Lessons from the Czech Exchange Rate Crisis." *Journal of Comparative Economics*, no. 4, 1998.

Bohm, A., ed. *Privatization in Central and Eastern Europe*. Ljubljana: CEEPN, 1992, 1993, 1994.

Desai, R. "Reformed Banks and Corporate Governance in the Czech Republic, 1991–1996." *Post-Soviet Geography and Economics*, no. 8, 1996.

Dimitrov, M. *State Enterprise Restructuring in Bulgaria, Romania and Albania*. Sofia: Gorex Press, 1997.

Estrin, S. *Self-Management in Theory and Practice.* Cambridge: Cambridge University Press, 1984.

———. *Privatization in Central and Eastern Europe.* London: Longmans, 1994.

Estrin, S., and P. Holmes. *Competition and Economic Integration in Europe.* London: Edward Elgar, 1998.

Estrin, S., K. Hughes, and S. Todd. *Foreign Direct Investment in Central and Eastern Europe.* London: Cassell, 1997.

Estrin, S., and X. Richet. "Industrial Restructuring and Microeconomics Adjustment in Poland. A Cross-Sectoral Approach." *Comparative Economic Studies,* no. 3, 1993.

Estrin, S., A. Gelb, and I. Singh. "Shocks and Adjustment by Firms in Transition: A Comparative Study," *Journal of Comparative Economics,* no. 2, 1995.

Genco, P., S. Taurelli, and C. Viezzoli. *Private Investment in Central and Eastern Europe: Survey Results.* European Bank for Reconstruction and Development, Working Paper no.7, 1993.

Gomulka, S. *Growth, Innovation and Reform in Eastern Europe.* Brighton: Wheatsheaf, 1986.

Jeffries, I., ed. *Industrial Reform in Socialist Countries: From Restructuring to Revolution.* Aldershot: Edward Elgar, 1992.

Kogut, B. *Direct Investment and Corporate Governance in Transition Economies.* Washington DC: World Bank Transition Economies Division, mimeo, 1994.

Lakatos, B., and G. Papanek. "Motivations for Establishing Enterprises with Foreign Participation in Hungary." *Economies Trends and Research Summaries,* no. 3, GKI, 1994.

Mejstrik, M. *The Privatization Process in East-Central Europe.* Dordrecht: Kluwer 1997.

Meyer, K. "Direct Foreign Investment in Central and Eastern Europe: Understanding the Statistical Evidence." CIS-Middle Europe Center, London Business School, Discussion Paper series, no. 1239, 1994 .

Pinto, B. et al. *"Transforming State Enterprises in Poland. Micro-Economic Evidence of Adjustment,"* Brookings Papers, 1993.

Richet, X. *Transnational Corporations, Foreign Direct Investment and Attractiveness of Central European Economies in Transition.* Helsinki: WIDER-UNU, 1995.

*Transition Report.* London: European Bank for Reconstruction and Development, 1994, 1995, 1996.

United Nations. *UNECE Economic Survey of Europe in 1994–1995.* New York: United Nations, 1995.

———. *World Investment Report 1995, Transnational Corporations, Employment and the Workplace.* New York and Geneva: United Nations, 1995.

World Bank. *Development Report.* Washington D.C.: World Bank, 1996.

# Foreign Direct Investment in Central Eastern Europe

# Part I

## Slovenia

# 1

# Kolektor

## Marjan Svetličič and Matija Rojec

### INTRODUCTION

This case examines the experience of the Slovenian firm Kolektor. This firm had been involved in a joint venture with the German firm Kautt and Bux for twenty-two years when the transition process in Slovenia began. It turned out, however, that it was not so much the local company that was in transition in the period 1990–94 as the foreign partner. The Slovenian firm actually saved the foreign partner from liquidation, and later, when the German company was taken over by the American company Kirkwood, Kolektor emerged more independent in terms of technology, managerial decision making, and marketing than it had been previous to the transition. There were really three distinct but interconnected transitions: of the German partner, of the Slovenian company, and of the whole market structure in this field. Kolektor turned out to be technologically the leading company in Europe in some lines of its business, shell commutators, for instance, an achievement that was possible due only to an ambitious local management that was able to seize the opportunity caused by the foreign partner's difficulties.

### HISTORY OF THE FIRM

Kolektor was established by the Idrija[1] municipality in 1963. The main objective was to provide employment for the women workers who could not find jobs in the old mercury mine that had operated in Idrija since 1492. Initially, Kolektor employed only twenty employees and operated in a rented facility. The opportunity to start such a firm arose

3

when Iskra, then one of the leading firms in Slovenia, started to transfer the production of some less important products to other companies. One of these products was the commutator, and it became the main product of the newly established firm in Idrija called Kolektor.

The technology and the product were then substantially different. The main buyer of these products was Iskra, which used commutators in household appliances and other products.[2] Because the technology was old, the costs were high, and the products were therefore hard to export, Kolektor started to look for ways to modernize production. In 1967, Yugoslavia adopted the first quasi–foreign investment (FDI) legislation, in the form of legislation allowing joint ventures between foreign and Yugoslav firms.[3] This was a new opportunity for Kolektor to modernize its technology and to penetrate foreign markets more aggressively so that it could have steady revenues from exports and decrease its dependence on Iskra, the almost exclusive buyer of its commutators at that time.

In 1968, Kolektor signed a joint-venture (JV) and a licensing contract with the German firm Kautt and Bux Gmbh. (K&B) located in Vaihingen near Stuttgart. Although K&B was a leading European producer of commutators, it was not the only potential partner. The German company was selected in a competition with the English company Watliff. The German technology and work mentality were considered by Kolektor as superior, and these were decisive elements in the selection. Overall strong economic cooperation between Slovenia and Germany, the small cultural distance between them, and the better knowledge of the German language on the part of Kolektor's staff may also have facilitated this decision. Kolektor's major motive was to get access to new technology and to change the production process from the original, very laborious technique of making commutators and of riveting commutators made of profiles, tubes, and bands. Newer types of commutators were already beginning to be made, and Kolektor thus felt the need to update its technology.

The arrangement with K&B was a usual mix of a JV and a licensing contract that was quite unique at that time in Slovenia. Foreigners had little confidence that they would be able to comanage a Yugoslav joint-venture partner on the basis of the JV legislation. Therefore, they preferred to have a licensing contract in addition to the JV contract because a licensing agreement was a more effective way to protect K&B's interests. On the other hand, the new technology was also

Table 1

**Major Development Landmarks**

| Year | Development |
|---|---|
| 1963 | Kolektor established |
| 1968 | Long-term joint-venture and cooperation contract signed with German company Kautt and Bux (K&B) |
| 1974 | New production hall built |
| 1978 | New plant for copper profiles production opened |
| 1986 | New production hall (conveyor-belt production) |
| 1988 | Long-term joint-venture and cooperation contract extended with K&B |
| 1988 | Toolmaking plant modernized |
| 1989 | New firm's premises built |
| 1990 | K&B became 51% owner |
| 1990 | FMR d.o.o. Idrija established, company for finance, marketing, and development, and Kolektor transformed into a limited-liability company |
| 1992 | Joining of new partner, Financial Engineering |
| 1993 | Kirkwood took over K&B and became 51% owner of Kolektor |
| 1993 | Purchase of production hall of Gostol |
| 1994 | Erection of bridge over Idrijca River |
| 1994 | Privatization of FMR d.o.o. Idrija |
| 1994–95 | Winning recognition of its own brand name on the market |
| 1995 | New plant for shell commutators |
| 1995 | Opening of the representative office in Stuttgart |

regarded as an important impulse to the strengthening of the competitiveness of those Slovenian firms that would use these new commutators in their final products.

In 1973, Kolektor used the first major investment to enlarge its capacities, and consequently it started selling on the European market via K&B's marketing network and trade name.

In order to reduce inventories of insulation materials and to secure the right quality and specifications of copper profiles, an intermediate product in commutator manufacturing, Kolektor undertook a second major investment in 1977–78 to begin the production of such profiles. Previously they had been purchased from suppliers in France and Germany.

The third major investment took place in 1986, when the mass production of commutators started with the new building for conveyor-belt production, which resulted in a significant increase in output. Two years later, Kolektor extended the joint-venture contract with K&B. The initial contract had a term of twenty years. If the contract had not been prolonged, Kolektor would have had to pay back the "equity"

Table 2

**Sales Revenues, Number of Employees, and Gross Value Added per Employee in 1994 and Prospects for 1995**

| Year | Number of employees | Sales in thousand DM | Gross value added per employee |
|---|---|---|---|
| 1994 | 932 | 79,000 | 26,180 ECU |
| 1995 (planned) | 938 | 91,000 | 27,816 ECU |

Table 3

**Educational Structure of Employees in Kolektor** (December 31, 1994)

| Education | Number | Percentage |
|---|---|---|
| University degree | 35 | 4 |
| Higher degree | 26 | 3 |
| Secondary school | 153 | 16 |
| Professional qualification | 306 | 33 |
| On-the-job training | 32 | 3 |
| Primary school | 301 | 32 |
| Incomplete primary school | 79 | 8 |
| Total | 932 | 100 |

share of the foreign partner.[4] Simultaneously, Kolektor modernized its tool department (see Table 1).

## COMPANY PROFILE

By Slovenian standards, Kolektor is a large company, employing 932 employees. In 1994 it was:
- twenty-seventh among Slovenian firms in terms of export volume;
- thirtieth among the 300 largest companies in Slovenia in terms of profits (368 million Slovenian tolars [SIT], or 4.6 million DM);
- fifty-third in terms of employment;
- eighty-eighth in terms of turnover; and
- ninety-third in terms of assets.

Gross value added per worker was 26,180 ECU in 1994, which made it a high value-added company (see Table 2).[5] Kolektor is obviously a relatively profitable company, providing important employment with a relatively low capital-to-labor ratio, and it is very export oriented.

Figure 1. **Sales Plan in 1995 by End Use**

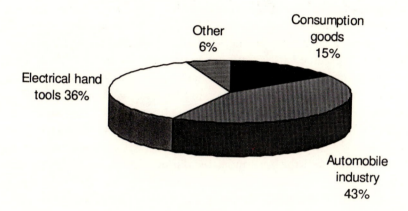

The employment structure of Kolektor is relatively good for its line of business (see Table 3). Among those with university degrees, 60 percent have technical training compared to the 40 percent trained as economists, lawyers, and professionals educated in other social sciences and liberal arts.

Although the educational structure is quite good, it is far from appropriate for the good of the company to introduce gradually leaner production and distribution. This goal demands more-educated workers who are able to make decisions on their own.

At the beginning, Kolector's objective had been the production of commutators for consumer goods such as household appliances. Today the major share of production consists of commutators for automobile production (42.5 percent) and tools (35.8 percent), while commutators for consumer products account for only 15.7 percent (see Figure 1). This is a natural consequence of the increased production of cars in the world and of the increasing use of commutators in automobiles. The modern automobile has as many as seventy commutators.

## ORGANIZATION AND MANAGEMENT OF THE COMPANY

At first, Kolektor's corporate structure as a joint venture had to conform to Yugoslavia's joint-venture and company laws. In 1990, Kolektor was transformed from a "socially"[6] owned firm into a private limited-liability company, with 51 percent equity share held by K&B and a 49 percent share held by FMR, a company for financing, marketing, and development that was established with the primary, if not the only, purpose of acting as the 49 percent shareholder of Kolektor. FMR itself remained in social ownership until the end of 1992, when the privatization law was adopted. The privatization of FMR also brought about changes in the ownership structure of Kolektor. In 1992, 300 employees of Kolektor established a company, FI (Financial Engineering), that bought a 26 percent equity share in Kolektor from FMR.[7] The 23 percent share that remained in FMR is owned mostly by various funds[8] and the remainder by the employees of Kolektor (see Figure 2).[9]

In the late 1980s, K&B started to lag behind global technology and marketing trends and ran into difficulties due to poor internal organization, an unsuccessful investment policy, and lack of attention to cost competitiveness.[10] To improve its creditworthiness, K&B wanted to incorporate Kolektor's balance sheet into its own consolidated balance sheet, which it could do only by becoming Kolektor's majority owner. In 1990, Kolektor agreed that K&B would become a 51 percent owner.[11] On that basis, K&B obtained a loan from German banks. However, this loan did not save K&B. In 1993, it was taken over by the U.S. firm Kirkwood.[12] Having a first option on K&B's share in the joint venture, Kolektor was seriously considering purchasing back this share, but Kolektor was unable to raise enough money to do so. Thus Kirkwood became the owner of 51 percent of Kolektor's shares.

Relations with the German partner had always been very good. Although the foreign partner had the right to name its own co-director, this director never interfered with the decisions of the local directors. The foreign partner was very tactful (Petri 1995), which is also one of the reasons why Kolektor sought to help K&B when it ran into difficulties in the beginning of the 1990s. The K&B crisis caused manifold production difficulties. The supply of raw materials was interrupted, and financing was difficult to obtain. Austria Bank, a subsidiary of the major Austrian bank in Ljubljana, nevertheless continuously financed Kolektor.

Negotiating the increase of K&B's share to 51 percent was also an opportunity for Kolektor's management to realize some of their strategic aspirations, that is, to get more autonomy, particularly in market-

Figure 2. **Capital Structure of Kolektor**

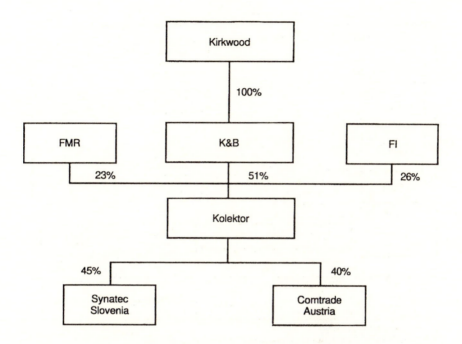

ing, and in this way to improve performance. According to the new contract, signed during the K&B crisis in 1991, Kolektor gained marketing independence and a high level of managerial independence. In spite of its 51 percent share, K&B agreed in 1993, that is, after its acquisition by Kirkwood, that a 75 percent majority would be necessary for major decisions to be made; practically speaking, three out of four members of the board would have to agree. Without a 75 percent majority, it is up to the management to decide on the company's policy. For all practical purposes, this means that, with a four-member board,[13] either partner's veto on some decision makes it possible for management to pursue its own policy. The distribution of share holding therefore only matters in terms of the distribution of profits. Even though the investment of the foreign partner is legally a form of foreign direct investment, in reality the foreign majority owner plays a role similar to that of a portfolio investor.

The organizational structure of the company has recently changed. The functional scheme was replaced by a hybrid combination of a

Figure 3. **Organizational Structure**

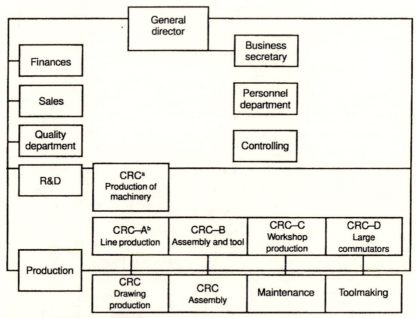

[a]Cost responsibility centers (CRCs).
[b]CRCs are organized on the basis of products and/or type of production.

functional and a divisional structure (see Figure 3).

Changes in the organizational structure are the result of the company's new position and its new ambitions. By becoming more independent in marketing its own products under its own brand name and by fighting to keep and to penetrate new markets, Kolektor became "leaner." It reduced costs[14] and improved its marketing and management. The primary emphasis was to cut costs. Therefore, special cost units, so-called cost responsibility centers (CRCs), were established. Their major purpose is production control, keeping down costs, and purchasing needed materials. They have no role in marketing. Therefore, marketing and, of course, R&D remain centralized. This is, to a certain extent, also a response to the needs of customers, who are not too keen on dealing with a number of new sellers, which would make their operations more complex and costly.

Perhaps the greatest asset or competitive advantage of Kolektor, apart from a well-defined strategy, is its homogeneous management team and the high stability of the management and personnel in general.[15] The managerial team has been working together for twenty years. The only newcomers are managers for quality assurance (QS) and for the financial division. In the transition process, the managers and the employees became shareholders, which provided additional motivation for even better performance.

The stability of the management team, however, also imposes some costs. In some cases, it is becoming a barrier to innovation because the same people are working too long at the same job. A manager who stays in one position for too long may become too autocratic and less flexible regarding innovations and changes in procedures.

The previous manager headed Kolektor for seventeen years. He was succeeded by the present manager, who was previously the director of marketing. The change was not easy because no member of the management team was very eager to take over from the former manager, who had been very efficient and influential. When he died in February 1994, the idea was to have a collective management team. Kirkwood, the majority owner, strongly opposed this idea. If a collective leadership were to be implemented despite Kirkwood's resistance to the idea, then Kirkwood wanted to appoint a vice-president. The present director, Mr. Petrič, then suggested another member of the existing management team for the post of director, but he himself was finally persuaded to accept the position. This was certainly a very good choice in view of the strategic reorientation Kolektor started to undertake. The major task of the new director was to put into practice Kolektor's newly gained independence in marketing. Mr. Petrič, an economist by training, was probably the best choice for such a strategic task, being responsible for marketing in Kolektor already.

Not only management but also many other employees have already been in the firm for thirty years. Labor turnover is insignificant. Geography promotes such high stability. Idrija is located in a valley where there are not many other opportunities for employment. Those who want to work where they were born, and this mentality is quite strong in Slovenia, where labor mobility is very low, have very few choices. Therefore, commitment to the company is very strong. For some, the firm almost represents a life-time employment opportunity.

On the basis of a special agreement signed with the trade unions, the salaries Kolektor is paying are 5 percent higher than the average in the same industry in Slovenia. Although many companies in Slovenia have had difficulties paying monthly salaries regularly, this has never been the case at Kolektor. The social services the company provides to its employees are also above the average for Slovenia. In the course of transition, it has not sold any of the quite numerous vacation apartments it bought in the past.[16] Not surprisingly, management relations with trade unions are good.

The management of the firm has always been highly committed to the local community. The employment level is higher than technological standards would demand. The same production could be achieved with fewer workers,[17] but lay-offs are few for social reasons. In keeping with the efforts to remain cost competitive, monthly cost reporting was inaugurated in 1993, followed by the streamlining of production and the improvement of the maintenance of equipment. The firm has also invested in the local infrastructure. In 1993, it built a bridge over the Idrijca River, which also contributed to the expansion of production to a new building on the other side of the river.

## PRODUCTION AND TECHNOLOGY

The main product of Kolektor is a commutator, which consists of two major components: the copper segment, along with the brush slide, and the supporting body holding the copper parts. Its function is to transmit electricity to the rotor of an electric motor and to commute electricity from one direction to the other. Although the commutator appears to be a relatively simple element, its functioning within an electric motor is subject to very complicated electrical, mechanical, thermal, and chemical processes. The interdisciplinary character of these processes is so complex that, even today, they are not fully understood. Thus building commutators is a demanding process, and their design is partly a science and partly an art based on past experience.

The commutator's complexity and therefore the additional components built into it depend on what the motor is used for. In order to attain the required commutator properties, the producer must use various technologies to build the commutator. Originally, riveting was the major production method. Subsequently commutators were made of profiles, tube, and band. The current technology is based on reshaping.

The product has a very wide use in consumer goods, in more sophisticated professional machines and tools, and, finally, and most signifi-

Table 4

**Turnover and Sales of Kolektor in 1990–94**

|  | 1990 | 1991 | 1992 | 1993 | 1994 | Index 1991=100 |
|---|---|---|---|---|---|---|
| Turnover (million SIT) | 466 | 1,357 | 3,496 | 4,558 | 6,589 | 486 |
| Sales (million SIT) | 448 | 934 | 3,111 | 4,249 | 6,452 | 590 |
| Sales (million DM) | 52 | 53 | 58 | 61 | 79 | 149 |

cantly, in all types of cars. Motors with built-in commutators are used in consumer goods such as household appliances and in high-technology professional machines and power tools. A major consumer is the automobile industry, offering a wide range of applications for commutator motors. Over ten commutators are built into a car of modern design and up to seventy into a car with the most advanced equipment.

Kolektor's production has increased in the past decade, particularly in the period 1991–94.[18] In nominal terms, turnover and sales increased almost fivefold. The increase in real terms, due to inflation and depreciation of the tolar exchange rate, was much more modest. Production volume, that is, the number of commutators produced, increased by 39 percent. Sales increased almost sevenfold nominally and 49 percent in DM terms (see Table 4).

This explanation of the product is important for understanding the process of technological transformation of the company from simple to more sophisticated production techniques and from a production technique totally dependent on the foreign partner to one based increasingly on its own R&D. The structure of the market was very important in forcing Kolektor to adapt technologically in order to be able to cope with the new trends in demand. Technological change was therefore market driven.

Kolektor is a typical case of the gradual growth of a firm from a simple to a more sophisticated technology and products. It started with a simple, labor-intensive technology based on low labor costs. With the assistance of a foreign partner, the firm gradually started upgrading technology and the quality of its products and, at the same time, increasing production and sales at home and on foreign markets. Through technology transfer, by acquiring knowledge from the foreign partner, and through the assimilation and adaptation of this knowledge, Kolektor gradually started to modernize its technology and products and to transform its marketing and management. Among these changes was the introduction of environmentally safer asbestos-free components in the production of commutators. Environmentally sensitive waste material is being sent for recycling to the United States. Kolektor introduced European environmental standards as early as 1990.

Although the company was started as a typical socialist firm with social objectives in mind, economic objectives became dominant rather early. Kolektor was among the first firms in Slovenia to realize that the best way to penetrate foreign markets and to modernize its technology and products is to establish long-term arrangements with foreign partners. The joint-venture contract was regarded as an instrument for the firm's technological and business modernization. Management realized that the foreign partner could not keep the local partner permanently in a position of simple standardized technological production, taking advantage of lower labor costs and that, in its own interest, it would have to transfer modern technology to its JV partner to remain competitive. As a result of this process, Kolektor's technology today is better than that of Kirkwood and equal to or better than that of K&B (Petrič 1995). In the cool transformation of copper and at making shell commutators, it is probably the best firm in Europe. In profile commutators, Italians are considered the most cost efficient.

Kolektor was the third company in Slovenia to receive the ISO 9001 standard in 1992, which was recognition of its high production quality and management standards. Kolektor could have received this award even earlier, but it was not seen as very important because the standards of the automobile industry, Kolektor's major customer, are even more demanding than the ISO 9001. Major buyers demand consistent quality and on-time deliveries. There were five audits of Kolektor by major buyers in 1994. The French company Valer nominated Kolektor as the supplier of the year, and Bosch gave it good scores as well.

In 1995, a major investment to expand and modernize the production facility was completed. Kolektor thereby increased the volume of output and introduced some new products or modified existing ones.

## RESEARCH AND DEVELOPMENT

Development started in Kolektor initially within the technical sector. Its own R&D department was established in 1976–77. It is still called the Development Department, since its main activities are the development of new products and new materials, the improvement of production/technological processes, and, finally, the development of new equipment and tools for the production of new products. In the second half of the 1970s, foreign knowledge became more of a complement and less of a substitute for local knowledge, as had been the case during the "infant" period after the establishment of the joint venture. Ambitions later increased in the direction of modest product, technology, and tools modifications. In the early 1980s, Kolektor filed its first patent application. Now Kolektor has four patents in Europe and the United States[19] and two patents at the application stage. They are process rather than product patents. These results were achieved with only ten employees in the R&D department.[20]

R&D expenditures are equal to 2.5–3.0 percent of Kolektor's sales, compared to 2.0 percent in 1991. If some other costs indirectly related to development activities were to be calculated as R&D costs, investment in R&D would increase considerably. As far as it knows, Kolektor spends more on R&D than does Kirkwood or K&B, which should improve Kolektor's competitive position on the world market in the future.

The aim of its own R&D activities was modest at first, mostly geared toward assimilating and adapting foreign knowledge. This goal was facilitated by the provision for the free transfer of knowledge[21] in the contract with the foreign partner. Kolektor's engineers and workers have had, apart from training on the spot, the opportunity for regular training by the foreign partner in Germany. Cooperation with the foreign partner in this way substantially contributed to the strengthening of the human-capital base of the company. At the beginning, the joint venture acted as a substitute for Kolektor's own ability to modernize production and upgrade technology to world market standards. The import of technology was clearly the major objective of the JV contract.

Kolektor gradually became more ambitious in developing its technological autonomy and started making more systematic adaptations and development of technology and products. This was facilitated by market demand, because customers demanded different commutators for their final products and by the fact that the head of the R&D department was a very experienced engineer, in charge of the R&D department for thirty years. To produce new models, in cooperation with its foreign partner, Kolektor was first forced to "invent" new equipment/tools[22] for the production of prototypes, to utilize new materials, and, finally, to modify products or change the technological process.

Progress was surprisingly good. By 1988, Kolektor already outpaced K&B in the number of patents. Up to 1988, technical knowledge flowed from K&B to Kolektor, while from 1988 on, it flowed more from Kolektor to K&B. From 1994 on, K&B has been producing on the basis of a Kolektor patent, although there was no contract stipulating that.

Such progress by Kolektor could not have been achieved without permanent contacts with the buyers of its products. Their needs are the decisive influence on product development in commutator production. The manufacturer has to develop a product according to customers' evolving needs. After a test period, which could be from six to eighteen months, depending on the product, the crucial issue is to provide standardized quality and performance in a product that fully meets the buyer's specifications. This is where differences among manufacturers occur; some are more capable of providing standardized quality than others. Those that can master the quality requirements can be sure that the buyer will purchase products from him. Competitors would need the same amount of time to develop a new product and to get it homologized, which creates a special kind of barrier to entry. So far, Kolektor has not established permanent links with universities or research institutes. This is one of their strategic tasks for the future.

This special characteristic of its industry requires that Kolektor develop its own R&D capacity and take more ambitious steps in the development of its own products. Obviously, the market structure is important for the development of the firm's strategy, together with ambitious management capable of realizing such a market structure and being able to make appropriate strategic decisions and to take the necessary risks.

The Kolektor case confirms the hypothesis that distance from the center, Ljubljana in this case, has turned out to be beneficial in the process of transition. Firms in the center prospered in the pretransition period due to good relations with politicians and bankers, who were mostly political appointees, and did not rely as much on their production and innovation/technological capabilities. Firms outside the center, not having daily contacts with politicians and bankers, had to rely much more on their own capabilities. After the collapse of the socialist system, such firms were better off. The managers of such firms also had acquired very strong local power, which had made them more independent of political interference. Therefore, they were free to follow economic rather than political objectives.

## TRAINING

Parallel to R&D efforts, Kolektor has also been giving increasing attention to training. It started by recognizing that better-trained workers and managers are a precondition for the improvement of the quality of products, for efficient marketing, and for effective management of the company. Training is not limited to only one type of workers, but, rather, it is evenly spread to all layers of the workforce. Managers do not have the time for regular MBA courses, but they participate in short-term training programs in communications, negotiations, and foreign languages. In 1993, Kolektor workers participated 204 days in different training programs abroad. The major objective of these programs was the transfer of specific technology to Kolektor.

Initially, training was limited to on-the-job training, while, in the 1990s, it became a more diverse activity. The major part of training took place after the introduction of new technology, when the contract with K&B was signed in 1968. It was performed mainly by the foreign partner in Idrija, at the company itself, and at K&B in Germany. The transition from technological dependence on K&B to a position of greater technological and marketing independence created a need for training in marketing, finance, and management. Training in these fields has now become one of the company's priorities.

## MARKETING

Based on production and sales in the amount of approximately DM 79 million in 1994, Kolektor is today the largest company in Europe in its field of operations, with a 20 percent market share. Competitors are Mam of Italy, with approximately DM 65 million; K&B of Germany, with DM 70 million; and Nettelhof, with sales of DM 55 millions in 1994. Kolektor is now the number one firm in Europe in sales of commutators and fifth in the world. Kirkwood is the dominant player in North America and Sugiama of Japan, in Asia.

Competition in the production of commutators is strongly influenced by the long period required for the development of a product prototype and its testing and by the need to manufacture the product to standardized quality and performance. These features create important first-mover advantages. A firm obtains a competitive edge, first, by realizing the emerging needs of buyers. This requires close and permanent interaction with customers. Second, firms can gain an advantage over competitors by speeding up the process of development of the new product, testing it, and beginning mass production. This is not possible without one's own R&D sector and one's own tool-manufacturing facilities. Without such in-house facilities and capabilities, the lead time would be too long and the firm would not be able to remain competitive in the sector. Second, firms such as Kolektor sell mostly in advance to long-term, known customers. This is why advertising expenditures are very low, constituting only 0.2 percent of sales. There is little room on the market for free sales that are not governed by long-term contracts.

Approximately 80 percent of Kolektor sales are to group A buyers, of which there are 22 in number. Otherwise the total number of buyers is as high as 116, meaning that there are some very small buyers.

It is not surprising that, in view of such a market structure, Kolektor's production was initially oriented toward the local market until 1968. Iskra was the major customer. Exports started a year after the JV contract was signed. All the export in that period was done through the K&B sales network and under the K&B trademark. In 1970, Kolektor exported only DM 100,000 worth of output. Planed export for 1995 was 710 times larger (see Figure 4).

The share of export has substantially increased in the past five years. In 1990, Kolektor exported over 69 percent of all sales, now already 80 percent. Exports also increased in real terms (see Table 5). Such rapid growth of exports is a combined result of technological modernization,[23] market trends, successful marketing efforts and direct contacts with customers, and, last but not least, an increase in the average DM exchange rate from 21 to 52 in the period 1991–92. Export expansion thus coincided with a more independent sales role for Kolektor.

The EU has traditionally been the major export destination. Nevertheless, this orientation even strengthened when Kolektor gained more marketing independence through the new contract with K&B when the latter was in crisis in 1991. Sales to Eastern Europe decreased substantially (see Table 6). This was partly a result of the transition crisis in

Figure 4. **Planned Export Structure for 1995**

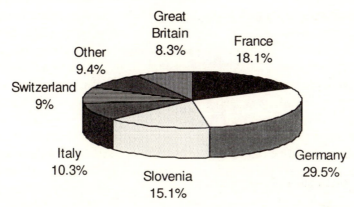

these countries, partly a result of German unification,[24] and partly a result of Kolektor's policy of increasing the EU market share when the firm got the opportunity to do so after gaining marketing independence. The fact that the company not only maintained the market share it previously achieved through the K&B trademark but even increased it is really an impressive result. There were some transitional difficulties in 1993, but 1994 was already a big success. This was a combined result of good management and marketing efforts, a good product that had received international recognition previously, and, last but not least, the economic upswing in Europe.

Initially, Kolektor's exports were totally dependent on its foreign partner. K&B allowed it to market its products on the markets of East European socialist countries, particularly in East Germany, at the beginning of the 1980s. By the mid-1980s, almost one-fourth of production was sold there. By the end of the 1980s, these exports decreased in view of economic difficulties in these countries. Even on these markets, Kolektor was not selling alone but through a big Slovenian foreign trade company, which had developed a good network there over the years.

In addition to becoming more self-reliant in its export activities, Kolektor also reduced its import dependence on its foreign partner. This had been almost total at the beginning of the relationship, and it was reduced to 57 percent after 1990. This does not, however, mean that imports were substantially reduced. It only means that now Kolektor is free to import from any supplier and no longer predominantly from K&B.

Table 5

**Export 1990–94 and Share in Sales**

|  | 1990 | 1991 | 1992 | 1993 | 1994 | 1995 (plan) |
|---|---|---|---|---|---|---|
| Export (million SIT) | 257 | 598 | 2,331 | 3,146 | 5,169 | — |
| Sales (million SIT) | 448 | 934 | 3,111 | 4,249 | 6,452 | 91 |
| Export (million DM) | 35.9 | 37.4 | 43.7 | 45.3 | 58.6 | 71.1 |
| Export/sales (%) | 57.4 | 64.0 | 74.9 | 74.0 | 80.1 | 78 |

Table 6

**Export by Destination** (in percent)

|  | 1990 | 1991 | 1992 | 1993 | 1994 |
|---|---|---|---|---|---|
| Foreign partner network | 74 | 90 | 94 | 46 | 18 |
| European Union | n.a. | n.a. | n.a. | 30 | 68 |
| Central and Eastern Europe | 26 | 10 | 6 | 2 | 3 |
| Other countries | 0 | 0 | 0 | 12 | 11 |

Marketing dependence on K&B held back the technological modernization of production and products. The lack of direct contacts with buyers, who provide information about the kind of products they need, is a major hindrance to development. Petrič (1995) even claims that technological independence is of no use without marketing independence. Therefore, strengthening the marketing function of the company and achieving a more independent marketing position became the most important strategic objective in the late 1980s. Since it developed its own technological capabilities and obtained its own patents, Kolektor has not signed any new contracts for the transfer of technology with K&B; previously such contracts stipulated an automatic transfer or a sharing of technology and knowledge by both partners. In this regard, Kolektor became an independent firm. Decisive steps toward this end were taken during the K&B crisis in October 1991–93.

The successful introduction of its own marketing activity was only possible because Kolektor gradually "became a mature firm capable of taking advantage of the new situation. In one year we achieved in marketing and in recognition of our own trademark as much as many firms cannot achieve in ten years" (Petrič 1995). Without such maturity, the high coherence of management, the support of employees as well, and, last but not least, a good reputation regarding the quality of products and the promptness of deliveries,[25] such an ambitious plan could not have been realized. Kolektor used the chance furnished by problems at K&B, one of the two external factors determining competitiveness (Porter 1990). Chance alone was not enough; it was perhaps a necessary but not a sufficient condition. Ambition and capabilities were the two additional necessary factors.

The development of Kolektor's own marketing network was initially based on its own local agents in Germany and France. In the future, Kolektor plans to establish its own subsidiaries. Their major tasks will be to gather information on the new needs of major customers and to market Kolektor's products. The first activity is as important as the second.

## FINANCING

Local banks were initially Kolektor's major source of finance. Kreditna banka Gorica was Kolektor's main source of funds, but the bank ran into difficulties by the late 1980s. Fear of the possibility of K&B's liquidation also emerged at the beginning of the 1990s. As a result of both these factors, Austria Bank in Ljubljana, a subsidiary of the largest Austrian bank, became Kolektor's bank. This move was facilitated by the good relations between Comtrade, Kolektor's Austrian affiliate, and Austria Bank in Vienna. In this way, outward internationalization strengthened the domestic market position of the company, an experience that is not limited to Kolektor alone. Some firms intentionally internationalize their activities in order to strengthen their domestic market position.

Depreciation, which is 8–10 percent of sales, and bank loans financed Kolektor's expansion. No major changes in financing took place in the 1990s. Management is quite independent in financing Kolektor's activities, with two important limitations:

(a) there is an upper limit for borrowing; and

(b) the sale of real estate above DM 700,000 is not permitted without a board decision.

## STRATEGY

From the very beginning, Kolektor's strategy has been very simple and clear:

- first, to modernize its technology and production program
- second, to upgrade its products and technology by assimilating and adapting foreign technology; and
- third, to gain more independence, particularly in marketing, and to strengthen its overall competitive position on the world market.

A logical consequence of such a strategy already in the 1990s was the desire to buy out K&B. Two factors prevented this. First, it was difficult to obtain the necessary financial resources, and, second, it was possible for Kolektor to attain its major strategic objectives within a joint venture with K&B. Foreign participation was not an obstacle, in view of the decision-making autonomy that Kolektor's management succeeded in obtaining.

After Kolektor became technologically strong[26] and achieved a high market share in Europe and in the world, it entered the fourth strategic stage, in which establishing a network, a strategic alliance with partners and customers, was an obvious next step. The internationalization of Kolektor's activities was organically built into such a strategy. The firm was transformed from a domestic to a more internationally oriented one, first by inward internationalization, through the import of technology and a JV contract. This was followed by greater export orientation, first using the foreign partner's marketing network and at later stages acquiring some niches that were not so interesting for the foreign partner, or, rather, where Kolektor was superior in marketing, that is, in Eastern Europe. To facilitate such an internationalization, Kolektor also established its own affiliate in Austria, Comtrade, with a 40 percent equity share, which was particularly instrumental in promoting export to Eastern Europe. It was also what we have elsewhere (Svetličič, Rojec, and Lebar 1994) called a system-escape type of outward FDI. Through such an investment, Kolektor became more able to import necessary materials even in the highly volatile foreign trade and exchange regime of the former Yugoslavia.

A network was formally proposed by Kolektor to K&B and Kirkwood. K&B welcomed it and so did Kirkwood, but only at first. Later it turned out that Kirkwood was unwilling to accept Kolektor as an independent and equal partner in the network. In addition, buyers did not favor such a network because they were afraid of monopoly pricing by such a strong group. Kirkwood wanted the network to operate on the principle of "governed competition." These views, of course, reflect a battle for a major share of the market, particularly in Europe, among

Kirkwood, its wholly owned affiliate, K&B, and Kolektor (Petrič 1995). Negotiations are still under way.

Independently, Kolektor is creating two of its own networks: (a) one of suppliers of raw materials; and (b) one of subcontractors for intermediate products.

Inputs are mainly imported. Slovenian producers supplied only 1.8 percent of Kolektor's materials and components purchases in 1994. Five major foreign suppliers, most of whom are from Europe, are responsible for 67 percent of total raw materials, while two Japanese firms supply 5 percent of total needs.

The network approach is part of a more ambitious outward internationalization strategy. Kolektor's management came to the conclusion that the specific advantages they acquired deserve to be exploited globally. Therefore, they are thinking of investing abroad, but not only for this reason. Another is to get closer to customers, to get information about their needs, to adapt Kolektor's products accordingly, and to adjust to new market trends as swiftly as possible.

Although Kolektor has been a European-oriented firm, after becoming independent in its marketing, its aspirations expanded. An already high European market share is difficult to increase. The financial position of former socialist countries, which would otherwise be an enormous potential market, is still weak.

Direct contacts with customers such as Bosch, Black and Decker, and Valeo that enable Kolektor to know more about their future strategies would facilitate Kolektor's new, more globally oriented strategy.

## SOME PROBLEMS

Perhaps the major problem of the company is the excessively high level of employment relative to the level of production. On this point, Kolektor's policy is a departure from the usual practice of its competitors. This is a consequence of a still rather strong social consciousness in the company's strategy. An excess of workers is at the same time also a barrier to taking more decisive steps in the direction of the automation of the production process. An excess of workers forces management to look for programs that would employ nonqualified workers.

The second problem has to do with strengthening incentives in the company and improving the attitude toward the product's quality. Cost awareness is also not yet very high at all levels. Improving cost competitiveness has to become a more dominant consideration in the future. The company is aware of this very pressing problem and is closely following the process of relocating some of the most labor-intensive parts of commutator production from Europe to locations with lower labor costs.

Strategically, the major problem is nondiversified production, which is highly exposed to technological changes on the market. The electronic revolution will not bypass this industry. Traditional commutators could be replaced by electronic commutation. Innovation in such a direction is very R&D intensive, and only very large companies can undertake it.

## CONCLUSIONS

Kolektor is not at all a typical foreign investment in a transition economy. Kolektor was already a successful company operating basically in a rather autonomous way before the transition; and, second, the transition has not had a major effect on the company. If anybody was in transition in the traditional sense, it was the foreign partner rather than Kolektor. Kolektor was in transition but in a different way: it was transforming from a basically marketing-dependent producer to an independent one. The main technological transformation had taken place before the transition process in the formerly socialist countries had started. Kolektor entered the 1990s as an already technologically well-developed company in its sector. By gaining an independent market position, it also strengthened its self-confidence and validated its long-term development strategy.

The Kolektor case also demonstrates that catching up is possible and is speeded up by the productive combination of own efforts and important assistance from a foreign investor if this assistance is part of an organic, gradual, but ambitious development strategy. Development was gradual, particularly in the field of technology, but it accelerated in the 1990s. In terms of marketing, however, the company achieved more in the past two years than in its previous history because it became an independent market player, selling its own products under its own brand name. This was possible only under two crucial preconditions: first, because the firm was from the very beginning very ambitious, aiming at the development of its own products and technologies, and developed its own high-quality products; and, second, because the management team was able to grasp the opportunity offered by the crisis at K&B.

Perhaps the most important message of the Kolektor case is the crucial importance of the management of the company, its stability, commitment, competence, and, last but not least, vision and risk-taking attitude. The Kolektor story could have turned out very differently if management had not had the vision and the courage to start climbing the "bumpy road" of marketing its own trademark "overnight."[27] The right combination of managerial capabilities, serendipity, courage, and vision has proved to be a precondition for such a transition.

All these changes could hardly be characterized as transition specific, meaning the transition from a socialist to a market economy. The major transition in Kolektor involved not changes in ownership but the taking over of the marketing of its own products and rounding out the technological transformation process. Ownership transformation only facilitated and speeded up this process, which would also have taken place without this ownership change.

Other changes that took place in Kolektor in the period 1990–95 were induced more by the achievement of a significant new market position. More than a major change of development strategy, this change meant a shift in strategy. By becoming an independent market player, marketing issues gained in relative importance. Quality considerations were the second related area calling for improvements. Company policy therefore focused on these two and related aspects, such as relations with suppliers and buyers. Developing mechanisms for managerial control and an internal information system also became important.

The case of Kolektor also supports the hypothesis that companies in the former socialist countries that were not located in the major (capital) city have proved to be in many instances much better suited to face world market competition. Those in the center frequently built their "competitive advantages" on good links with politicians and bankers, in this way acquiring various benefits and protection but thereby neglecting the strengthening of their own innovation, investment, and production capabilities.

Finally, the Kolektor case demonstrates the importance of managerial ambitions to use partners to improve autonomy and, last but not least, not to be afraid of associating with foreign partners of FDI.

## NOTES

This case study is part of the ACE Project 94–0622–R, "A Comparative Study of Foreign Direct Investment in Bulgaria, the Czech Republic, and Slovenia," coordinated by Saul Estrin, London Business School.

The authors greatly appreciate the help in preparing this case study kindly provided by S. Petrič (general manager), Natasa Lusa Kren (legal adviser), and Anica Ursič Vončina (comptroller) of Kolektor.

1. Idrija is a small town in Slovenia (population 17,221) approximately 60 kilometers northwest of Ljubljana, the capital of Slovenia.

2. For instance:
• electrical motors for household appliances, such as vacuum cleaners, washing machines, and so forth;
• electrical motors for electronic hand tools, such as grinding machines, circular saws, and drilling machines, and electrical motors for the automotive industry, such as starters for cars and trucks, windshield wipers, fans, window openers, and so forth;
• electric motors for special machines, such as locomotive engines, and so forth.

3. Quasi because it did not enable foreigners to own their part of the company. A foreigner could participate in management, but his share was in fact a kind of long-term credit arrangement. The important point was that it enabled participation in management and a sharing of profits. Management was shared with a so-called workers' council with strong worker participation.

4. This was before the adoption of new FDI legislation in what was then Yugoslavia at the end of 1988, which was the first real equity FDI legislation. Only under this new law could foreigners become real co-owners or even 100 percent owners of domestic firms. Kolektor first wanted to conclude a new equity joint venture, but debates about this legislation took so long that the management of the company felt it would be better to prolong the existing contract.

5. Value added decreased from DM 17.6 million in 1991 to DM 14.2 million in 1993.

6. This was a special type of ownership in the former Yugoslavia that was not classic state ownership.

7. The decision to buy a 26 percent share was connected with the fact that this is exactly the percentage that gives veto power in Kolektor and thus enables management to put forward its own decisions.

8. According to the Slovenian Privatization Law, in the process of privatization, each company should transfer 10 percent of the equity to the pension fund, 10 percent to the restitution fund, and 20 percent to the development fund. The latter then sells these shares to the so-called authorized investment funds, which pay with the "ownership certificates" collected from Slovenian residents.

9. They became owners partly by exchanging ownership certificates for shares and partly by the so-called internal buyout of shares.

10. K&B probably became too large, too centralized, and very formalized, which reduces initiatives at all levels. Transformation from a limited-liability partnership to a joint-stock company was attempted but failed.

11. This way claims on K&B were also resolved. Such a transaction represented a

recapitalization of Kolektor, which is very important in view of the usual under-capitalization of Slovenian firms.

12. Kirkwood Industries is a U.S. multinational company established in 1944 in Cleveland, Ohio. Kirkwood has four divisions: Kirkwood Commutator, Kirkwood Carbon Co., Midwest Mica and Insulation, and Coaxial Dynamics.

13. Synatec Slovenia is a joint venture of Kolektor (45 percent), Synatec from Germany (45 percent), and two managers of the company with 5 percent each. The Synatec production program consist of the development of programmable logical controllers (PLGs) for Kolektor and for the general market. Synatec Slovenia is also an agent for Kloeckner and Mueller selling PLGs and switching technology. The company was developed out of the team formed in Kolektor in the 1980s dealing with computer programming. The group was progressing well and cooperated closely with the German partner, Synatec, which later became a JV partner. The board is composed of two of Kirkwood's representatives and two Slovenians. As a rule, they meet and evaluate annual, three-, six-, and nine-month results and development reports.

14. Costs in 1993–94 in fact increased, which was the consequence of higher copper and some other input prices on the world market. The accounting system in Slovenia also changed in 1994, which inflated costs, including some formerly excluded extraordinary expenses now included in costs.

15. The company has had only four general managers since its establishment. The first two were there for five and nine years, respectively, while the third one stayed for seventeen years (Jaklič and Česen 1995, p. 12).

16. These apartments, eleven at the seaside, three at a mountain ski resort, and two in spas, are now owned and managed by FMR.

17. One can estimate that a reduction of fifty workers would increase efficiency.

18. This period is taken as a basis because Slovenia became independent in 1991 and more reliable statistics are available for that period. Inflation before was also so high that it makes comparison very unreliable anyway.

19. The first was filed on August 12, 1982. It refers to the method for manufacturing unfinished parts of pressed material commutators. Patent protection is granted in Bulgaria, Denmark, European patent countries, Russia, Romania, Spain, the United States, and Slovenia. The second patent was applied for on August 13, 1982. It refers to the method of producing a semifinished commutator. Patent protection is granted in Germany, Romania, Spain, the United Kingdom, the United States, and Slovenia. The third one was applied for on December 24, 1991, and refers to the method for the production of a molded plastic flat rotary switch. Patent protection is granted in European patent countries, Germany, the United States, and Slovenia. The fourth one refers to the method of preparation and production of commutators and was applied for on May 18, 1992. The patent protection was granted for European patent countries, Germany, and Slovenia.

20. The machine-making unit, employing twenty-seven workers, could be added, at least partly, to R&D activities as well. It develops new machines for new products.

21. Actually a provision on free mutual exchange of knowledge and the equal sharing of it.

22. They do not produce tools themselves due to lack of capacities.

23. This year, the production of the commutator profile substantially increased, as did the production of large commutators and the assembly of switches.

24. Export to former East Germany, which was Kolektor's major buyer among the

socialist countries, became export to the EU. Second, the East German market started to be supplied from what was now Germany. At the same time, some products were discontinued.

25. Director Petrič even claims that Kolektor is not alone in this. Many Slovenian companies are better than many firms from Italy, France, or Spain regarding prompt deliveries (1995).

26. In view of the fact that its investments in R&D are twice as big as those of Kirkwood and K&B, the latter firms may lag behind technologically in the future (Jaklič and Česen 1995, p. 17).

27. Such a transition was facilitated by the fact that it was not difficult for Kolektor to convince its buyers that it was already producing commutators before, sold under the K&B trademark. The situation would have been much more difficult if Kolektor were producing for customers whom it did not know.

## BIBLIOGRAPHY

Dahlman, C.; B. Ross-Larson; and L. Westphal. 1989. "Managing Technological Development." WB Staff Working Papers No. 717.

Jaklič, M., and T. Česen. 1995. *Poskus kooperativne internacionalizacije*. Ljubljana: Kolektor.

———. 1995. *Internationalization Through Strategic Networks and Equality of Partners*. Kolektor. 1995. Basic Information on the Company.

"The Largest 300." 1995. *Gospodarski vestnik* (Ljubljana). June 22: 44.

Petrič, S. "Včasih tudi bankrot prav pride." *Delo*, Saturday supplement, June 10, 1995: 34.

Porter, M. 1990. *The Competitive Advantage of Nations*. New York: The Free Press.

Svetličič, M., and M. Rojec. 1994. "Foreign Direct Investment and the Transformation of Central European Economies." *Management International Review*, 1994, no. 4: 293–312.

Svetličič, M.; M. Rojec; and S. Lebar. 1994. "Internationalization Strategy of Slovenian Firms; German Market Case, High Speed Competition in Europe," ed. K. Obloj. *Proceedings of the 20th Annual Conference of EIBA*. Warsaw.

# 2

# Sarrio Slovenija Ltd.
*Cartonboard-Producing Company in the Control of Saffa S.p.A. from Italy*

Matija Rojec and Marjan Svetličič

## INTRODUCTION

The acquisition of Sarrio Slovenija, which at the time of its acquisition was named Papirnica (Papermill) Količevo, by Sarrio S.A. from Spain, in which Saffa S.p.A. of Italy has 65 percent majority ownership, was one of the first, and is still among the largest, foreign privatizations and foreign investments in general in Slovenia. Under the terms of the acquisition agreement signed on July 27, 1992, Sarrio S.A. acquired a 76 percent equity share in the then socially owned Papirnica Količevo. The remaining 24 percent remained in the hands of the Development Fund of Slovenia; of that, 14.4 percent was intended for subsequent distribution to the employees on the basis of the pending privatization legislation. Subsequently, in 1994 these employees sold their shares to Sarrio S.A., and they were the first workers in Slovenia to have cashed in their ownership certificates at the nominal value. By February 1995, Sarrio S.A. had acquired the remaining shares from the Development Fund. In March 1995, the EBRD, as a part of the terms of DM 19.6 million financing, acquired 3.94 percent of the company's share from Sarrio S.A., subject to clearly defined conditions and restrictions. The share of Sarrio S.A. was thus reduced to 96.06 percent.

## HISTORY AND GENERAL CHARACTERISTICS OF SARRIO SLOVENIJA

Sarrio Slovenija is a limited-liability company for the production of coated cartonboard, predominantly from recycled fibers, with 385 employees. Total production in 1994 was 94,669 tons, and net sales were DM 80 million. In 1995, total production was 95,873 tons, and net sales were DM 99.9 million. Plans for 1996 were for 100,371 tons and DM 99.0 million. According to the firm's balance sheet, on December 31, 1994, the assets of Sarrio Slovenija were DM 169 million, of which 75.2 percent was financed by equity capital and reserves and 13.6 percent by medium-term loans. In 1994, Sarrio Slovenija was the seventy-fourth largest Slovenian enterprise by sales and thirty-eighth by assets (*Gospodarski vestnik* 1995b). In the first half of 1994, Sarrio Slovenija exported goods with a value of DM 25.1 million and imported goods with a value of DM 20.5 million, which put it in thirty-ninth place among the largest Slovenian exporters (*Gospodarski vestnik* 1995a). Its major foreign market is Germany, but exports to other EU countries are increasing as well. Sarrio Slovenija also has important customers in Egypt, Croatia, and the Czech Republic.

Papirnica Količevo was established in 1920. The first cartonboard machine was installed in 1927 and the first paper machine in 1930. In 1947, the company was nationalized. In 1961, the second cartonboard machine was installed and in 1979 the third. At the time of privatization, the company was a medium-sized producer of cartonboard with 640 employees, 90,000–100,000 tons of annual production, and annual sales between DM 50 million and DM 60 million. Thirty percent of cartonboard production was sold in Slovenia, and the rest was exported, 10 percent to other parts of the former Yugoslavia and 60 percent elsewhere.

There was a major increase in production capacities in Papirnica Količevo in 1979, when the installation of the third cartonboard machine increased daily production from 100 to 400 tons of cartonboard. The investment in new capacities was almost entirely financed by foreign credits and by a contractual joint venture with Andritz/Siemens. The amount of foreign liabilities originating from this investment was approximately DM 99 million. These liabilities were regularly serviced until 1982. From then on, repayments became an increasingly heavy burden for Papirnica Količevo. Before the acquisition, Papirnica Količevo's foreign liabilities were DM 50 million.

Prior to its privatization, Papirnica Količevo faced two major problems, undercapitalization and excessive debt.

• Due to the unfavorable financial situation, almost no investments or production modernizations occurred in Papirnica Količevo in the few years before privatization; all efforts were concentrated on resolving the accumulated financial problems, such as servicing debt and financing current operations. Nevertheless, the company was no longer able to service its foreign liabilities.

• This inability to service foreign loans became even more of a problem when, due to the loss of the former Yugoslav market, the only possible solution for Papirnica Količevo proved to be to direct much more of its production to foreign markets. Such an effort, however, required additional investments and an intensification of contacts with potential buyers abroad due to the intensive competition in the cartonboard industry. Papirnica Količevo could afford neither.

• During the general rescheduling of Yugoslav foreign credits in 1982, the major part of Papirnica Količevo's foreign credits was transferred to the local bank LB Banka Domžale. Consequently, the bank had a considerable part of its total loans tied up in Papirnica Količevo, which distorted the bank's portfolio structure and limited its ability to diversify its loans, thus posing the threat that the bank would be unable to service Papirnica Količevo adequately in the future.

The management of Papirnica Količevo realized that attracting a strategic foreign investor who would recapitalize the company was the only feasible solution. Consequently, in 1989 Papirnica Količevo started discussions with potential foreign investors.

## CARTONBOARD INDUSTRY AND MARKET STRUCTURE

Cartonboard is a material that is used for the most part in the packaging industry:

(a) Cartonboard is coated or uncoated. The major difference between the two, as far as their use is concerned, is that only the coated cartonboard can carry print. Coated cartonboard is used mostly in the packaging of food, pharmaceuticals, cosmetics, detergents, small household appliances, sports products, and cigarettes. The Sarrio Group produces exclusively coated cartonboard.

(b) Cartonboard is produced from virgin fibers or from recycled fibers (waste paper). Fifty-seven percent of world production of cartonboard is accounted for by cartonboard produced from recycled fibers. In the case of the Sarrio Group, this share is as high as 91.6 percent.

Until the end of 1992, the cartonboard industry was characterized by growth and stability, which was not typical for the paper sector in general. In 1993, world consumption of cartonboard was 25.1 million tons, of which Western Europe's share was 6.6 million tons. In the 1981–93 period, the average annual growth rate of world consumption was 2.6 percent. However, in 1993 the European demand for cartons made from recycled fibers decreased by 4 percent. The most difficult year for the European producers of coated cartonboard since the oil crisis of 1974 was 1993. The reason for the sluggish demand was the widespread economic recession, which led to reductions in inventories of consumables and of durable consumer goods and consequently to a reduction in the demand for coated cartonboard. In this major contraction in the general demand for cartonboard materials, the products of the Sarrio Group, being made predominantly of recycled fibers, were among those that have seen much less of a reduction in consumption compared with products from other fungible materials and particularly those made of virgin fibers.

At the end of 1993, signs of an increase in demand for coated cartonboard made of recycled fibers were evident. The crisis that characterized the sector from the end of 1992 through almost all of 1993 receded. The principal signs that confirmed this trend were (i) the increase in prices, which in the case of coated cartonboard made of recycled fibers was over 20 percent in 1994 and 14 percent from the end of 1994 to the end of 1995; (ii) the high level of growth of demand in Europe and globally as well; and (iii) substantial back orders, which should allow for increased efficiency in the management of the factories.

There are also other recently emerging trends that could favor cartonboard producers in the future, and especially the Sarrio Group, which is characterized by production using recycled fibers:

(a) the switch within the packaging industry from nonrecyclable materials, such as plastics, to recyclable, "environmentally friendly" forms of packaging, such as cartonboard;

(b) within the cartonboard industry, a shift from virgin fiber–based grades toward recycled fiber–based grades made from waste paper;

(c) increasing pressure from environmentalists and legislators alike to reduce the absolute volume of packaging to encourage the use of materials made of recycled fibers.

Therefore, the future competitive position of cartonboard, and in particular the coated cartonboard made of recycled fibers, should improve relative to that of other products used in packaging, especially in view of environmental considerations. In addition, the strategy of the producers of consumer products to reduce packaging, which was one of the causes of the reduced demand for cartonboard, is being reconsidered due to the increase in consumer protests against the fall in the efficiency of packaging systems.

The European coated-cartonboard industry for general packaging is dominated by four major manufacturers; the remainder are small producers.[1] At this moment, the total production capacity of coated cartonboard both from virgin (FBB) and recycled (WLC) fibers in Western Europe is 4.6 million tons, over 60 percent of which is supplied by four producers. The largest of these is Mayr Melnhof from Austria, with approximately 1.06 million tons; the second is Sarrio S.A., together with affiliated companies, with 844,000 tons of annual production; the third is Stora, with approximately 670,000 tons; and the fourth is Enso Gutzeit, with approximately 570,000 tons. In recent years, concentration in the cartonboard industry has become noticeable. Based on the forecasts of European cartonboard consumption to the year 2000, the industry is expected to experience a consolidation phase over the next few years, which will provide considerable opportunities for efficient low-cost producers. The concentration of the cartonboard industry will continue, with a number of small producers being acquired by larger producers or merging with one another. The reasons for the concentration strategy can be found in the size of investments required to maintain efficient production, the cost of new production capacity, the resources required to develop products, the effort required to develop a worldwide marketing strategy, and the complexity of producing coated cartonboard from recycled fibers derived from a wide range of recycled materials.

## SAFFA AND THE SARRIO GROUP AND THEIR MOTIVATION TO ACQUIRE PAPIRNICA KOLIČEVO

Saffa S.p.A. began its activities as a producer of matches. In 1955, it entered the production of coated cartonboard, with the intention of producing boxes for the matches it produced. In successive years, Saffa increasingly concentrated its resources on the production of car-

Figure 1. **The Saffa Group** (December 31, 1995)

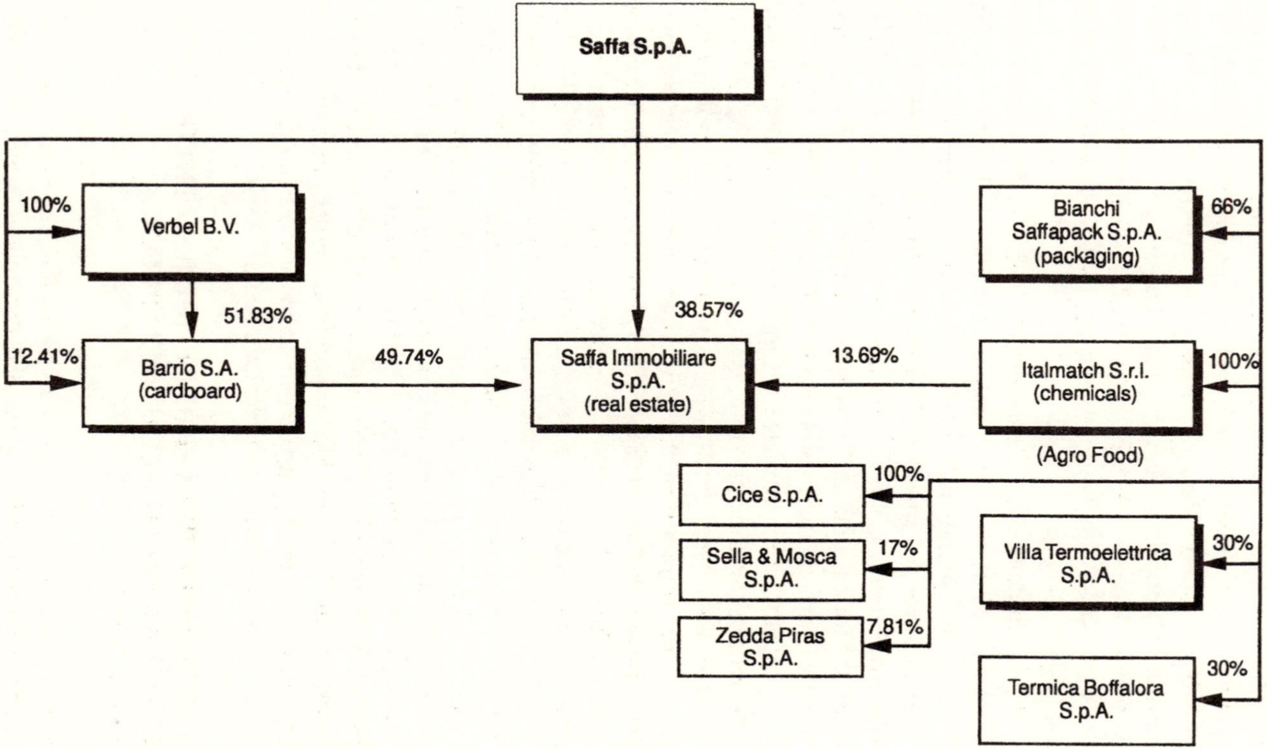

tonboard and later on packaging production. In the 1983–94 period, the cartonboard production capacity of Saffa increased from 183,000 to 844,000 tons annually, of which 773,000 tons were of coated cartonboard from recycled fibers. By 1994, the Saffa Group became the seventh largest cartonboard producer in the world and the second largest producer in Europe of cartonboard from recycled fibers after Mayr Melnhof of Austria.

On January 1, 1988, after a series of acquisitions, Saffa was transformed into a diversified industrial holding, with consolidated annual sales of approximately 800 billion lira in 1994[2] and over 1,000 billion lira estimated in 1995, operating in five sectors: cartonboard, packaging, chemicals, agro-food, and real estate (see Figure 1). The cartonboard sector represents the core business of Saffa; in 1994, it accounted for 72.5 percent (584.6 billion lira) of Saffa's overall sales, and predictions for 1995 forecast a further increase to 77.2 percent (783.4 billion lira).

Sarrio S.A. is the major company in the sector of production and distribution of coated cartonboard in the Group. It is 65 percent owned by Saffa (see Figure 1) and directly owns six production sites, two in Spain, three in Italy, and one in Slovenia, in which eight production lines are installed. Coated cartonboard made from recycled fibers makes up 91.6 percent of production. The productive capacity of the Sarrio Group is 25 percent of that available for coated cartonboard from recycled fibers in Europe. Sarrio S.A. also owns minority interests in the Italian producer of coated cartonboard from recycled fibers, Reno De Medici S.p.A., the second Italian producer, and in a Tunisian company, Cartonnerie Tunisienne S.A. (see Figure 2). If the production of these two companies is aggregated with that of the factories of Sarrio S.A., the combined productive capacity for coated cartonboard from recycled fibers would be more than 30 percent of that available in Europe.

Eighty-seven percent of the production of the Sarrio Group is destined for European markets. In addition to the markets of the countries where Sarrio has production capacities, Sarrio's market position is particularly strong in Germany, France, and Belgium. The geographical position of Sarrio's production sites particularly facilitates distribution because they are equidistant from the markets of Western and Eastern Europe and near major European ports. Sarrio's production sites are situated along a line that runs along the whole south of Eu-

Figure 2. **The Sarrio Group** (December 31, 1995)

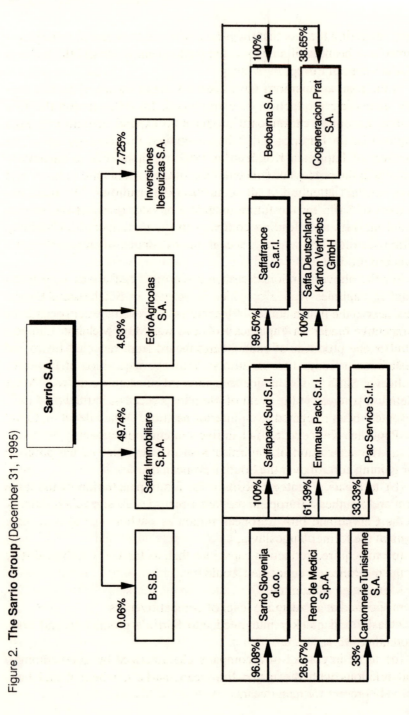

*Source:* Saffa S.p.A.

rope, reflecting the fact that the production and commercial strategies of Sarrio have been, until now, oriented predominantly toward the markets of south-central Europe.

In the past, acquisitions have been the major means of Saffa's rapidly increasing production of cartonboard. In 1983, it was the first leading European cartonboard producer to expand activities through acquisitions in Europe, and it has continued this strategy up to the takeover of Papirnica Količevo in 1992. Saffa intends to participate actively in the process of concentration of the cartonboard industry and pays constant attention to all acquisition opportunities. The main objectives of Saffa for the future include a broader presence on international markets as a leading company in the cartonboard and folding carton sector, with the major accent on environment-compatible materials and products.

For the above-mentioned strategic reasons,[3] Saffa was very interested in Papirnica Količevo, which is situated in Southeastern Europe very near to the Italian border.[4] This interest was even greater because the competitive bidder for Papirnica Količevo was Mayr Melnhof, Europe's number one producer of coated cartonboard from recycled fibers and Saffa's major competitor in Europe. With the acquisition of Papirnica Količevo, Saffa took a major step forward in catching up with Mayr Melnhof, whereas in the event of Melnhof's success, Saffa would have definitely been relegated to an inferior pasition.[5] When deciding to bid for Papirnica Količevo, Saffa had five strategic objectives:

(a) the acquisition of Papirnica Količevo was part of the program for gaining control over the South European market;

(b) to create a strategic position for future penetration of the large East and Southeast European markets because of Količevo's proximity to the Central and East European region as a whole and also to other parts of the former Yugoslavia;[6]

(c) to acquire production capacities that, as far as the technical state of the machinery is concerned, could be:

• expanded substantially;

• operated at an adequate level of competitiveness;

• easily and quickly integrated into Sarrio's production and commercial network;

(d) to be in control of a company characterized by good commercial relations with the major European markets, where it had been actively present for many years;

(e) to make further and important steps forward in the realization of increasing the expansion of Sarrio's production potential and in the improvement of its competitive position.

## PROCESS OF NEGOTIATION AND
## ACQUISITION OF PAPIRNICA KOLIČEVO

The case of the foreign privatization of Papirnica Količevo is an example of a direct sale through a combination of the acquisition of existing social capital and immediate additional investment. This was one of the first cases in which the Development Fund of the Republic of Slovenia, hereafter referred to as the Fund, transferred all the social capital of Papirnica Količevo to the Fund and assumed an ownership position in the target company before the transaction. In other words, from the formal legal point of view, the seller of the equity capital of Papirnica Količevo was the Fund.

Papirnica Količevo was sold through a competitive bidding between two major European cartonboard companies, Mayr Melnhof and Saffa. It was a complex transaction that involved acquisition of a part of the social capital transferred to the Fund, additional investment in, that is, recapitalization of, Papirnica Količevo, the solution of the denationalization problem, and an attempt partially to rehabilitate the local bank, which was jeopardized by its extensive loans to Papirnica Količevo.

In September 1991, Papirnica Količevo announced a public tender in which interested buyers were invited to submit offers for the recapitalization of Količevo. Although Saffa had signed a letter of intent for the recapitalization of Papirnica Količevo in 1990, it did not react to the tender. Mayr Melnhof was the only firm that submitted an offer. The reason was the feeling at Saffa that Papirnica Količevo had already more or less settled the deal with Mayr Melnhof or at least that the management of Količevo was more in favor of Mayr Melnhof. Indeed, the management of Papirnica Količevo was in favor of Mayr Melnhof.

Papirnica Količevo continued its negotiations with Mayr Melnhof, which made two subsequent offers. Both were rejected by the Agency of Privatization of the Republic of Slovenia, hereafter referred to as the Agency, which had to approve any such transaction, mostly because the value of Papirnica Količevo implied by the offer was too low. At that moment, negotiations were in a rather ambiguous situation, but in March 1992, Reno De Medici, in which Sarrio S.A. has a minority interest, suddenly expressed its interest in investing in Količevo and prepared an informal offer. The result was that the workers' council of Papirnica Količevo rejected the last offer of Mayr Melnhof and re-opened the bidding process. Before that, the Development Fund had assumed a 100 percent ownership position in Papirnica Količevo.[7]

The reopened bidding process based on a restricted tender via letters of invitation was prepared and managed by the Agency/Fund. Letters of invitation were sent to Saffa, Mayr Melnhof, and Reno De Medici. Only Saffa and Mayr Melnhof submitted offers. The invitation letter structured the proposed transaction in detail. It set out financial and commercial arrangements through which a bidder would take a stake in Papirnica Količevo and set out a scheme of minority shareholders' rights. It also required the submitted proposals to pay considerable attention to issues of the future, postacquisition development of Papirnica Količevo along the following lines:

(a) In view of the required capital equipment imports if Papirnica Količevo were to realize development plans, bidders were invited to put forward their proposals regarding capital expenditures and the development of the company. The investment plans were to identify the steps that would be taken to modernize the plant and equipment and the necessary guarantees that would ensure the implementation of these plans. Bidders were also asked to quantify the level of capital investment proposed in the next five years and its impact on the financial structure of Papirnica Količevo.

(b) The management of Papirnica Količevo and the Agency/Fund were aware of the need to reduce employment in certain areas and to establish an up-to-date organizational structure in the company. The invitation letter asked the bidders to address these issues in their proposals, including indemnities provided for the reduction of redundant workers. The invitation letter, however, especially stressed that proposals that created new jobs in Slovenia would be particularly welcome.

(c) A continued commitment to the development of staff, the maintenance of employment, and the improvement of the living standards of employees were also important areas to be covered in the proposals. Investors were also required to address training issues for all grades of employees in their proposals.

Invited bidders were told in the invitation letter that, "in evaluating proposals, the price offered for the company, its future prospects under

Table 1

**Evaluation of Bids for Acquisition of Papirnica Količevo**

| Criterion | Maximum number of points | Number of points attributed to | |
|---|---|---|---|
| | | Saffa | Mayr Melnholn |
| A. Price offered | 30 | 30 | 0 |
| B. Immediate additional equity investment | 20 | 0 | 20 |
| C. Medium and long-term investments in fixed assets | 10 | 10 | 0 |
| D. Employment policy[a] | 10 | 10 | 10 |
| E. Protection of minority shareholders | 10 | 10 | 10 |
| F. Financial, market, and production status of buyer | 5 | 5 | 5 |
| G. Premature repayments or assuming credit liabilities of Papirnica Količevo | 5 | not applicable | |
| H. Other criteria according to the discretion of the committee | 10 | not defined | |
| Total number of points | 100 | 65 | 45 |

[a]Additional employment, retaining the existing level of employment, reduction of employment (indemnities).

changed ownership arrangements, and other aspects of the arrangements in the light of the priorities set out in the invitation letter will be taken into account. The overall economic implications of the acquisition for Slovenia will be considered as well. Price will be an important factor but not the sole or necessarily the main criterion for deciding the winning bidder."

On the basis of criteria for the final evaluation of offers (see Table 1) announced in advance, the bidding committee, consisting of representatives of Papirnica Količevo, the Agency/Fund, and the local bank LB Banka Domžale, decided to select Saffa as the winning bidder. The committee felt that Saffa's offer would ensure the development, competitiveness, and financial prosperity of Papirnica Količevo. Saffa's offer included the immediate purchase of equity capital, immediate increase of equity capital (recapitalization), as well as additional medium and long-term investments in fixed assets. The final contract also contained the system of minority shareholders' rights proposed in the letter of invitation.

According to Saffa, they won the bid "probably because, together with an adequate and better price offered, we also proposed a midterm development plan of the company that we gave assurances would realized and that we, in fact, are already realizing." This plan defined not only the technical investments to be made, but also provided (i) criteria in the field of employment and human-resource management, with the methods to be used for the resolution of the problem of redundant workers; (ii) a program of computerization of accounting; (iii) activities in the field of environmental conservation; and (iv) the mode by which Papirnica Količevo would be integrated into the Sarrio Group.

On July 27, 1992, Sarrio S.A. and the Development Fund signed the agreement by which Sarrio S.A. became the 76 percent owner of Papirnica Količevo. The agreement also stated that the share of Sarrio S.A. would progressively increase to achieve 100 percent by February 1995. The total cost of the acquisition for Sarrio S.A. was DM 106.2 million. Besides, Papirnica Količevo was recapitalized in the amount of DM 30 million.

## CHANGES IN PAPIRNICA KOLIČEVO AFTER THE ACQUISITION

After making a detailed audit of organizational structure, of production efficiency, of product quality, of the relations between the factory and the environment, of the commercial position on various markets on which Papirnica Količevo operated, Sarrio S.A. prepared a first program of intervention in Sarrio Slovenija that was intended to improve rapidly the general efficiency of the company. Sarrio's major objectives in the reorganization of the company were (i) a significant reduction of employment; (ii) the elimination of activities not directly connected with the production of cartonboard; (iii) streamlining of the central functions of the company; and (iv) improvement of the quality of management. To realize these objectives, Sarrio started immediately to do the following after the acquisition:

(a) to change the company culture in Sarrio Slovenija in order to bring its operating mode and management style, as soon as possible, up to the level of the Sarrio Group. This operation, called "homogenization of culture," meant the preparation of Sarrio Slovenija to be able to apply the common management practices of all of Sarrio's companies. The aim was to integrate Sarrio Slovenija organizationally in every

Figure 3. **Organizational Structure of Saffa's Cartonboard Sector**

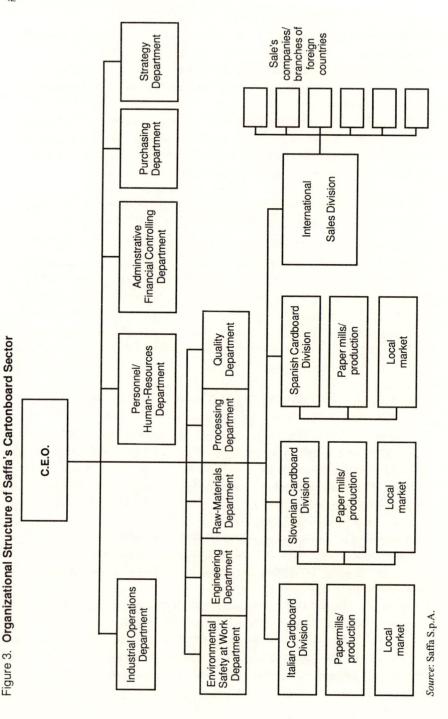

*Source:* Saffa S.p.A.

detail into the cartonboard sector of Saffa, which is managed centrally from Milan;

(b) to reduce employment and unbundle noncore activities;

(c) to improve efficiency and the competitiveness of the production system in Sarrio Slovenija.

The realization of these measures has been supported by investments of DM 23.6 million in the 1993–95 period: DM 5.7 million in 1993; DM 11.8 million in 1994; and DM 6.1 million in 1995. Most of the investment financing has been provided by Sarrio S.A.[8]

### The Position of Sarrio Slovenija in the Organizational Structure of the Group: "Homogenization of Culture"

Figure 3 presents the organizational structure of Sarrio's cartonboard sector. The main characteristic is that the management of all the country's cartonboard divisions is maintained directly from Sarrio's headquarters, that is, by the chief executive officer in Magenta (Milan). The organizational structure of Sarrio's cartonboard sector is centralized in a typically divisional manner, and its organizational philosophy is "We are a group; the rules are the same for everyone, for Sarrio S.A. as well as for Sarrio Slovenija." In this context, the so-called "homogenization of culture," that is, that all divisions are capable of using the same business procedures and techniques, is of crucial importance for running the Group as a whole.

In the context of the organizational structure of the Sarrio Group, Sarrio Slovenija assumes the position of one of the country cartonboard divisions (Italian, Slovenian, Spanish) that have the status of profit centers. The management of each profit center has full responsibility regarding production efficiency, sales, administration of financial resources originating from cash flow and from shareholders' capital, human-resource management, safety at work, and the environment.

Communications between Sarrio Slovenija and Sarrio are based on a divisional principle. Chiefs of departments in Sarrio Slovenija have appropriate contact persons in the respective departments of Sarrio; for instance, the production manager in Sarrio Slovenija with a person or persons from the Industrial Operations Department in Sarrio, the chief of the financial department in Sarrio Slovenija has a contact person in the Administrative/ Financial/Accounting Department in Sarrio, and so forth. These contacts are on a continuous basis, at least once a week.

For Sarrio as a centrally managed group, the most important post-acquisition problem was to integrate Sarrio Slovenija as quickly as possible into its organizational structure. To harmonize the operating and management style in Sarrio Slovenija with that of the Group as a whole, Sarrio began to change the company culture in Sarrio Slovenija. "Homogenization of culture" had the aim of preparing Sarrio Slovenija to adopt the common management style of all the Sarrio companies.

To speed up the "homogenization of culture," Sarrio has made intensive efforts to integrate Sarrio Slovenija into the Group, that is, to establish intensive cooperation between Sarrio Slovenija and the other companies of the Group. This was done via a speedy transfer of all the know-how and procedures, administrative, budgeting and performance analysis, purchasing/procurement, human-resource management, quality control, and customer service, in use in Sarrio S.A. to Sarrio Slovenija. The management and staff of Sarrio Slovenija have had full freedom in visiting any unit of the Group and to have contacts on all organizational levels to get information and knowledge of any kind relevant for the cartonboard sector. The "homogenization of culture" process began with managers and then spread downward.

The first "homogenization of culture" measure applied immediately after the acquisition was the introduction of a new management control system. Sarrio introduced standard methods for its companies abroad. Sarrio's management control system is composed of two major elements: the annual budget (plan) and detailed monthly reports:

(a) Every Sarrio company and division has its annual budget/plan. The budget/plan is prepared in the following phases: (i) headquarters provides the major elements for the preparation of the annual budget/plan to the companies; (ii) on this basis, the companies prepare their draft annual budgets/plans; (iii) the draft budget/plan is then discussed with headquarters, and after two or three rounds of discussions the final annual budget/plan is adopted. In 1994, Saffa introduced three-year planning periods; every company has to prepare a three-year plan. During the next year, the plan would be a real budget/plan; during the second year, it would be more of a forecast; and during the third year, it would be more of an indication.[9]

(b) The second element of Sarrio's management control system consists of detailed monthly reports. Every Sarrio company or division has to send very detailed monthly reports on sales, production, working capital, and finance to headquarters by the eighth day in the following month.

Monthly reports have the following basic elements: (i) profit–loss statement for the current month; (ii) profit–loss statement for the period from the beginning of the year until the end of the current month; (iii) deviations from the budget/plan; (iv) analysis of reasons for the deviations, for example, trends in the price of cartonboard, deviations of the geographical or product mix of sales, structure of transport costs, deviations from the standard efficiency of the production process, the trend in the prices of raw materials, and so forth. On that basis, the management of Sarrio Slovenija, in cooperation with headquarters, prepares the appropriate policy to eliminate the negative deviations.

Parallel to the introduction of the new management control system, the training of people to execute the new system was initiated. Training was in Italy and in Slovenia. Approximately twenty people from Slovenia were trained for a month each. Sarrio's experience is that, in the case of Sarrio Slovenija, the transfer of the controlling and organization system was quite rapid and successful.[10] Within seven or eight months after the acquisition, Sarrio got the first monthly report from Sarrio Slovenija.[11] Headquarters considers the successful introduction of the mew management control system to be one of the most important objectives achieved to date. Nevertheless, Sarrio considers further improvements in this field as necessary if Sarrio Slovenija is really to be made competitive on the international cartonboard market. That is why Sarrio constantly motivates the staff of Sarrio Slovenija to go to its factories in Italy for training, especially to a twin factory in Belluno, near Venice. Although this factory is very near, the staff of Sarrio Slovenija has not been too eager to take advantage of this opportunity very often. Probable reasons are language, although Sarrio offers to provide translators, and differences in style.

Purchases of raw materials from abroad and all the exports of Sarrio Slovenija and the other Sarrio companies are handled centrally by the respective departments for Sarrio as a group:

• all the purchasing of raw material from abroad for all the Sarrio companies is handled by Sarrio's Raw Materials Department (see Figure 3);

• all the nonlocal sales of Sarrio Slovenija and other Sarrio companies are managed by Sarrio's International Sales Division, which has a number of companies and branches abroad (see Figure 3).

The sales and purchasing department of Sarrio Slovenija is totally integrated into Sarrio's purchasing and sales network and system.[12]

Sarrio Slovenija handles only sales and purchases on the local market, that is, in Slovenia. However, this does not mean that Sarrio Slovenija just delivers certain quantities of products to the International Sales Department of Sarrio, which then handles the sales. Although all the sales and purchases go via Sarrio companies responsible for purchasing and sales, country cartonboard divisions in Spain, Italy, and Slovenia behave like independent companies. The general manager of Sarrio Slovenija is responsible for the profit-and-loss statement of the company and must negotiate with Sarrio's International Sales Department about the price of his cartonboard to be sold and about the commission that Sarrio Slovenija will pay to the International Sales Department. The same is true about purchasing.

In short, international purchasing and sales in the Sarrio Group are centralized and coordinated on the group level, but individual divisions otherwise behave as independent companies, and they negotiate the price and commission. The same principle would apply to maintenance and other services provided by Sarrio's Engineering Department to Sarrio Slovenija.

Therefore, although Sarrio is organized in divisions and is strictly coordinated from the center, headquarters encourages individual divisions, such as Sarrio Slovenija, to act like companies.

### Reduction of Employment and Unbundling of Noncore Activities

Low labor productivity was one of the major problems of Papirnica Količevo before its acquisition. Given the total output of Papirnica Količevo and organization structure of similar companies abroad, the number of employees, 664 at the time of acquisition, was far too high. The reduction of employment in Papirnica Količevo was anticipated already in the acquisition agreement between Sarrio and the Development Fund.

Excessive employment in Papirnica Količevo was partly due to traditional overstaffing in socialist enterprises and partly due to technological problems, the production of outdated products and services, and a low level of automatization in administration but was above all due to the organization of the company. A number of activities were carried out in the factory that were not directly connected with the production of cartonboard. Papirnica Količevo had its own cafeteria, a large maintenance workshop, and its own unit for the production of pallets for transporting cartonboard that employed 51 people. Sarrio took the following immediate steps:

(a) Activities that were not directly connected to the production of cartonboard were "privatized" and in such a way eliminated. The pallet production unit, the maintenance workshop, and the cafeteria were separated from the mill and taken over by the employees of these units, in the case of the maintenance workshop in combination with some external partners. They are all now in private hands. They provide part of their services to the mill but also to other potential customers, and they are now better managed than before. For instance, the new owners of the cafeteria built a very nice new restaurant that is patronized not only by employees of Sarrio Slovenija but also by the general public.

(b) The cleaning and security staff were spun off in similar fashion. They were dismissed from the company, but, at the same time, they were hired on a contract basis to provide cleaning and security services.

(c) Another method for the resolution of the redundancy problem was that the company paid a certain amount to the pension fund to fund early retirement to employees who were near retirement.

In this way, the number of employees in Količevo was cut from 664 to 385 in less than two years. Comparisons with other cartonboard factories in the Sarrio Group show the need for further reduction of labor costs. Sarrio is gradually introducing the computerization of production and administrative processes and new production technology in Sarrio Slovenija. This will reduce the number of employees to 368 in the near future.

### Improving the Efficiency and Competitiveness of Production

The improvement of the efficiency and competitiveness of the production system was also addressed after the acquisition. These problems were tackled and partly resolved by the management staff of Sarrio Slovenija. Among the problems addressed were the following:

- costs of production, including the use of raw materials, energy, and people according to predetermined standards;
- delivery of production;
- quality of products;

• customer service, including accuracy of delivery and technical assistance;

• efficiency of the plant and machinery as a basic condition for assuring the efficiency, quality, and low costs of production.

Basically, the above issues could be grouped under two headings, quality and variable cost.

*Quality Problem*

In the cartonboard industry of today, quality is a "religion." Sarrio paid a great deal of attention to the quality issue after the acquisition because low quality, in the broadest sense of the word, was the crucial problem at Papirnica Količevo before the acquisition. For instance, they were not in a position to tell costumers when they would be able to produce something, and they almost never delivered goods on time. There were three major reasons for quality problems in Papirnica Količevo. The first was related to technological problems, which existed because indebtedness prevented new investments for many years. The second related to the problems of internal organization of the company, and the third related to the fact that Papirnica Količevo had a bad payment record and, therefore, bad relations with its suppliers. Suppliers would not deliver raw material on time, and the raw material delivered was not of good quality. This had an adverse impact on the quality of products.

There are two modes of quality control in the cartonboard industry. The first is the control at the end of the production line when the controller simply tries to find inadequate products and to eliminate them. This is a rather costly method of quality control. The inadequate products are either thrown away or put back into the production process to make them acceptable. In both cases, substantial additional costs cannot be avoided. The second mode of control is the control of inputs and of the production process itself. The idea is to find out why there is a low percentage of products of acceptable quality and to establish a control system consisting of a continuous checking of the production process itself. Quality improvement by this second method cannot be obtained through the improvement of inadequate products but rather through the improvement of technology and human resources, that is, through the elimination of reasons for inadequate quality.

Immediately after the acquisition, Sarrio began to introduce qual-

ity control in production and to eliminate reasons for low-quality products. The changes introduced in the production process and technology
included the following:

(a) Sourcing high-quality raw materials by improving relations with
suppliers. One of the major determinants of quality in the cartonboard industry is the type of raw materials used. Only high-quality
raw materials should be used. Prior to the acquisition, Papirnica
Količevo had a bad payment history with its suppliers and was not able
to get high-quality raw materials on time. The intervention of Sarrio
stemmed the cash-flow problems in Sarrio Slovenija and eliminated its
image of a bad payer. This enabled the company to get high-quality
inputs on time.

(b) Introduction of differential treatment of different kinds of waste
paper. After the acquisition, a considerable improvement was made in
the treatment of raw materials. This has been of major importance for
improving quality since Papirnica Količevo uses a large amount of waste
paper collected in towns as its raw material. Waste paper from industry
is of good quality, but waste paper collected in towns is of low quality.
For the latter, special treatment is needed to assure the quality level of
the final product.

(c) Investing in new machinery. In the production of cartonboard,
there are a number of delicate steps that jeopardize the quality of the final
product. First, the cartonboard production process is characterized by
intensive use of water, which can easily deform the product. The second critical point for the quality of the final product is in the drying
process; the third is the coating, and the fourth is the final cutting of
the cartonboard rolls.[13] All these stages in the production of cartonboard are rather sophisticated, and in the whole process there are many
possibilities to make mistakes and thus reduce the quality of the final
product. To reduce these mistakes and consequently to improve quality, there was no other choice but to invest in new machinery. In 1993–
95, Sarrio invested DM 23.6 million in the machinery for Sarrio Slovenija
and another DM 26 million in the 1996–97 period. This was necessary in
order to ensure good quality of products.

To improve the quality of products, Sarrio will invest an additional
DM 50 million in Sarrio Slovenija. The quality of production has
improved considerably in recent years, but it has to be improved further. Sarrio and the management are pretty clear about what should be
done to increase the quality to an adequate level. Sarrio plans to raise

Table 2

**Major Performance Indicators of Sarrio Slovenija in 1993–96**

|  | 1993 | 1994 | 1995 estimation | 1995 budget |
|---|---|---|---|---|
| Production (tons) | 86,572 | 94,669 | 95,873 | 100,371 |
| Sales (tons) | 84,615 | 96,364 | 93,484 | 100,371 |
| Net sales (thousand DM) | 67,896 | 79,970 | 99,870 | 99,029 |
| Gross income[a] (thousand DM) | 5,165 | 6,383 | 6,309 | 15,344 |
| Gross income/net sales (%) | 7.6 | 8.0 | 6.3 | 15.5 |

*Source*: Sarrio Slovenija d.o.o.
[a]Before depreciation, interest, and taxes.

the quality in Sarrio Slovenija to that achieved in its plant in Belluno near Venice. In Sarrio's development strategy, Sarrio Slovenija and the plant in Belluno are treated as twin factories. In the future Belluno is to specialize in low-grade cartonboard and Sarrio Slovenija in high-grade cartonboard, but first they have to achieve the same quality.

*Variable Cost Problem*

Before the acquisition, Papirnica Količevo had very high variable costs due to high costs of raw materials[14] and of energy, which, in Slovenia, is related to the high costs of natural gas. Lowering costs is one of the priority tasks in Sarrio Slovenija. Due to the lack of waste paper in Slovenia,[15] its price doubled in the past two years. The problem of high costs of raw materials has been resolved to a certain extent by the integration of Sarrio Slovenija into Sarrio's purchasing network, but it still remains one of the serious obstacles to better performance. On the other hand, nothing has been achieved with respect to the costs of energy. This remains an important problem, even more so knowing that the paper industry is very energy intensive. In Slovenia the costs of energy are especially high because natural gas is very expensive.[16] In principle, Sarrio has a technical solution to reduce the energy costs through the "cogeneration of energy," which would reduce the costs of thermic energy being intensively used in the cartonboard production process. However, the investment to do this is very high, and there is no adequate legislation regarding cogeneration in Slovenia.

## PERFORMANCE

Results achieved by Sarrio Slovenija in 1993 and 1994, preliminary results for 1995, and the budget for 1996 are shown in Table 2. Compared to 1993, production in 1994 increased by 9.3 percent and sales by 13.9 percent in physical terms (tons) and by 17.8 percent in value terms. For 1995, a slight reduction of sales in tons notwithstanding, sales in value terms increased by 24.9 percent; the strong increase is due to an exceptional increase in cartonboard prices, which followed an even more extraordinary increase of prices of raw materials for cartonboard production. Approximately 76 percent of sales in 1995 was realized through exports. According to plans, in 1996 Sarrio Slovenija will increase sales in physical terms by 7.4 percent, expecting to contribute approximately 16 percent to the consolidated sales of the Sarrio Group.

The years 1993 and 1994 saw intensive restructuring in Sarrio Slovenija, causing operating losses, and 1995 was characterized by variability of world demand for coated cartonboard and an exceptional change in the trend of the price of basic raw materials. Consequently, Sarrio Slovenija could not achieve financial results commensurate with its higher productive and organizational efficiency. Nevertheless, 1996 should bring a major increase in profits and also a considerable improvement in the gross income–net sales and operating income–net sales ratios. This is mostly due to the following factors:

• a higher share of total production consisting of coated cartonboards of higher quality, which obtain higher prices on the market;

• the use of better raw materials in production and improved treatment of raw materials;

• an organizational restructuring of the company and the introduction of a new management control system;

• new investments that have improved the quality of production.

## SOME OTHER ISSUES

### *Management*

In accordance with the acquisition agreement, Sarrio retained the entire Slovenian management of Papirnica Količevo. This included the general manager and four directors responsible for administration and finance, for production, for sales, and for human-resources management and organization, respectively. The general director kept his post although he had favored Mayr Melnhof in the acquisition process, and he proved to be loyal to the new owners. Sarrio wanted to keep him as the general manager because he was a rather good production manager and thus was important in the context of the centralized divisional organization of the Sarrio Group. However, after some time, he resigned due to health reasons, contrary to the general belief in Slovenia that he was forced out of his position. The next general manager appointed by Sarrio was a former director of Nova Banka—Creditanstalt, and he was brought in by Sarrio Slovenija because Sarrio considered the financial problems of the company to be important. Despite the belief that a financial expert would be the most appropriate choice, it soon became clear that this was a wrong judgment about the kind of person Sarrio needed as a general manager. In a system such as Sarrio's, where decision making on financial and most other issues is centralized, one really does not need a general manager who is a financial expert but rather a manager who is strong in technical and production issues.

On September 1, 1995, Sarrio Slovenija obtained a new general manager, the former director of the factory Gorenje Tiki. Like some other staff in Sarrio Slovenija, he was recruited through a corporate recruiter from Trieste. Sarrio considers it very difficult to find adequate management in Slovenia. The reasons may be in the small size of the country where everybody knows everybody.

The commitment of the management of Sarrio Slovenija to the company has been very high. Yet, its understanding of commitment does not lead it to take initiatives to improve the operation of the firm. This is probably connected with the fact that they still do not feel that "they are a company responsible for itself."

### Research and Development

In Sarrio Slovenija, there are no R&D department and R&D activities. The situation before the acquisition was the same, that is, there was no R&D in Količevo. In the cartonboard section of Sarrio, R&D activities are going on in three subdepartments of the Industrial Operations Department; that is, in subdepartments for raw materials, processing, and quality. They find new raw materials, how to produce better products from the same or worse raw materials, how to improve the coating system, what to do to improve quality, and so forth. The R&D staff in Sarrio has links with universities in Italy, Germany, and the United Kingdom. The idea is to establish cooperation with the University of Ljubljana as well and, in the long run, perhaps to established an advanced school for the paper industry in Slovenia.

## FUTURE DEVELOPMENT PLANS

In the short term, Sarrio will insist on further improvements in corporate culture, increased labor productivity, and efficient and competitive production, as well as on resolving the problem of waste water in Sarrio Slovenija. Sarrio's long-term aim is to bring production in Sarrio Slovenija to the level of efficiency and quality that will be fully comparable with Sarrio's best factories. This is necessary if Sarrio Slovenija is to compete with the most competitive producers on the cartonboard market. The predictions are that the market of cartonboard for packaging will be increasingly competitive. The realization of this program depends, on the one side, on finding the financial resources necessary for the realization of investments and, on the other, on the eagerness and determination of the management of Sarrio Slovenija.

In 1993–95 investments in the amount of DM 23.6 million were realized. In the 1996–97 period additional investments in the amount of DM 26 million are budgeted,[17] devoted to:

• increasing production capacity to 130,000 tons annually (more than 20 percent increase in capacity);

• improving the productivity per employee by approximately 30 percent;

• constructing a purifying plant for the waste water from the mill to contain no more pollutants than allowed by Slovenian legislation;[18]

• computerizing administrative, commercial, and production processes and procedures.

Sarrio Slovenija has a key role in the development plans for Sarrio's cartonboard sector. In the 1998–99 period, Sarrio plans investments in Sarrio Slovenija to increase its production capacity further, in order to improve the potential of supply and to reduce the costs of production. The increase in production capacity will enable Sarrio Slovenija to reach standards of efficiency in line with the best plants in the Sarrio Group.

Sarrio considers the development of production in Sarrio Slovenija as its priority cartonboard project. This is because the cost structure and geographical position of Sarrio Slovenija is considered strategic for

Sarrio's penetration of the markets of Central and Eastern Europe.[19] The development of consumer product distribution in these markets, which is expected to bring about a major increase in the consumption of coated cartonboard, is inevitable and probably fairly imminent. Planned additional and improved production capacities in Sarrio Slovenija are synchronized with these processes.

## CONCLUSIONS

Geographical and strategic considerations were crucial in Sarrio's decision to acquire Papirnica Količevo. Its proximity to Central and Eastern Europe and to the former Yugoslavia on the one hand and to Italy on the other, prospects of further concentration in the industry through merger and acquisitions, and the interest of a major competitor for Papirnica Količevo stimulated Sarrio to acquire Papirnica Količevo.

The assessment of the domestic actors involved in the sale of Papirnica Količevo is that the transaction brought about good results, to a large extent due to the competitive bidding approach. With the entrance of a strategic foreign investor, Papirnica Količevo has considerably improved its development and business potential. The following aspects of the transaction for individual actors on the Slovenian side can be listed:

(a) Papirnica Količevo obtained a strategic investor who assured further development, business, and employment possibilities. From the financial point of view, the sale of the company also resulted in its recapitalization. From a strategic point of view, the sale included a development and investment plan to accelerate development.

(b) For the Development Fund, the transaction meant the influx of additional foreign capital that could be used for investment in other projects and for the restructuring of other domestic companies.

(c) Many of the employees kept their jobs and their ownership share according to the then forthcoming privatization law and also special minority shareholders' rights. A reasonable scheme for the resolution of the redundancy problem was adopted. Recently the employees sold their minority share to Sarrio S.A., and they are the first ones in Slovenia who were able to sell their ownership certificates at their nominal value.

(d) The Slovenian state got a functioning enterprise that is able to fulfill its tax and other obligations, that assures employment, and that supports the development of the local community.[20]

(e) The managers retained their positions and received additional benefits and the possibility of additional training.

(f) The former owners of Papirnica Količevo, whose ownership was nationalized in 1947, received compensation.

Three years after the acquisition of Papirnica Količevo by Sarrio S.A., the major preacquisition objectives of the management of Papirnica Količevo and of the Development Fund had been realized to a considerable extent. The company regularly services its debts, production has been modernized, a new organization scheme has been introduced, exports have increased, and the issue of redundant employees has been resolved.

Finally, there is no doubt that the takeover by Sarrio S.A. of Papirnica Količevo ended the long-lasting agony of the firm and assured good prospects for the future. It is also clear that there was no other solution than bringing in a strategic foreign investor. The fact that Sarrio is a divisionally organized group where the managing of the group is rather centralized may disturb public opinion in Slovenia, which is not very much in favor of foreign direct investment, but in fact does not make much difference. Be it centralized or decentralized, the majority owner always decides on the major issues.

## NOTES

The authors would like to thank Mr. Cesare Bianconi, vice-president of Saffa S.p.A., and Mr. Dario Fumagalli for their time, readiness to cooperate, valuable information, and kindness during the preparation of this case study. The paper *Presentazione della Societa SARRIO SLOVENIJA d.o.o.* prepared by Mr. Bianconi, *Saffa —Annual Report* and *Financial Statements 1993* and *Saffa Group Press Kit*, Ljubljana, July 25, 1992, have been extensively used in the preparation of this case study.

1. The ten largest cartonboard manufacturers in the world, International Paper, Mayr Melnhof, Enso Gutzeit, Federal Paper Board, Stora Billerud, Westvaco, Sarrio Group, Riverwood, Honshu, and Mead, meet approximately 38 percent of world cartonboard needs.

2. Approximately DM 800 million according to the average exchange rate for 1994.

3. Two additional factors were also relevant. The first was that good prospects in the cartonboard industry offer possibilities for the improvement of individual producers' positions. None of the major producers could afford not to participate in the race for a better position. The second was that, in the cartonboard industry, an acquisition is much less expensive than a greenfield venture.

4. Saffa could not allow Mayr Melnhof to locate "on the Italian border."

5. Mayr Melnhof was the first potential buyer of Papirnica Količevo. A natural "oligopolistic reaction" of Saffa was to be alert about the moves of its major competitor. For more on that, see section 5.

6. In the words of Mr. Bianconi, "opening up the markets of the other parts of the former Yugoslavia would be of huge importance for Saffa."

7. From the legal point of view, this was the only way to realize the transaction, because the law required the Fund to be the seller of social capital that has no "known owner."

8. One can say that the real bank of Sarrio Slovenija is Sarrio S.A; Sarrio Slovenija does not have any correspondent bank in Slovenia apart from small, short-term financing for salaries, and so forth.

9. For instance, in 1995, Sarrio Slovenija prepared a detailed budget/plan for 1996, a forecast for 1997, and indications for 1998. In 1996, the forecast for 1997 will become a detailed budget/plan for 1997, indications for 1998 will become a forecast for 1998, indications for 1999 will be introduced, and so forth.

10. Much faster than in the case of the Spanish cartonboard mills.

11. Initially, the reports for a new firm were simpler than for the other firms in the group. In 1994, the format of the monthly reports of Sarrio Slovenija was already the same as for all the other companies.

12. Before the acquisition, all the international purchases and sales of Papirnica Količevo were made through Hago, an Austrian company established by Slovenian paper manufacturers.

13. Cartonboard comes from the coating section in the form of rolls. Since it is sold in sheets, the rolls are cut. In the cutting process, a lot of dust appears, which reduces the quality of consequent printing. This is crucial since coated cartonboard is usually printed.

14. Waste paper, Količevo's major raw material, is 62 percent imported.

15. Before 1991, Količevo was purchasing waste paper mostly from other parts of the former Yugoslavia.

16. Much more than in Italy, for instance.

17. Of that, DM 19.6 million relates to the loan provided by the EBRD that will be used for the construction of a biological purifying plant, for financial restructuring, and to cover the increased need for working capital due to the higher volume of production.

18. The completion date set for this project with the help of the EBRD loan was 1995, but it was contingent on obtaining the construction permit in time.

19. Also, the reopening of the Yugoslav market would be a huge opportunity for Sarrio Slovenija and Sarrio itself.

20. Instead of the enterprise being unable to settle its liabilities, it would, like many others in a similar situation, ask for government assistance to survive.

## REFERENCES

Bianconi, Cesare. 1995. *Conferenza Stampa per la Presentazione della Societa Sarrio Slovenija d.o.o.* Mimeograph.

*Gospodarski vestnik*. 1995a. Vol. 44, no. 4.

*Gospodarski vestnik*. 1995b. Vol. 44, no. 24.

Saffa. 1994. *Annual Report and Financial Statements 1993*. Milan.

Saffa. 1993. *Annual Report and Financial Statements 1992*. Milan.

Saffa. 1992a. *Annual Report and Financial Statements 1991*. Milan.

Saffa. 1992b. *Saffa Group Press Kit*. Ljubljana, July 25. Mimeograph.

# 3

# Tobačna Ljubljana, d.o.o.
## *Cigarette-Producing Company with the Majority Share of Reemtsma, Germany, and Seita, France*

### Matija Rojec and Marjan Svetličič

## BASICS

Tobačna Ljubljana, d.o.o. (hereafter referred to as TL)[1] is the first direct foreign privatization in Slovenia. By direct foreign privatization, we mean the direct sale of a majority share of a socially owned Slovenian company to a strategic foreign investor. With the acquisition agreement signed on October 7, 1991, the German firm Reemtsma[2] acquired a 58.8 percent and the French firm Seita[3] a 17.7 percent equity share in the then socially owned TL. The remaining 23.5 percent remained in the hands of the Development Fund of Slovenia to be distributed among TL's employees during the privatization of the Slovenian economy.

TL is a limited-liability company for the production and distribution of tobacco products, predominantly cigarettes. TL's equity capital in 1994 was DM 68.2 million, and it had 1,117 employees. In 1994 it sold 5,045 billion cigarettes, for a total gross revenue of DM 371.1 million, of which taxes accounted for DM 217.5 million. TL ranks among the largest Slovenian enterprises,[4] and it also had a dominant position in the Slovenian cigarette market, accounting for 83.8 percent of sales in 1994.

On the other hand, Reemtsma, the majority owner of TL, is Europe's largest independent cigarette manufacturer. Reemtsma's annual sales amount to DM 8,786 million, its assets total DM 3,397 million, of which 40 percent is equity capital, and it employs 8,311 people. In 1993, Reemtsma's sales of cigarettes amounted to 74.2 billion cigarettes;[5] of that, 31.2 billion were sold in Germany and 43.0 billion abroad. Most of the international sales, some 27.7 billion cigarettes, are produced in Reemtsma's foreign production facilities. Although Germany is still the major market for Reemtsma, its cigarette market share in Germany is 24.3 percent, the company is becoming increasingly international. In 1993, for the first time in Reemtsma's history, the volume of foreign sales exceeded domestic sales.

With the exception of affiliates in Hong Kong and the United States, Europe is the major area of internationalization of Reemtsma. Having strengthened its position in Western Europe, Reemtsma was quick to seize the new market opportunities that emerged in Central and Eastern Europe (CEE) after 1990. From the very beginning of the transition of the former socialist countries, the tobacco industry has been one of the primary objectives of foreign investors. Besides the giants Philip Morris, RJ Reynolds, and BAT, Reemtsma is the only cigarette producer that has been actively engaged in the CEE countries, perhaps in more of these countries than any other cigarette producer. Reemtsma has cigarette production capacities in Hungary, the Slovak Republic, Slovenia, and Ukraine. Reemtsma also has sizeable sales organizations in the Czech Republic and in Poland. Local market shares of these companies are 36 percent in Hungary, 75 percent in the Slovak Republic, 83.8 percent in Slovenia, 25 percent in Ukraine, and 12.6 percent in the Czech Republic (Reemtsma: Annual Report 1993).

Seita, the other foreign shareholder in TL, is the largest French producer of tobacco products. It is in the process of privatization.

## HISTORY AND SOME GENERAL CHARACTERISTICS OF TOBACCO COMPANY LJUBLJANA: MOTIVATION FOR ATTRACTING STRATEGIC FOREIGN INVESTOR

TL was established in 1871 as a state monopoly for the production of cigars, pipe, chewing tobacco, and snuff. The production of cigarettes began in 1877, and, in 1957, as the first in the former Yugoslavia, TL introduced the production of the oriental-type filter cigarette called "Filter 57." Until 1986, Filter 57 was the most produced and sold cigarette in the former Yugoslavia; it was priced the same as 85 mm cigarettes, although its actual length was only 80 mm. In the period between 1974 and 1986, when its production amounted to between 6 and 8 billion cigarettes, Filter 57 accounted for approximately 90 percent of TL's total cigarette sales. In addition to Filter 57, TL produced three other brands of cigarettes, Astor Mild, Ibar, and Morava, all with the soft type of packaging. Before 1984, TL had more than 15 percent of the market in Yugoslavia and the highest productivity level of all Yugoslav tobacco factories. With the exception of 1982, TL earned profits,[6] salaries were under the Slovenian average, and business assets were up to 60 percent sourced by equity ("social capital") and long-term sources. The number of employees in that period was approximately 2,200; of that 1,800 were in Slovenia and the rest in two tobacco production units in Vojvodina and Bosnia and Hercegovina and in two sales units in Serbia and Vojvodina. Activities in Slovenia encompassed production of cigarettes, production of small leather goods, wholesale and retail trade, and business administration.

In 1987–88, TL realized that the taste of consumers had changed considerably toward lighter cigarettes with less nicotine and lower tar, in taste similar to the American blend, and in a box package. Although TL at that time had sufficient production capacities and financial resources to adjust its production to these changes in consumers' taste, it continued to produce the oriental-type Filter 57 and missed the right moment to invest in the development of new cigarette brands as well as in the development of the necessary human resources and knowledge. At the same time, other Yugoslav producers increased their production of much more attractive foreign cigarette brands produced on the basis of license agreements. As a result, TL's Yugoslav market share decreased from more than 15 percent in the early 1980s to less than 9 percent in the second half of the 1980s.

The long-running success of Filter 57 had a crucial impact on the way of thinking in TL before the transition. This way of thinking and of doing business had three major features:

The first was that, due to very successful sales of Filter 57 for a very long period of time, there was no need for "market-oriented thinking" in TL; there were no modern marketing activities in the company. The competition took advantage of this.

The second was that the success of Filter 57 offset losses from some of TL's other activities. TL was earning enough on Filter 57 so that it was able to cover losses in two other activities, leatherware production (unbundled in the process of acquisition of TL by Reemtsma/Seita and now an independent company called Inini) and Maloprodaja, a retail sales unit. The leatherware unit was launched to broaden the assortment of goods in Maloprodaja. Both units made losses, but Maloprodaja was important because it generated a steady cash flow. In an environment of high inflation and uncertain payments, this was extremely important since any delay in payments meant losses.

The third was that TL produced only oriental cigarettes and failed to develop technology for the production of American-blend and extra-light cigarettes.

All these problems led to a realization that TL could not base its future only on Filter 57 and that something should be done with the unsuccessful parts of the company business. The management and the planning department were eager to introduce changes, but the former managing director did not agree. Finally, in 1988, with the appointment of a new managing director, who was recruited internally, a new development concept was adopted by TL. It had three major objectives:

(a) to develop new brands of cigarettes with the major stress on quality and to introduce technological changes in the production process;

(b) to promote sales and to develop a modern marketing concept;

(c) to reorganize TL into an efficient modern enterprise.

This new development concept was supposed to be realized by concentrating resources, expert staff, and decisions and by recruiting new skilled staff while increasing salaries above the Slovenian average.

In short, the new development concept was based on a quality cigarette suited to the consumer's taste, meaning a cigarette of superior quality. In practice, this development concept led to the following operational objectives as defined in 1990 by then socially owned TL:

(a) to develop own new brands and to acquire attractive international brands;

(b) to attract fresh capital to restructure the production technology and to acquire know-how;

(c) to establish appropriate sales and marketing activities;

(d) to find new markets for existing and new brands;

(e) to modernize the internal organization;

(f) to develop the human resources needed to realize the aforementioned objectives.

TL's management was aware that the realization of the above development concept, denoting a thorough transformation of the company, could be realized only in parallel with the privatization of the company. A number of approaches to privatization had been considered by the management, but most of them, like a management and employee buy-out or selling the company to financial institutions or individual investors, could not solve the company's fundamental problems. The new owners would simply not be in a position to implement the objectives of the new development concept (Korže and Simoneti 1992, p. 3). That is why TL's management came to the conclusion that the best, if not the only, way to assure the long-term prosperity of the company was to attract a strategic foreign investor in the form of an important international cigarette manufacturer.

## SECTORS AND MARKETS

The international tobacco industry is increasingly dominated by a handful of large multinational companies, such as Philip Morris, BAT (British American Tobacco), RJ Reynolds, and Rothmans. Brand names such as Marlboro, Winston, and so forth, increasingly dominate all over the world and gradually replace a large number of local brands whose sale was traditionally limited to their local markets. Besides large multinational tobacco companies, there is a small number of the so-called independent cigarette manufacturers, independent in the sense that they are not affiliated with the largest multinational companies in the branch, like Reemtsma and Seita, who, however, are mostly concentrated in their domestic markets, while their international involvement is of a relatively limited scope. Reemtsma is to a certain extent an exception to this characterization.

One could predict that the future development in the tobacco industry would bring further internationalization; that is, the gradual acquisition of independent national cigarette manufacturers by big cigarette multinational corporations and, maybe, the entry of a few independent manufacturers, such as Reemtsma, for example, into the club of big cigarette multinationals. National legislation is the only obstacle to such a development; that is, countries having a traditional tobacco monopoly and state-owned tobacco industry may oppose such a trend. However, overwhelming privatization processes in the world will definitely tackle state ownership in the tobacco industry as well.

Quick and intensive involvement of the big tobacco multinationals, and also of Reemtsma, in the CEE countries after the beginning of transition is the best illustration of the above-mentioned processes in the tobacco industry. The tobacco industry is among the industries that attracted a disproportionately high share of foreign direct investment in CEE countries compared to its importance in the host economies. Philip Morris, BAT, R.J. Reynolds, and Reemtsma have bought a considerable, if not the majority, part of the tobacco industry in CEE countries. The major cigarette manufacturers of the world are fighting for control of state tobacco companies in a number of CEE countries, where people smoke 550 billion cigarettes annually. Although Reemtsma is much smaller than the big multinational tobacco companies, it is engaged in no less than six CEE countries, and it is, besides Philip Morris and BAT, definitely among the leading foreign investors in the CEE countries' tobacco industry.[7]

## REEMTSMA'S MOTIVATION TO ACQUIRE TOBACCO COMPANY LJUBLJANA

Three factors influenced Reemtsma's decision to acquire TL. The first two factors, to strengthen Reemtsma's position in the CEE region and to increase its market share in the former Yugoslavia, were strategic. The third facilitating factor was the previous cooperation between Reemtsma and TL. The determinants of Reemtsma's motivation for acquiring the majority share of TL should be traced to its efforts to strengthen its position as a European cigarette manufacturer faced with increasingly aggressive penetration of the European cigarette market by the leading United States–based cigarette multinationals. At the end of the 1980s, Philip Morris had begun to penetrate the European market intensively. There were also clear indications that other major multinationals from the cigarette branch, especially BAT and R.J. Reynolds, would follow Philip Morris. To cope with this, European cigarette manufacturers tried to strengthen their position and to organize mutual cooperation. Reemtsma was the leading European cigarette manufacturer in this effort. These processes coincided with the opening up of the former socialist countries, which suddenly became an obvious new target for Philip Morris and BAT but also for Reemtsma in its efforts to realize its strategy of strengthening its position and organizing the cooperation of European cigarette manufacturers.

Thus, the acquisition of TL was only one of the bricks in building this strategy. Not surprisingly, Reemtsma's competitor in acquiring TL was Philip Morris. Crucial for Reemtsma's decision to buy TL was the fact that, at that time, the acquisition of TL would provide access to the entire 20 million–strong market of Yugoslavia. Before the acquisition, Reemtsma already had twenty years of experience in cooperation with TL through a contractual joint venture. Positive experience in this cooperation contributed to the choice of Reemtsma as a strategic foreign investor in TL.

Seita's involvement in TL is a result of Reemtsma's initiative to strengthen cooperation among European cigarette manufacturers. At one time it seemed that Reemtsma and Seita would acquire an equity share in each other. This never happened, but it was the major reason for Seita's involvement in TL, that is, to demonstrate the coordinated strategy of the major European cigarette manufacturers. The rather passive involvement of Seita in TL is characteristic for the whole period after the acquisition; its attempts to take a more active approach are inconsistent and usually superficial.

## PROCESS OF NEGOTIATION AND THE
## ACQUISITION OF TL BY REEMTSMA/SEITA[8]

Slovenian privatization is a decentralized process. A privatization is initiated and structured by the company to be privatized, that is, by its management and workers' council.[9] It is important to note that in 1990, when TL decided to initiate its privatization by selling the company to a strategic foreign investor, there was no legal or any other incentive or pressure for companies to privatize. The decision of the TL management and of the workers' council to attract a strategic foreign investor was, thus, entirely their own, motivated exclusively by the need for faster development of the company. This step was not forced by any deadlines of privatization legislation. TL would have decided to attract a strategic foreign investor even if there were no privatization involved.

The objective of TL's management in this privatization was twofold: (a) to assure the development and marketing of top-quality cigarettes according to the latest standards of the tobacco industry; and (b) to keep a part of the company in Slovenian ownership to enable subsequent participation of the employees in the ownership of TL.[10] In its search for potential strategic investors, management soon focused on two potential investors who expressed strong interest in purchasing the company: Reemtsma, in alliance with Seita, and Philip Morris. In mid-1990, TL began to negotiate with the two potential foreign investors and to define detailed objectives and conditions to be contained in the bid of the foreign investor regarding technology, market, and organization.

At the beginning of 1991, the Agency for Restructuring and Privatization of the Republic of Slovenia, hereafter referred to as the Agency or the Privatization Agency, and the Development Fund of the Republic of Slovenia, hereafter referred to as the Fund or the Development Fund, were invited by the management of TL to advise on the anticipated transaction. The two government institutions had a double role in this deal. The staffs of the Agency and the Fund served primarily as consultants in preparing the privatization plan, designing tender procedures, analyzing the offers, and negotiating the deal with the successful bidder. At the end of negotiations, the legal role of the Agency was to approve the transaction, whereas the Fund was one of the parties who signed the contract with the foreign investor. This was because before the transaction all TL's social capital had to be transferred to the Fund and the Fund then acted as the seller. In cases of social ownership without a known owner, this was the only way to effectuate the transaction.

TL's management saw advantages to the active involvement of the Agency and the Fund, not only in providing professional support but also in minimizing the danger of speculation that a transaction had been structured "under the table" to benefit the existing managers. Foreign investors were also pleased to work with the Agency and the Fund because they had confidence that all steps would comply with legal requirements and that the problems of getting the necessary approvals and guarantees would be minimized.

After the two potential acquirers completed their analytical work on TL, they were given a formal invitation to submit their bids and to explain the financial and commercial arrangements through which they would take a stake in the company. They were also asked to prepare a detailed program on how they could contribute to the fulfillment of TL's development objectives by developing new products, modernizing technology, developing marketing strategies, introducing changes in internal organization, developing human resources, and stabilizing local supplies of raw materials. They were also told explicitly that the price would be important but not necessarily the main criterion for deciding on the preferred bidder. They were also informed that, in evaluating proposals, the future prospects of the company and the overall economic implications for Slovenia would be taken into account as well.

The Selection Committee, consisting of the representatives of TL, the Fund, and the Agency, unanimously decided that Reemtsma/Seita made a better bid. Although from the macroeconomic point of view, employment generation, additional investment in Slovenia, fiscal implications, and immediate impact on foreign exchange generation, the bid of Philip Morris was stronger, the decision was in favor of Reemtsma/Seita. The reasons were the following:

(a) From the point of view of the future development of the company, the advantage was on the side of Reemtsma/Seita because they proposed a partnership that would preserve the identity of TL and continue the business tradition of one of the oldest Slovenian companies.

(b) The bid of Reemtsma/Seita enabled TL to retain all its major business functions.

(c) The price offered for the company and the proposed payment arrangements made by Reemtsma/Seita were better.

A detailed investment program assuring new technology and modernization of the existing facilities for the next five years was included in the acquisition agreement between the Fund and Reemtsma/Seita. For the purchase of the majority share in TL and for further development of the company, the foreign buyers invested nearly DM 120 million (Korže and Simoneti 1992, p. 9).

The shareholders' agreement defined specific provisions for corporate governance and minority shareholders' rights to protect the position of the remaining minority Slovenian shareholders. For example, no liquidation procedure could be started for five years after acquisition, and consent would be required for any modifications of statutes, for capital reduction, and for admission of new partners. The Fund, in principle, agreed to accept new shareholders. Foreign partners got the right of first refusal for the remaining shares of the Fund, with the limitation that the Fund was free to transfer these shares to workers, the general public, and its subsidiaries or to make any other transfer as required by law (Korže and Simoneti 1992, p. 10).

Although not decisive, one should not neglect the importance of rather subjective factors in deciding for one or the other bidder. In the

Figure 1. **Ownership Structure of Tobačna Ljubljana, d.o.o.**

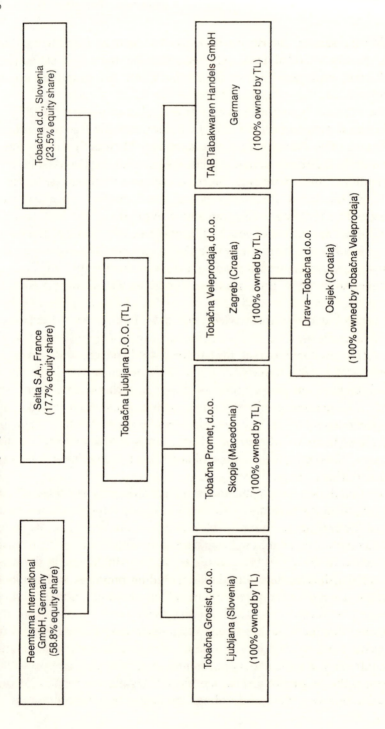

*Source:* TL.

case of the sale of TL, Reemtsma proved to have an important advantage, twenty years of successful cooperation with TL, established relations, and personal contacts between the management of Reemtsma and TL.

The contract between the Fund as the seller of TL and Reemtsma/ Seita was signed on October 7, 1991. The transaction was structured in such a way that the socially owned company TL was first transformed into a limited-liability company, TL, d.o.o., with the Fund as the only shareholder. Then Reemtsma/Seita purchased a 76.5 percent share of TL from the Fund, Reemtsma getting 58.8 percent and Seita 17.7 percent. The remaining 23.5 percent was retained by the Fund for subsequent privatization by the employees of TL (see Figure 1). Reemtsma/Seita were willing to accept employee share participation only on the condition that employee shares stayed indivisible. A special joint-stock company Tobačna d.d. was set up for this purpose. Its only purpose was to hold the 23.5 percent share of TL. Tobačna d.d. is still in the ownership of the Fund, but in September 1995 the process of exchanging the ownership certificates of the employees of TL for the shares of Tobačna d.d. started. In 1996, Tobačna d.d. would be owned by the employees of TL.

Negotiations on and the signing of the acquisition agreement took place in an extremely unstable situation because Slovenia had declared independence on June 25, 1991, and, on the next day, the Yugoslav Army intervened to prevent the disintegration of Yugoslavia. This was important from the point of view of concluding the agreement because of the inherent political risk to the foreign investor and also because the disintegration of Yugoslavia severely weakened the market position of TL. At the time the agreement was signed, TL still counted on the Croatian and Bosnian markets, but, with the disintegration of Yugoslavia, TL lost markets that had accounted for approximately half of its total sales in the late 1980s. Besides, TL lost its assets in the other republics of the former Yugoslavia, including premises and stocks of cigarettes, and TL was forced to write off its claims on customers from that area.

In the negotiations Reemtsma/Seita demanded that access to the cigarette markets of Croatia and Bosnia and Hercegovina remain unrestricted and that sales should not be discriminated against by customs duties, taxes, or quotas. During the war in Croatia, this request became a major threat to the execution of the entire transaction, especially when Slovenia and Croatia introduced different taxation policies. The problem was resolved only after the signing of the contract because the foreign partners eventually relied on the letter of intent of the Slovenian government regarding this subject (Korže and Simoneti 1992, p. 11). Nevertheless, the subsequent development of the situation ended more or less with total loss of TL markets in the other republics of the former Yugoslavia. This became a significant problem for TL and its new owners, who were attracted by the markets of at least Croatia and Bosnia and Hercegovina if not of those of the whole former Yugoslavia.

## ORGANIZATION/MANAGEMENT STRUCTURE OF TOBACCO COMPANY LJUBLJANA

The organizational structure of TL is basically divisional (see Figure 2). In developing its organization, TL has followed the example of other European companies. The major feature evident from Figure 2 is that TL has retained all crucial business functions. The request that TL retain all the major business functions and not be restricted only to certain functions defined by the foreign partner was one of the explicit conditions put forward to potential foreign investors during negotiations. TL's management was of the opinion that this was the only way to develop the Slovenian market further and to enable the development of the management and employees. The basic idea of TL's management regarding relations with a strategic foreign partner was "to walk separately but to act jointly, to upgrade domestic knowledge with foreign knowledge and not just simply to transfer foreign knowledge into the local environment." Thus, after the acquisition by Reemtsma/Seita, TL has not only retained but even further upgraded all crucial business functions and also organizationally introduced and integrated some new business functions, such as controlling production, production analysis as an extension of controlling, and technical organization of projects. In recent years, a considerable development in the organization, specialization, and working methods in TL is evident, especially in marketing, sales, and distribution. Direct communication between experts from TL and those from Reemtsma/Seita is the major vehicle of the development of all business functions in TL; even more, TL's experts have access to and apply the output of the comprehensive and expensive research capacities of Reemtsma and Seita.

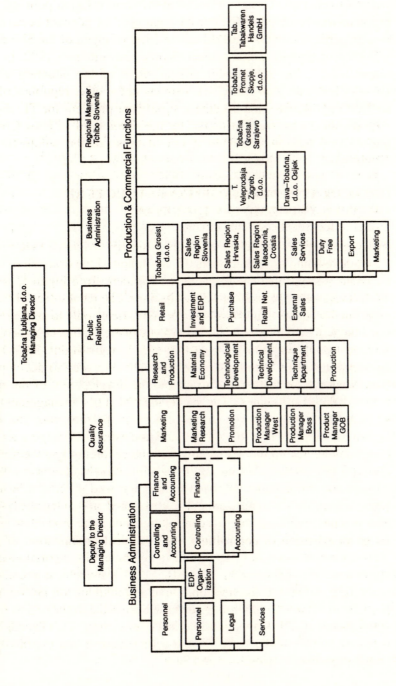

Figure 2. **Organizational Structure of Tobačna Ljubljana, d.o.o.**

69

*Source:* Saffa S.p.A.

TL is treated like are other Reemtsma companies and subsidiaries in other countries. The business language in TL is Slovenian, with English as a neutral language for the German, French, and Slovenian partners.

After the signing of the acquisition agreement, a new eight-member advisory board[11] was nominated, chaired by the chief executive of one of the foreign partners. Interestingly, the foreign partners have nominated for one of their board representatives a distinguished Slovenian economist (Korže and Simoneti 1992, p. 12). Four members were nominated by Reemtsma, one by Seita, and the other three were divided as two representatives of the employees and one representative of the Development Fund. Advisory board meetings are normally held three times a year. In order to speed up the meetings of the advisory board, the members meet informally one day before the meeting and discuss most of the issues of the agenda. This practice has proved to be very effective.

The managing director of TL had been appointed in 1988, long before the presence of Reemtsma/Seita. There have been no attempts by the new majority shareholders to replace him. His appointment, not accidentally, coincides with the commencement of major changes in the company. Before, these changes could not be made, although there had been some efforts to introduce changes in TL's strategy. The managing director was recruited internally within TL. Before he had been the director of TL's sales and retail department. This is probably also one of the reasons why he strongly emphasizes the marketing aspects of TL's activities. One of the most important tasks of the managing director is maintaining relations between TL and its staff and Reemtsma/Seita and their staffs. Although a number of TL's employees are in daily contact with their counterparts from Reemtsma and Seita, it is usually the managing director who intervenes whenever problems arise.

The activities of TL are defined in detail in the annual plan that is adopted every year by the shareholders. The role of the annual plan is very strong. The plan is very detailed, and it identifies by name the person responsible for the implementation of every activity defined in the plan. Subsequent changes in the plan are not allowed. The idea behind this is to make the plan as precise as possible in spite of frequent and volatile changes in the external environment. Nevertheless, the strategy of achieving the planned objectives can be changed if the circumstances change sufficiently. Within the limits of the plan, it is the managing director who is the major decision maker. Reemtsma/ Seita do not interfere in the realization of the plan as long as some substantial negative deviations from the plan do not appear. If they do, the managing director must have a sound explanation for the deviations.

TL must make monthly reports on the realization of the plan. Reemtsma's planning system does not allow any adjustment of the plan's objectives even in the event of unpredicted external or other occurrences that change the situation considerably. The opinion of TL's management is that, in such cases, it would be much better to adjust the objectives accordingly rather than to make reports on the deviations from objectives that are no longer feasible.

TL can be regarded as a relatively autonomous company. Interventions from Reemtsma are rare. Once the annual plan is approved, the management has a relatively free hand in its realization. The only limitations are important financial decisions, with relatively large amounts involved, and regarding some important positions, such as head of divisions and above, that must be coordinated with Reemtsma. In other words, the segment of decision making in which Reemtsma would like to be absolutely in control at any time are decisions on investments and on key personnel.

Contacts among Reemtsma/Seita on one side and TL on the other are carried out by contact persons within Reemtsma/Seita and TL for the major fields of cooperation. This scheme does not always work very smoothly. Much depends on the contact persons designated, and it also differs between Reemtsma and Seita. Communication with Reemtsma is very good. Reemtsma seems to be a relatively decentralized type of multinational company, not interfering much in the daily operations of its subsidiaries if they perform according to the plan. Communications with Seita more frequently encounter problems. Seita is a state-owned company, rather rigid, more than companies in Slovenia had ever been, and with very strong and hierarchical internal relations. The issue of very strong hierarchical relations in Seita increases the problems in everyday contacts between TL and Seita staff.[12] The concept that TL is relatively autonomous in a number of decisions somehow does not fit into Seita's business philosophy. TL's staff is much more satisfied with the contacts and the contact persons from Reemtsma.

The major organizational and management problems in TL are as follows:

(a) some departments in TL are already organized according to Reemtsma's system and some not yet, which creates certain coordination problems;

(b) there is still too much overhead;

(c) there are still reserves in the organization field; many activities are going on that are not necessary;

(d) there are still reserves in the field of work discipline.

The fact that there are two foreign partners present in TL does not create major problems. Although there is an agreement that Reemtsma should take care of production and marketing and Seita of retail sales and distribution, it is Reemtsma who actually plays the role of the strategic foreign investor while Seita's efforts are mostly sporadic, less active, and auxiliary. However, the problem with two different partners is different decision-making processes and reaction times in decision making, particularly if one of the partners is a state-owned company, as Seita is.[13] Its decision-making process is much slower, less flexible, and more bureaucratic.

## Business Information and Changes in Organization and Decision Making

Up-to-date information is increasingly important for the organization and decision making in a company. Furthermore, business information dictates to a certain extent changes and adjustments in the company's organization and decision making. There is an increasing need for information in TL.[14] TL's present information system is linked to "Mehanografski center," a data-processing service established by a group of companies, TL being one of them. The major disadvantages of this system are that it is relatively outdated, is only partly integrated into the company,[15] and is too slow in developing new applications without a clear idea of the system's further development. In short, the costs of the present information system are too high relative to its performance and quality.

Therefore, TL has began to introduce its own, new information system, which will eliminate the deficiencies of the present information system and will be based on the idea of the "satisfied user." The new information system will increase management efficiency and reduce the so-called auditing costs of TL. It will also improve the qualification structure of people working in the information system. In order to introduce such an information system TL has already taken the following steps:

(a) searching for the appropriate organization of the information users;

(b) partly eliminating and partly integrating the existing system in TL;

(c) introducing new Slovenian accounting standards that are harmonized with international standards.

The introduction of the above-mentioned steps has been possible only as a result of substantially increased need for information in TL. The latter has come with the introduction of Reemtsma's planning concept. This concept substantially increased the need for more information because:

(a) it increased the responsibility and commitment of TL's management on all decision-making levels; and

(b) due to their responsibility for negative deviations from the plan, it has made all decision makers more actively involved in planning and in assessing business operations.

The information system is becoming an increasingly important issue in TL. There is an increasing awareness in the company that the successful development of TL requires exact planning and assessing of the volume and structure of business operations, expected profits, business opportunities and risks, and so forth. Management wants accurate information for strategic decision making and as an instrument for controlling operations. Information is needed daily. Adequate information is increasingly considered to be one of the most important instruments for strengthening TL's competitive position.

In cooperation with Reemtsma, TL has set up a system of business reporting that has brought a more systematic and thorough approach to monitoring results and the realization of planned objectives. Controlling and internal auditing in accounting was also introduced. Recently, TL, in cooperation with Reemtsma, decided to introduce a new integral information system, SAP/R3, used also by Reemtsma in the SAP/R2 version. The introduction of the SAP/R3 system enables TL to be more compatible with Reemtsma's system of operation. SAP/R3 is not only an information system, it is also the information system that dictates changes in organization and decision making. The advantages of the SAP/R3 for TL are twofold: (a) it meets the need for harmonized and centralized data for decision making, and (b) it is compatible with the information system of the strategic partner. Compared with the previous information system in TL, SAP/R3 is 2.5 times less expensive and at the same time more flexible, more integrated, and simpler to use.

The major feature of SAP/R3 is that it offers strong support for decision making in each business area, especially the controlling module,[16] which originates from other modules such as financial accounting, sales and distribution, material management, controlling, and planning of production. Thus it is the most powerful instrument in the hands of the management.

Initially, the new information system, introduced after the acquisition, was based completely on Reemtsma's standards. Later, it became obvious that, for the time being, this was too demanding for TL because the hardware and human capacities at TL were not on the necessary level yet. The application of the new system is now more adjusted to the Central European application of Western standards, which means a selective, not a complete application. To enable the introduction of the SAP/R3 in TL, TL staff was trained at Siemens–Nixdorf's training center in Brussels. Eight people from TL were trained in Brussels, four for one month, four for two weeks, seven in Ljubljana for two weeks, and two in London for one and a half weeks.

## TECHNOLOGICAL DEVELOPMENT, PRODUCTION, AND PERFORMANCE AFTER THE ACQUISITION BY REEMTSMA/SEITA

The major objective of TL in searching for a strategic foreign investor was "to produce and market cigarettes of superior quality according to the latest standards of the tobacco industry" and to develop its technological capabilities further. To achieve these objectives considerable investments, introduction of new brands of cigarettes and transfer of technology were necessary.

### Investments and Technological Development

According to the acquisition agreement between Reemtsma/Seita and the Development Fund, Reemtsma/Seita were bound to invest an additional DM 37 million in TL. TL's investment plans for 1992–96 amounted to DM 53 million, 75 percent in the production of cigarettes (of that 20 percent in technological modernization), 14 percent in sales and marketing, and the remaining 11 percent in upgrading the information system. This considerably exceeds the amount set out in the acquisition agreement. By the end of 1994, DM 32 million of investments were already made, that is, an average of DM 10 million annually. This figure was increased by DM 12 million, which was the value of technology and know-how transferred from Reemtsma/Seita to TL. The above investments resulted in the introduction of the following technical changes in TL's manufacturing process:

(a) new-generation machinery in the production and packaging of cigarettes, such as Protos 70 in the production of cigarettes, FPZ 400 in the packaging department, a tobacco-leaf dryer and refrigerator in the primary department;

(b) own perforation of cigarette paper;

(c) own casings production;

(d) use of the most up-to-date systems and quality control in the preparation of tobacco, such as dosage of casings;

(e) regular servicing of production machinery.

The realization of investment plans for 1995 and 1996 was frozen due to the risks associated with the tax claims for the period before the presence of Reemtsma/Seita (see section 11, "Relations with Slovenian Authorities").

Since the current technology in TL was transferred from Reemtsma, it is very similar to the one used by Reemtsma itself, and the production process in TL is not more labor intensive than the one in Reemtsma. The new technology is more environmentally friendly than the old one. Also, better work-safety measures were introduced, but noise caused by the machinery remains a problem.[17]

A major preacquisition objective was to retain all the crucial business functions in the company. Thus TL kept its R&D department after the acquisition by Reemtsma/Seita.[18] There are twelve people employed in the R&D department, and they played a key role in accomplishing the objective of "producing and marketing cigarettes of superior quality according to the latest standards of the tobacco industry." TL's R&D department staff quickly mastered the new technology of ventilated cigarette filters and specific technological processes of tobacco processing to yield lower tar and nicotine values in cigarettes. They studied technologies transferred from Reemtsma and introduced them into TL's manufacturing process. This not only enabled the manu-

Table 1

## Chronology of Introducing New Cigarette Brands by Tobačna Ljubljana

| Cigarette brand | Date of introduction |
|---|---|
| Production: | |
| 1. Boss | |
|     Internally called "box" | October 1987 |
|     Renamed Boss Classic | March 1994 |
| 2. 57 Mild | February 1988 |
| 3. Set | December 1988 |
| 4. Boss soft | February 1990 |
| 5. Macho | December 1990 |
| 6. Extra 91 | September 1991 |
| 7. West | February 1992 |
| 8. Gauloises Blondes | September 1992 |
| 9. Boss Lights | September 1993 |
| 10. Milde Sorte | March 1994 |
| 11. West Lights | March 1994 |
| 12. Gauloises Legères | May 1994 |
| 13. Boss Super Lights | February 1995 |
| Imported cigarettes: | |
| 1. West 25 | May 1993 |
| 2. Davidoff Classic | June 1995 |
| 3. Davidoff Lights | June 1995 |

*Source*: TL.

facture of high-quality cigarettes in TL but has also improved working conditions in the factory.

## *New Production Program*

With the above investments, technical improvements, and transfer of technology and know-how, TL was able to begin the production of new, high-quality cigarettes corresponding to the taste of consumers and to the latest standards of the tobacco industry (see Table 1):

(a) TL developed its own new American-blend cigarette family, Boss. The Boss family covers three cigarette brands, classic, lights, and super lights.

(b) TL has complemented its own brands of cigarettes with the production of light cigarettes from Reemtsma's cigarette family West and Seita's cigarette family Gauloises.

(c) Two new cigarette brands on average are introduced to the market annually. In 1994, three new brands were introduced.

(d) TL has increased the number of packaging versions from eighteen in 1991[19] to as many as eighty-two in June 1995. This indicates a high flexibility of production. Packaging in TL made a major breakthrough by radical transition from the soft to the box type of packaging. The latter now accounts for 50 percent of TL's production. Box packaging is increasingly becoming a standard among smokers.

### Some Performance Indicators

The major success of TL in its transformation process was that it was able to retain and even slightly increase the volume of sales and to almost retain the level of net turnover (gross turnover minus taxes; for more on that, see section on "Sales and Marketing"). This is regarded as success because it was achieved in spite of the following:

(a) the loss of the former Yugoslav market, which in 1991 accounted for 47.6 percent and in 1994 for only 5.9 percent of TL's total sales;

(b) a considerable increase in cigarette prices due to a tremendous increase in taxes, which, in 1991, accounted for 42 percent and in 1994 for 66 percent of the retail price of cigarettes;

(c) the fact that only in 1990 did TL really begin to restructure its production and introduce new trademarks.[20]

Although TL had started to introduce changes and to restructure production before the acquisition, the take-over of Reemtsma/Seita made this transformation and restructuring process faster and deeper.

The new investments, new production program, new technology, and new organization resulted in the improvement of the following performance indicators of TL:

(a) Productivity increased from 10.5 million cigarettes per worker annually in 1991 to 12.5 million in 1994. For 1995, the planned target was 14.4 million.

(b) Machine capacity utilization increased (i) in cigarette production from 61 percent in 1991 to 77.3 percent in 1994 and 79.3 percent in May 1995, and (ii) in packaging from 60 percent in 1991 to 80.3 percent in 1994 and 80.8 percent in May 1995.

(c) The percentage of waste in cigarette production and packaging decreased from 6.3 percent in 1991 to 4.4 percent in 1994 and to 4.1 percent in May 1995. The losses of tobacco in the production process decreased even more, from 15 percent in 1991 to 7.25 percent in 1994 and 6.5 percent in May 1995.

(d) Tobacco stocks have increased from 8 to 14 months of production needs. This assures constant quality of cigarettes and reduces TL's vulnerability to fluctuations in the tobacco market.

Before the disintegration of Yugoslavia, TL was buying tobacco from the other republics of the former Yugoslavia. Now the majority of tobacco is imported from Reemtsma and from Zimbabwe, Malawi, the United States, Greece, and Thailand.[21] For its supplies to TL, Reemtsma uses transfer pricing. However, Reemtsma has little leeway in pricing because tobacco prices are very transparent. TL buys tobacco when it is the cheapest, and Reemtsma must take this into account with its supplies to TL.

### Quality Assurance Policy

One of the most outstanding features of the postacquisition development in TL is the increase in the quality level of its products (see Figure 3 on page 80). Although quality control was introduced in TL in 1988, real quality improvements have been achieved only recently. The European cigarette industry grades the quality of cigarettes by quality levels: Q1 marks the best quality, followed by the decreasing level of quality Q2, Q3, and so on. In 1991, TL's cigarettes did not even achieve the Q3 quality level, in either their physical or their attributive characteristics. By June 1995, TL's cigarettes made a remarkable development toward the Q2 quality level. The situation is even better with light cigarettes. As far as physical characteristics are concerned, including the standard deviation of cigarette weight, the Q2 quality level was exceeded; in attributive characteristics, quality is between Q2 and Q1. Now TL is able to assure more or less the same quality as its major competitors Philip Morris, R.J. Reynolds, BAT and Rothmans, which was not the case in 1991.

The higher quality level was achieved thanks to the following activities and measures:

(a) TL's suppliers were integrated into the production process by introducing quality standards for all the suppliers. These quality standards define the necessary level of quality of all components, reducing quality problems as far as inadequate material is concerned.

(b) Technical documentation was drawn up for the regulation and monitoring of the production process.

(c) With the permanent training of employees, TL gradually passed from a concept of product and service quality to a concept of labor and operation quality. If the former concept was based on the control of final products, the elimination of inadequate products or their return into the production process for improvement, the idea of the latter concept is "make it good the first time around." The advantage of the latter concept is that it saves costs and time by reducing the frequency of failures and not, as was the case before, by subsequently eliminating deficiencies.

(d) New information methods and techniques were introduced for accurate and high-quality collecting and processing of data as well as reporting on that basis. In short, a new information system gives better and more abundant information for making decisions.

(e) New and improved measuring equipment was introduced that enables better monitoring of the physical and chemical characteristics of cigarettes.

All the above activities to increase the quality level are in conformity with the ISO 9001 standard.

## FINANCIAL ISSUES

TL is a highly solvent company without any liquidity problems. The current financial needs of the business operations are financed by internal funds. TL takes short-term credits only sporadically. Investments are also financed from internal resources, and no credits have been taken for these purposes. One indicator of the good financial situation of the company is that in the past fifteen years it has never failed to pay monthly salaries on time, a situation that was quite rare in the transition period in Slovenia when many companies had difficulties in maintaining an adequate cash flow.

Although TL was financially sound before its acquisition by Reemtsma/Seita, a number of improvements in the field of financial policy have been made in recent years that have further improved the financial situation of the company:

(a) planning financial flows, especially cash flows;

(b) monitoring the realization of the plan;

(c) increasing the payment discipline of customers (by the introduction of a strict database of nonpayers despite the large number of new retail and distribution companies and the collapse of old ones in the transition period);

(d) coordination of the financial field with the fields of accounting, sales, and purchasing;

(e) improving cash management.

Figure 3.  **Trends in Various Indicators of Quality Level in Tobačna Ljubljana, d.o.o., in 1992–June 1995**

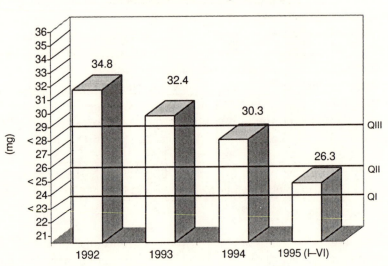

Standard deviation of cigarette weight

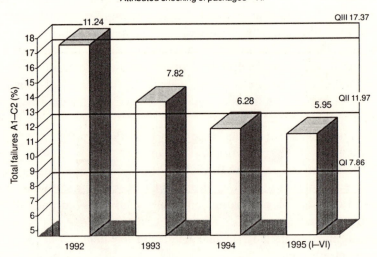

Attributed checking of packages—KF

Attributed checking of cigarettes

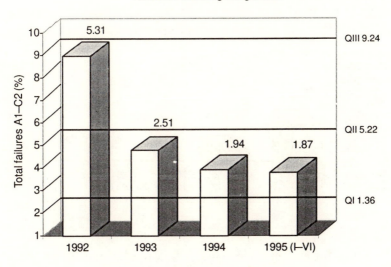

*Source*: TL.

Attributed checking of packages—PB

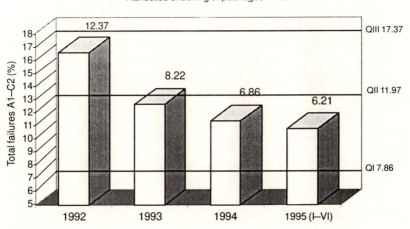

Table 2

**Geographic Distribution of Tobačna Ljubljana, d.o.o., Sales in 1991–95**

|  | 1991 | 1992 | 1993 | 1994 | 1995 (plan) |
|---|---|---|---|---|---|
| 1. Slovenia |  |  |  |  |  |
| billion cigarettes | 2,460 | 3,383 | 3,674 | 3,670 | 3,700 |
| share (%) | 50.5 | 59.3 | 77.7 | 72.7 | 71.4 |
| 2. Former Yugoslavia |  |  |  |  |  |
| billion cigarettes | 2,317 | 771 | 428 | 297 | 700 |
| share (%) | 47.6 | 13.5 | 9.1 | 5.9 | 13.5 |
| 3. Export |  |  |  |  |  |
| billion cigarettes | 93 | 1,548 | 624 | 1,078 | 780 |
| share (%) | 1.9 | 27.1 | 13.2 | 21.4 | 15.1 |
| Total |  |  |  |  |  |
| billion cigarettes | 4,870 | 5,702 | 4,726 | 5,045 | 5,180 |
| share (%) | 100.0 | 100.0 | 100.0 | 100.0 | 100.0 |

*Source*: TL.

TL plans further improvements in this field in the future. By up-grading the SAP/R3 information system, TL expects to improve the integration of all business functions in the company and that of customers and suppliers with the financial department in the company.[22] In view of TL's plans to penetrate new markets (see section 9, "Sales and Marketing"), TL will have to seek barter arrangements and to organize coping with the unstable conditions in these new markets. To do that, TL needs strict control and efficient payments collection.

TL performs its financial operations with four Slovenian banks: Nova Ljubljanska banka, SKB, ABanka, and Nova Kreditna banka Maribor. There is no need for TL to try to use some financial lines abroad, via Reemtsma for instance, because the aforementioned Slovenian banks are fully competitive as far as interest rates and accuracy are concerned.

Financial control is probably the most strictly prescribed element in the relations between TL and Reemtsma. In the financial area, reporting to Reemtsma occurs monthly. The rules of the game in compiling monthly, semi-annual, and annual financial reports are very strict. However, Reemtsma would interfere only when the indicators in the reports show worse results than those defined in the annual plan. Day-to-day financial decisions are made without interference from Reemtsma. Therefore, within the framework of the plans, the financial director is quite independent in managing financial matters. Only for large amounts of money is he supposed to seek the consent of the managing director, who would probably consult with Reemtsma.

In the initial period following the acquisition, there were problems with the comparability of TL's accounting data with Reemtsma's. This was due to the specific accounting system then being used in Slovenia. After Slovenia adopted international accounting standards and decreased the inflation rate, these problems mostly disappeared. Now Slovenian and German accounting systems are more or less comparable.

## SALES AND MARKETING

In recent years, TL's sales underwent significant changes in three major aspects: the change in the market structure when it lost the former Yugoslav market; the change in cigarette brands by the introduction of new, especially its own (Boss), light and superlight American-blend brands; and the change in the structure of cigarette prices in the main market, where the share of taxes increased tremendously.

### *Changes in the Geographical Distribution of Sales*

The main reason for changes in TL's market structure was the collapse of the Yugoslav market in 1991 (see Table 2). In 1991, only 50.5 percent of TL's total sales of 4,870 million cigarettes was absorbed by the Slovenian market, as much as 47.6 percent by other countries of the former Yugoslavia, while 1.9 percent was exported. By 1994 this structure totally changed; the share of Slovenia in TL's total sales of 5,045 million cigarettes increased to 72.7 percent, the share of the other countries of the former Yugoslavia decreased to only 5.9 percent, and the share of exports increased to 21.4 percent.

Although the increase in exports in the period 1991–94 was remarkable, the collapse of the former Yugoslav market was compensated mostly by the increase in TL's sales in the Slovenian market. TL's sales in Slovenia in 1991–94 increased from 2,460 to 3,670 million cigarettes, that is, by 49.2 percent. As a result, TL's market share in Slovenia increased from 56.2 percent in 1991 to 83.8 percent in 1994. In spite of this increase, exports remain a less important segment for TL; in 1995, a certain decrease in exports was planned. Relatively high exports in 1994 and especially in 1992 seem much more a reflection of Reemtsma's assistance in compensating for the collapse of the Yugo-

Figure 4. **Sales of Cigarettes of Tobačna Ljubljana, d.o.o., in 1960–95**
(billion cigarettes)

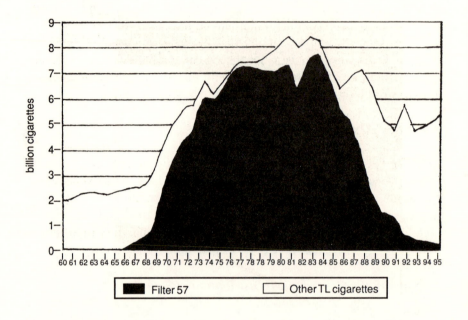

slav market than a self-sustained long-term trend. In 1992, 53 percent; in 1993, 31 percent; and in 1994, 48 percent of TL's exports went via Reemtsma's network. The rest was exported to CEE countries. A customs duty of 90 percent on cigarettes in the EU region prevents any export to EU countries.

### Changes in the Sales Structure of Cigarette Brands

TL had the highest output of cigarettes in the first half of the 1980s, when annual production was almost 8.5 billion cigarettes, of which approximately 7.5 billion was Filter 57. After 1984, TL's production and sales entered a long downward trend due to the sharp and rapid decrease in the sales of Filter 57; the sales of Filter 57 decreased to less than 1.5 billion in 1990 and to less than 0.5 billion in 1994 (see Figure 4). In 1987–88, TL began to increase the share of other cigarette brands in its sales. The major turnover in the structure of cigarette brands in TL sales, however, occurred only after 1990, especially after the take-over

Figure 5. **Market Share of Tobačna Ljubljana, d.o.o., in the Slovenian Cigarette Market in 1990–95** (in %)

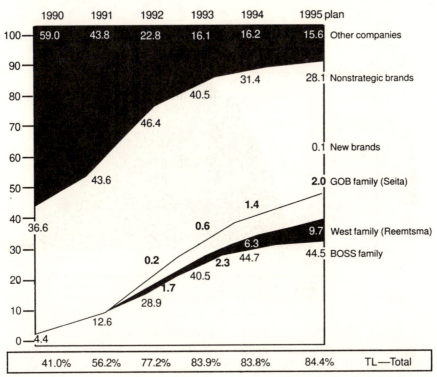

*Source*: TL.

by Reemtsma/Seita. In 1991, the nonstrategic brands still accounted for 77.6 percent of all TL sales in Slovenia and the new, modern Boss family for only 22.4 percent. In 1994, cigarettes of the Boss family amounted to 53.3 percent of all TL sales in Slovenia, 7.9 percent of sales represented cigarettes of Reemtsma's West family, 1.7 percent of Seita's Gauloises family, and 37.5 percent by nonstrategic brands of cigarettes (calculated from Figure 5).

### Changes in the Structure of Cigarette Prices

While the number of cigarettes sold by TL in the Slovenian market in 1991–94 increased by 49.2 percent, from 2,460 to 3,670 million ciga-

Table 3

**Gross and Net Turnover and Taxes in Tobačna Ljubljana, d.o.o., in 1991–95** (DM million)

|  | 1991 | 1992 | 1993 | 1994 | 1995 (plan) |
|---|---|---|---|---|---|
| 1. Gross turnover | 234.6 | 239.9 | 284.3 | 371.1 | 414.8 |
| 2. Taxes | 73.4 | 107.5 | 136.6 | 217.5 | 245.5 |
| 3. Net turnover (gross turnover − taxes) | 161.2 | 132.4 | 147.7 | 153.6 | 169.3 |
| 4. Taxes as percentage of gross turnover (%) | 31.3 | 44.8 | 48.0 | 58.6 | 59.2 |
| 5. Share of taxes in cigarette retail price in Slovenia (%) | 42 | 52 | 54 | 66 | 64[a] |

*Source*: TL.
[a]The decrease in the share of taxes compared to 1994 is planned due to a different product mix.

rettes, and the gross turnover by 58.2 percent, from DM 234.6 million to DM 371.1 million, the tax paid by TL in the same period increased almost threefold, from DM 73.4 million in 1991 to DM 217.5 million in 1994. This is not surprising because in Slovenia the share of tax in the retail price of cigarettes increased tremendously between 1990 and 1994, that is, from 42 percent to no less than 66 percent. The consequence is that the share of taxes in TL's gross turnover increased from 31.3 percent in 1991 to 59.2 percent in 1994 (see Table 3 for details).

Taking into account the problems and challenges TL has faced in recent years,[23] retaining and even increasing production and maintaining the level of net turnover (gross turnover minus taxes; see Table 3)[24] is definitely a success. In spite of the loss of a large part of its market and a considerable increase in cigarette prices, TL succeeded with new brands of cigarettes to keep its existing consumers in Slovenia and to attract the new ones in Slovenia and abroad.[25] Reemtsma's contribution to that was very important, especially in two aspects:

(a) in assisting and supporting TL experts in more rapidly developing and promoting TL's own Boss cigarette, which is now by far the company's best-selling cigarette. The introduction of Reemtsma's West and Seita's Gauloises cigarettes also contributed to the success, only less;

(b) in opening up some export markets to TL, especially in

1992, immediately after the collapse of the Yugoslav market. Reemtsma exported TL's cigarettes via its own sales network abroad and, for instance, allowed TL to export to the Czech Republic and to compete with its subsidiary there.

Last but not least, one of the major changes that enabled TL to overcome the difficult transition period and to make profits in all these years was the strict elimination or scaling down of loss-making activities and products.

### Changes Introduced in the Sales and Marketing Activities of TL

TL's sales activities were intensified only after 1988, when the decreasing production and sales of Filter 57 no longer allowed for a sence of comfort and after the new managing director had been appointed. Before the acquisition, warehousing and commissioning were centralized; now everything is operated from a center in Ljubljana. The distribution process was automatized and computerized. A "calling center" was organized for regularly monitoring the situation in the market. Using so-called preliminary calls, the "calling center" secures the orders of customers and their regular supply.

Although a kind of marketing was introduced before 1988, real marketing activities began only after the take-over by Reemtsma/Seita. The following are the most outstanding changes that occurred in the sales and marketing area after the acquisition by Reemtsma/Seita:

(a) In the field of sales and marketing, a promotion service was introduced. The service assures regular sales and the promotion of TL's products in the entire Slovenian market. Considerable progress was achieved in the monitoring service, which is also computer backed. Thanks to this service, management is now familiar with all the sales data, which promotes faster communication and information flow. Management is aware that the high quality of their product is not enough for its success if it is not accompanied by quality service supporting the sale of the product.

(b) The retail sales network, with its more than 165 sales spots in bars, tobacco shops, and so forth, all over Slovenia is extremely important for TL. Because of irrational organization and very extensive assortment, the retail sales department was losing money in the past. Narrowing down the number of items in the sales assortment from 5,225 to 700 and the number of retailers from 350 to 200, investments in the modernizations of shops and in the information system, the centralization of management and warehousing activities, and the elimination of unprofitable sales spots resulted in the elimination of losses in retail sales. TL's management is preparing a new strategy of development of the retail sales department; not only the retail sales department as a whole but each individual shop is supposed to be profitable. Shops should be a showcase for TL's cigarettes; a new name ("3DVA") will be launched for the shops. Resolving the retail sales issue is important also because this unit employs more than 30 percent of all TL employees.

### The Vision of Future Development in the Field of Sales and Marketing

In 1994, Reemtsma initiated a project called "Vision 2000" in which the managements of Reemtsma's companies abroad elaborated, along the lines of the standardized questionnaire prepared by Reemtsma, their views on the development of their companies by the year 2000. "Vision 2000" for TL was prepared entirely by TL's staff in Ljubljana, and Reemtsma adopted the document. TL's objectives in "Vision 2000" are quite high. In recent years, after the collapse of the former Yugoslav market, TL's efforts were concentrated on retaining and improving its position in the Slovenian market. The major marketing efforts in "Vision 2000" are of a much more aggressive character, and they are export oriented, calling for the penetration of new markets, especially in the other countries of the former Yugoslavia, in the countries of Eastern Europe, Russia, the Middle East, and Africa.

Although TL's exports increased considerably after 1991, exports are still of a more or less ad hoc character, with great annual fluctuations. Reemtsma played a very important role in increasing TL's export in recent years. Reemtsma's corporate network markets are divided among its foreign affiliates, and TL cannot export to the EU and to countries where Reemtsma has affiliates.[26]

TL's management regards higher quality, lower costs, more flexible production, and know-how in the organization of sales and distribution as the competitive advantages that assure the realization of the objectives of "Vision 2000." In spite of higher risks existing in such markets as the former Yugoslavia, Eastern Europe, Russia, the Middle East, and Africa, TL has no other choice if it wants to achieve the necessary increase in production and subsequent lowering of costs per unit. The penetration of new markets is also necessary in order to retain and promote TL's strategic brands, whose isolation in the small Slovenian market would mean their slow but sure disappearance. TL's objective is to increase annual production to 7 billion cigarettes and to achieve a 12 percent market share in the markets of the former Yugoslavia. TL's planned investments will not increase production; they will only modernize it. To access foreign markets, TL will have to make additional investments abroad in its own sales and distribution network, in information systems and human resources, and above all in the marketing support of TL's brands. An increased presence in foreign markets will require changes in TL, especially as far as the mastering and managing of a large number of tobacco blends, brands and types of packaging is concerned. Also, all of TL's departments will be faced with the need to provide a number of new services as a support to sales and marketing activities in foreign markets. The target export markets, defined in TL's "Vision 2000," are characterized by low labor costs. Consequently, TL will have to decrease costs to remain competitive with local cigarette manufacturers. Considerable changes in the level and structure of the costs of TL's facilities and headquarters in Ljubljana should be expected.

## EMPLOYMENT, SALARIES, AND TRAINING

Probably the major and the most interesting feature of TL's development in the period after 1988, and especially after the take-over by Reemtsma/Seita, is the investment in human-resource development, that is, the training of the existing staff and employment of new, highly skilled staff. If TL's development after 1988 is characterized by investments in modernization, it can be said that the investments in people had priority. TL's transformation was accomplished through the upgrading of its own staff, supplemented by new experts.

As a consequence of new technology, rationalization, a new structure of operations, and a modified and reduced market, the number and structure of employees in TL changed dramatically in the past four years.[27] The major objective of these changes was to renew the human-resource potential of the company in accordance with the overall restructuring of TL. Renewing the human-resource potential was based on the following principles:

(a) to develop TL's staff and to increase the economic security of employees;

(b) to employ new, young, skilled people;

(c) to assure social security for the redundant workers.

### Structure of Employees

From 1991 to June 1995, the share of unskilled and semiskilled workers decreased from 40 percent to 33 percent, while that of skilled workers and technicians increased from 54 percent to 56 percent and of university graduates from 6 percent to 10 percent.

The changes in the structure of TL's employees are the result of (a) redundancies (the number of employees was reduced by 216 persons since 1991), when mostly low-skilled or unskilled employees left the company, on the one hand, and (b) of new employment, where higher educational levels prevail, on the other. Since 1991, TL has hired forty-nine new university graduates; twenty of them came directly from the university, and most of them had been receiving scholarships from TL. Of the secondary-school level, TL hires ten new people on average annually.

### Recruitment Policy

The recruitment policy of TL has two major characteristics:

(a) In the case of executive staff, especially directors, TL strongly prefers internal recruitment. Wherever possible, new executives and directors are recruited from within TL. Being employed in TL has at least 50 percent weight in selecting a new director. Until now, external recruitment occurred almost only in the case of new departments and where there was a lack of adequate internal manpower, for instance in marketing and accounting.

(b) In the external recruitment of new, high-skilled personnel, TL concentrates on young people coming from the University of Ljubljana mostly with no previous experience. Many of them had TL scholarships. TL traditionally provides a number of such scholarships in different fields. At the moment, TL gives twenty scholarships to students at the University of Ljubljana.

The number of permanent foreign staff in TL is only three: the marketing director, from Reemtsma, the retail sales director, from

Seita, and another person from Reemtsma to help in the introduction of new technology and production. The managing director retained his job after the acquisition, but some new executives were nominated. With the exception of the marketing director, no foreign staff was hired immediately after the acquisition (Korže and Simoneti 1992, p. 12).

## Redundancy of Workforce and Reduction of Employment

In the acquisition agreement, a development plan for TL was prepared with the supposition that the modernization would require no redundancies (Korže and Simoneti 1992, p. 10). However, like most other companies in the process of privatization and transition, TL was not able to avoid redundancies. Before, during, and after the acquisition, TL considerably reduced the number of employees. In the 1991–June 1995 period, the number of employees was reduced by 216 persons or by 16.8 percent, from 1,286 in 1991 to 1,070 in June 1995. The biggest percentage reductions were in production, in sales and marketing, and in retail sales. The reductions in business administration were smaller. On the other hand, the number of employees in quality control and in R&D increased (see Table 4 for details).

The process of redundancies in TL is not yet finished. In order to increase efficiency, a necessary condition for survival in the extremely competitive cigarette market, TL will not be able to avoid some more reductions in the workforce in the future. To reduce the number of people in the administrative area, TL has already introduced a new information system.

TL has traditionally been a company with a lot of feeling for the social problems of its employees. Therefore the issue of redundant workers was handled very carefully. This standpoint was also affirmed by the acquisition agreement's stipulation that the company should not reduce the workforce due to modernization. TL therefore used a soft approach and invested a lot of money and effort in resolving problems associated with redundancies. The methods used have been the following:

(a) The company paid off the employees who were close to retirement, enabling them to retire immediately.

(b) There were a lot of individual discussions with employees to clarify the situation and to avoid dismissals in cases where grave social

Table 4

## Number of Employees in Tobačna Ljubljana, d.o.o., in 1991–95

| Field of employment | 1991 end | 1992 end | 1993 end | 1994 end | 1995 June | Change in 1991–95 Number | % |
|---|---|---|---|---|---|---|---|
| 1. Business administration | 140 | 130 | 130 | 124 | 119 | −21 | −15.0 |
| 2. Retail sales | 441 | 431 | 396 | 381 | 360 | −81 | −18.4 |
| 3. Development and production | 498[a] | 538 | 485 | 418 | 398 | −140[b] | −26.0[b] |
| —Direct production[c] | n.a. | 380 | 328 | 283 | 270 | −110 | −28.9 |
| —R&D | n.a. | 10 | 12 | 11 | 12 | +2 | +20.0 |
| —Other activities in the development and production department | n.a. | 148 | 145 | 124 | 116 | −32 | −21.6 |
| 4. Quality assurance | n.a. | 30 | 26 | 27 | 26 | −4 | −13.3 |
| 5. Marketing and sales | 207 | 172 | 160 | 167 | 167 | −40 | −19.3 |
| Total | 1,286 | 1,301 | 1,197 | 1,117 | 1,070 | −216 | −16.8 |

*Source*: TL.
[a]Figure for 1991 includes quality assurance.
[b]Decrease in 1992–95 because figure for 1991 is not comparable. See Note a.
[c]Blue-collar workers.

problems would appear.

(c) The company tried to find alternative jobs for redundant employees.

(d) The company has encouraged people and helped them start their own businesses.

## *Training*

Intensive training has been the key element of TL's transition before and especially after acquisition by Reemtsma/Seita. An extensive training program to raise productivity and introduce new quality standards for employees was proposed in the acquisition agreement itself (Korže and Simoneti 1992, p. 10). Training embraces all fields of operations: technical, organizational, and commercial. Reemtsma and TL participated in the training approximately equally.

In recent years, two thirds of TL employees were involved in various training courses. The percentage of employees involved in the training process increased especially in 1992, that is after the acquisition by Reemtsma/Seita (for details, see Table 5). This coincides with

Table 5

**Number of Tobačna Employees Involved in Training Processes in 1991–95**

| Type of training (I–VI) | 1991 | 1992 | 1993 | 1994 | 1995 |
|---|---|---|---|---|---|
| 1. Training of business administration and production management | 16 | 22 | 45 | 200 | 75 |
| 2. Professional training | 130 | 548 | 357 | 196 | 120 |
| 3. Training abroad | 27 | 42 | 79 | 87 | 44 |
| 4. Computer training | 211 | 91 | 148 | 201 | 35 |
| 5. Foreign-language training | 98 | 74 | 83 | 75 | 68 |
| Total: | | | | | |
|   (a) Number of employees involved in training | 482 | 777 | 712 | 759 | 342 |
|   (b) % of total employees | 37.5 | 59.7 | 59.5 | 67.9 | 32.0 |
| | | | | | |
| (a) Average number of training days per employee involved in training | 4 | 4 | 4.5 | 3.5 | 3.9 |
| (b) % of training out of working process | 42 | 57 | 49 | 44 | 60 |

*Source*: TL.

the introduction of new technology, marketing and business administration techniques in TL. The following types of training have been applied in TL:

(a) Education and training in business administration and production management for the highest, higher, and middle executive levels with active work in workshops. For example, TL management is continuously trained in Mercury International management courses in Ljubljana. Also, one of TL's staff is attending an MBA course in Slovenia.

(b) Professional education and training for executive and expert staff at home and abroad, and training of staff in Reemtsma and Seita and within their business partners abroad for technical, marketing, and computer experts. Training in Reemtsma is concentrated in marketing, development, and production. Recently, training for the introduction of the new information system gained particular importance. Reemtsma helped TL in organizing SAP/R3 training for TL's staff at Siemens-Nixdorf's training center in Brussels. By special request, Reemtsma provided TL with training experts for TL's management.

(c) Computer training in their own computer workshop to introduce the new information system and to increase general computer literacy.

(d) Education of employees in schools and faculties in Slovenia (twenty employees); work with new employees coming from schools and universities, with TL scholarship holders, and with students in their regular annual practical training in TL.

## Salaries

Before the acquisition, the salaries in TL were under the Slovenian average. After the acquisition, the policy of TL has been to keep salaries approximately 10 percent above the Slovenian average, depending on the business results of the company. All fringe benefits were preserved. Thus, it was not surprising that there was no active opposition to the deal from the trade unions both within and outside the company (Korže and Simoneti 1992, p. 10).

In May 1995, the average salary in TL was DM 1,411 (SIT 114,792) in gross terms and DM 899 (SIT 73,093) in net terms, while in 1991 it was only DM 520. In any case, this is a rather high increase, although one should take into account that this is a general trend in Slovenia.[28] The salary in TL was 5 percent above the Slovenian average.

## Company Climate

TL has traditionally been known for good relations among employees, for the trust employees feel toward the executive staff, and for their high level of commitment to the company. In spite of the change of ownership, TL retains its traditionally good working atmosphere. The level of identification with the company and trust in the company remained very high among the employees after the acquisition by Reemtsma/Seita. However, in spite of the salary increase, discontent arose among employees in the first period after the acquisition because the work load, especially as far as quality is concerned, substantially increased. This was due not so much to increased export orders as to quality problems in introducing new brands. Very probably, the issue of the increased workload would have appeared even if there were no foreign acquisition. Nevertheless, the workers did not join the general strike organized by the trade unions in 1992.

In any case, interviews among employees demonstrate that the increased workload has resulted in increasing alienation among employees. Personal contacts are fewer and fewer. Many feel this as a deterioration compared to strong personal relations before. Nevertheless, the climate in the company is good.[29] To retain the high level of commitment of the employees to the company, TL is undertaking a number of measures in the areas of (i) training and development of employees; (ii) salaries depending on results; (iii) improving internal communications; and (iv) improving labor conditions, discipline, and mutual relations to improve the "climate." The following are some of the activities that were undertaken in recent years:

(a) Sixty-four percent of employees are trade union members. Even before the respective Slovenian legislation on employees' participation in management was adopted, the Staff Committee[30] was organized in TL. Employees directly elected their representatives to the Committee. The influence of employees on management is assured through their participation in the advisory board. In the advisory board, composed of eight members, employees are represented by two members. These two were elected directly and represent a link between the interests of employer and employees in the most important decisions of the company. After the conclusion of the privatization process, when the employees of TL will own 23.5 percent of the company, they will be able to exercise their influence as owners.

(b) TL ascribes increasing importance to the area of internal communication, that is, to informing employees comprehensively and adequately about the development concept of the company, about business plans, and so forth. This improves the working commitment and cooperation with and among employees. Internal communication develops in various directions and especially through representatives in the Staff Committee and trade unions.

(c) TL also invests in the social standard of the employees. TL has a canteen, a general practitioner and a dentist, vacation facilities, additional health insurance, a program for sending employees to health resorts, a vacation program for children of employees, and so forth. Social standards were not reduced after the acquisition.

## RELATIONS WITH SLOVENIAN AUTHORITIES

Two aspects of TL's relations with Slovenian authorities are especially relevant. One can say that TL's experience in that respect are not quite satisfactory.

The first aspect is the involvement of Slovenia's government through the Agency for Privatization and the Development Fund in the sale of TL to a strategic foreign investor. In the acquisition process both institutions were involved.[31] One can say that the experience of the Agency's and the Fund's involvement has been positive for TL and for Reemtsma/Seita and that both institutions played a positive role in the successful accomplishment of the transaction. As a result of that transaction, the Fund is still a 23.5 percent owner of TL in the form of Tobačna d.d. until the privatization of Tobačna d.d. by the employees of TL. With regard to its role as part owner, TL's management is not very happy about the rather passive attitude of the Fund, which "does not seem to care much about what is going on in TL."

This reproach of TL's management seems to relate especially to TL's problems with the Agency for Payments, in regard to which the government has not given any support to TL. The problem is the following. Slovenia has an institution called the Agency of the Republic of Slovenia for Payments, Supervision, and Information, hereafter referred to as the Agency for Payments, which is a left-over from the former socialist system and is in the process of undergoing transformation. Its function is to effectuate payments among companies and to make audits of companies in the process of privatization. The Agency for Payments is responsible directly to Parliament and not to the government. The Agency for Payments is politically backed by the opposition in Parliament. In 1994, the Agency for Payments made a privatization and financial audit of TL. The conclusion of the audit report was that in 1991, that is, just before the sale of the company to Reemtsma/Seita, TL had calculated the sales tax incorrectly. The Agency for Payments ignored the fact that all tobacco companies in the former Yugoslavia had done the same according to the instructions of the then Federal Ministry of Finance. The reproach of the audit report was also that the write-off of TL's claims toward customers from the other republics of the former Yugoslavia should be treated as a gift and that a corresponding tax should be paid. The amount to be paid by TL to the state according to the audit report (unpaid taxes plus interest for four years, where the value of interest is five times the actual amount of the taxes) seriously jeopardizes TL's further development since it will have to delay planned investments for the next five years.

Reemtsma fully supports the management of TL and its managing director in this case and is of the opinion that the management had acted correctly while neither the Fund nor the government have given any support to TL. Nevertheless, these problems have consequences in Reemtsma's attitude toward TL. Until the appearance of these problems,

TL was more independent than other Reemtsma subsidiaries in Slovakia and Hungary. Now Reemtsma is showing a tendency toward monitoring TL's operations more closely.

The impression is that the government would support TL in this case, but it does not like to enter into a discussion with a strong parliamentary opposition that needs such "affairs" for political reasons. The fact is that the whole acquisition of TL by Reemtsma/Seita took place in a situation of a radically changing political, economic, and legal environment and that requests to pay taxes not paid due to the disintegration of Yugoslavia, taxes that would never end up in the Slovenian budget, does not seem reasonable. The government should take a much firmer stand in this regard for at least three reasons:

(a) There are not many legal, and certainly no economic, grounds for the Agency's claims;

(b) Government agencies sold the company to Reemtsma/Seita and gave certain guarantees about hidden liabilities to the purchasers:

(c) Last but not least, the government should not jeopardize the future of TL and kill the "goose that lays the golden egg." TL is the second biggest taxpayer in Slovenia.[32] In 1994, its sales-tax contribution to the Slovenian budget was DM 217.5 million, and the amount is constantly increasing.

## UNBUNDLING OF BUSINESS AND SOCIAL ASSETS

Reemtsma and Seita were not interested in the purchase of TL's company apartments and other nonbusiness assets. Therefore, these were transferred free of charge to the Slovenian Housing Fund. The employees were guaranteed all privileges the new Housing Law granted to the tenants and buyers of state-owned apartments. The housing stock was successfully transferred, and much of it was privatized.

Similarly, the foreign partners were not interested in the leather-goods producing unit Inini. This unit was not ready to be sold prior to closing; so a special arrangement was made with the Development Fund in which TL accepted the obligation to consolidate, temporarily manage, and then sell the unit within one year on behalf of the Development Fund. But TL would bear no risk for its financial performance. As the guarantee against such risk, the Development Fund was obligated to extend to TL a one-year deposit against which the potential current losses of the leather business could be offset; and, at the same time, the Development Fund reserved the right to audit TL's financial records. Inini was reorganized and consolidated, and it showed positive financial performance, against all expectations (Korže and Simoneti 1992, p. 12). By now Inini is an independent company.

## CONCLUSIONS

TL began the process of its transformation already in 1988. In 1990, the new development concept of TL based on quality cigarettes adjusted to the consumer's taste was defined by the then socially owned TL. Finding a strategic foreign investor was a part of this strategy. When Reemtsma/Seita took over the company, they also adopted most of the existing development concept since they found it adequate.

The major conclusion of the TL case is that, although TL had an adequate development concept and was on the way to implementing it, the presence of Reemtsma/Seita has made this transformation and restructuring process easier, faster, and deeper because Reemtsma/Seita:

(a) transferred technology and know-how and enabled experts in TL to master the production of light and super-light American-blend cigarettes much faster, including the Boss brand, which was developed by TL's experts;

(b) invested the necessary capital for the modernization of production by reinvesting TL's profits;

(c) opened export markets to TL in 1992, when TL sales in other markets of the former Yugoslavia collapsed;

(d) decisively intensified the introduction of a number of new activities in TL that have considerably improved the organization and performance of the company. Reemtsma/Seita also considerably contributed to the intensification of training processes in TL.

The changes introduced after the acquisition required extraordinary efforts by the employees and especially by the executive staff. Overnight, the company became, as some observers claimed, a Western company with no "socialistic" easy-going ways. Effective working hours increased substantially. Commitment to the company, being strong already, strengthened. The transformation is not yet completed, but the most intensive changes took place in the first two years after the acquisition.

TL as a part of Reemtsma's international network could be regarded as a relatively autonomous company. Interventions from Reemtsma are rare. Once the annual plan is approved, the management has a relatively free hand in its realization. The segment of decision making in which Reemtsma would like to be absolutely in control of at any time are investments and key personnel.

According to TL's management, TL is currently facing three major problems:

(a) After the independence of Slovenia in 1991, the antismoking campaigns and the movement supporting smoking restrictions spread from Western Europe to Slovenia. The tobacco industry is considered detrimental by the state, although the sales tax on cigarettes and the profit tax represent a rather important source of budget revenues. In such circumstances, the development strategy of TL has a negative connotation and is increasingly limited in spite of its efficiency, profitability, efforts, and money invested into the reduction of the tar and nicotine content of its cigarettes.

(b) A special problem represents the sale of TL, which was a socially owned company when sold, to Reemtsma/Seita. The case is rather unique. On the one hand, the state collected the purchase money, and, on the other hand, the same state, through its institution the Agency for Payments, subsequently ascertained that the goods sold had a fault in the form of unpaid sales taxes, suggesting that its price was too high. The risk, that is, the liability to the state, amounts to some DM 20 million according to the decision of the Supreme Court of Slovenia in January 1996 and means a potential danger for the company.

(c) One of the major objectives of TL, that is, selling TL cigarette brands in the former Yugoslav market, is not realizable due to the disintegration of Yugoslavia in 1991. TL expects this will be possible in the future, but things are moving forward very slowly or not at all. Besides, compared to the situation before 1991, market conditions in the former Yugoslavia will be changed. Although Reemtsma decided to penetrate the former Yugoslav market through TL, it began to condition this decision on a satisfactory solution of the above-mentioned dispute with the Slovenian authorities.

TL is an example of foreign investment that definitely contributed to the faster and better development of the acquired company. Credit for the successful foreign privatization of TL can go to both sides: (a) to Reemtsma/Seita, since they contributed a number of "ingredients" that speeded up and facilitated the TL transition process; and (b) equally to TL's management, which had a vision and concept of TL's transition and future development, a clear idea why the company needed the involvement of a strategic foreign investor and, above all, of its staff, which was capable of realizing the transition. The dispute with Slovenian authorities should not threaten the further development of a sound company.

## NOTES

The authors would like to thank the management of Tobačna Ljubljana for its time, readiness to cooperate, valuable information, and kindness during the preparation of this case study. The analyses "Razvoj podjetja Tobačna Ljubljana, d.o.o. s poudarkom na učinkih privatizacije" (The development of Tobačna Ljubljana, d.o.o., with emphasis on the effects of privatization) prepared by the staff of TL and edited by Barbara Trenc and Majda Novak has been widely used in the preparation of this chapter.

1. In 1994, TL was the tenth largest Slovenian enterprise by total turnover, the twenty-fourth by assets, and the thirty-sixth by employment (TL data and *Gospodarski vestnik* 1995).

2. In 1993, Reemtsma also sold 3.9 billion units of tobacco rolls.

3. In 1982, the Yugoslav government set an inadequate retail price for cigarettes, which caused problems for most Yugoslav cigarette producers that year.

4. Philip Morris is the leader in acquiring tobacco companies in CEE countries. In 1991, Philip Morris acquired an 80 percent share of the Egri Dohangyar Cigarette Factory in Hungary for USD 60 million. In April 1992, it bought the Czech company Tabak for USD 400 million; in June 1993, it paid USD 60 million for the Krasnodar factory in Russia; and in September 1993, it bought the Almaty Tobacco Company in Kazakhstan for USD 200 million. It has also bought factories in Lithuania and Ukraine. In total, Philip Morris spent USD 1 billion developing its cigarette business in the CEE region. BAT has made four strategically important acquisitions. The first was in 1991, when it acquired a 51 percent share of the Pecsi Dohangyar Cigarette Factory in Hungary for USD 60 million. In July 1994, it acquired a 75 percent share of the Saratov Tobacco Factory in Russia. In December 1994, BAT bought an 85 percent share of Yavac Tabac from Moscow and a 51 percent stake in the Uzbek Tobacco Company. BAT has invested USD 500 million in the CEE region. Reynolds has made a USD 104 million greenfield investment in tobacco manufacturing in the Czech Republic and USD 10 million in tobacco processing and sales capacities in Poland. Rothmans made a USD 36 million greenfield investment in the Rothmans Nevo plant for cigarette production. (Data sources: *Central European* 1995, p. 26; *Business Central Europe* 1995, pp. 32–33; *Financial Times Budapest* 1993; PAIZ [State Foreign Investment Agency of Poland]; *Business Eastern Europe* 1994, pp. 10–11).

5. This part of the paper is mostly based on Korže and Simoneti 1992.

6. In the self-management concept, managing directors and heads of various organizational units were formally elected by the workers' councils, which were elected by employees. The workers' council was formally the highest body in a com-

pany, but traditionally the workers' council did not interfere in management decisions and almost always agreed to proposed policies. The privatization of companies also meant the elimination of workers' councils.

7. At that time, privatization legislation was not yet in effect, but according to the drafts then in existence, it was obvious that employees would be able to participate in the privatization of their companies.

8. With the functions of a supervisory board according to the Slovenian Company Law.

9. The problem is that the contact person in Seita holds a high position and cannot therefore devote enough time to handling the simple operational issues that arise every day.

10. Seita is now also in the process of being privatized, which could have some impact on its management practices.

11. In 1988, there were only 3 personal computers in TL, while at present there are more than 200.

12. For instance, in spite of a considerable increase in the number of personal computers in TL, personal computers were bought according to the individual needs of users and without a general coordinating plan of computerization in the field of business information.

13. Modules are individual complex segments of the information system related to individual business functions.

14. Workers are not keen on following safety instructions regarding noise, which results in sick leaves.

15. The letter of intent specifically stipulated that TL would keep its development department.

16. In 1986, TL was producing four different brands but in only one packaging version.

17. In 1990, the Boss brand had only a 4.4 percent market share in Slovenia, but in 1994 the market share was 44.5 percent.

18. TL's total imports, not only of tobacco for production and various intermediates but also of machinery and equipment, spare parts, promotional material, finished goods, especially other cigarette brands for wholesale, amounted to DM 33.9 million in 1994, representing 30 percent of TL's total purchases. The share of imports from Reemtsma in total purchases was 13 percent. The share of imported tobacco and intermediates in TL's total purchases of tobacco and intermediates was much higher, around 74 percent. The share of imports of tobacco and intermediates from Reemtsma in total TL purchases of tobacco and intermediates was 22 percent.

19. TL has 3,500 suppliers and 6,000 customers.

20. The loss of the Yugoslav market, a tremendous increase in taxes and a consequent price increase, and a major transition to the production of new brands of cigarettes.

21. In spite of a tremendous increase in taxes, net turnover decreased only from DM 161.2 million in 1991 to DM 153.6 million in 1994.

22. A very comprehensive advertising campaign was an important integral part of TL's efforts to attract new consumers.

23. Reemtsma's permission for TL to compete with Reemtsma's affiliate in the Czech market is an exception.

24. The average age of employees is 36.6 years, 70.4 percent of TL's employees are women, and the average length of employment is 15.5 years.

25. Partly because of a real increase in salaries but even more because of exchange-rate trends. Due to an excessive supply of foreign exchange in recent years in Slovenia, the inflation rate in 1993 and especially in 1994 was higher than the depreciation of the Slovenian tolar (SIT) against foreign currencies. For example, in 1994, the inflation rate was 18.6 percent, while the SIT depreciated against the DM only by 6.3 percent. This made salaries, as far as they followed the inflation rate, higher if expressed in DM.

26. All these conclusions are based on a survey questionnaire administered in TL on the "climate" among the staff in 1992.

27. Staff committees as defined in the new legislation on workers' participation in management have nothing to do with the previous workers' councils of the self-management period.

28. See in section 5 on the negotiation process and the acquisition of TL by Reemtsma and Seita.

29. After the national oil company Petrol.

30. Only after the acquisition did executives' responsibility for implementing the plan really come to the fore.

## REFERENCES

"Foreign Investment–Visegrad: Investing by Numbers." 1995. *Business Central Europe* (London) 3, no. 21 (May): 32–33.

Korže, Uros, and Simoneti, Marko. 1992. "Case Study Privatization of Tobacco Company Ljubljana (TL)." Kenan Institute of Private Enterprise, The University of North Carolina at Chapel Hill, Chapel Hill. Central Europe Working Paper No. 1 (June).

PAIZ (State Foreign Investment Agency of Poland). *List of Major Foreign Investors in Poland.*

"Profiting from Direct Action." 1995. *Business Central Europe* (London) 5, no. 4 (April): 23–26.

Trenc, Barbara, ed. 1995. "Razvoj podjetja Tobačna Ljubljana, d.o.o. s poudarkom na učinkih privatizacije" (Development of Tobacco Company Ljubljana, Ltd., with emphasis on the effects of privatization). Ljubljana: Tobačna Ljubljana, d.o.o., June.

*Reemtsma: Annual Report 1993.*

"300 Največjih" (The largest 300). 1995. *Gospodarski vestnik* (Ljubljana) 44, no. 24 (June 22).

"The 40 Biggest Western Deals in EE." 1994. *Business Eastern Europe.* July 18: 10–11.

"Top 100 Foreign Investments in Hungary." 1993. *Financial Times Budapest.* June 17.

# 4

# Biterm d.o.o.
## Thermostat-Producing Company of Gorenje GA (Slovenia) and Danfoss International A/S (Denmark)

### Matija Rojec and Marjan Svetličič

## BASICS

Biterm d.o.o.,[1] located in Bistrica ob Sotli,[2] is a 64-employee mixed company with Slovenian-Danish capital that was established on January 18, 1994. The founders of Biterm d.o.o. are the Slovenian company Gorenje GA[3] d.o.o., with a 75 percent share in equity capital, and Danfoss International A/S from Denmark, with a 25 percent share in equity capital.

Gorenje GA is one of the largest Slovenian enterprises,[4] whose major activity is the manufacture of household appliances, such as refrigerators, washing machines, dish-washing machines, and kitchen ranges. Gorenje exports more than 95 percent of its production[5] and has considerable market shares in a number of European countries, especially in Austria. Gorenje also has a number of companies abroad.

On the other hand, Danfoss is a well-known Danish multinational enterprise with activities all over the world. Danfoss is one of the leading producers of thermostats in the world. Its production is between 6.5 and 7.0 million thermostats a year. Besides the Biterm facility, Danfoss also has production capacities for thermostats in Turkey and in Thailand.

Formally, Biterm is registered for the production of thermostats and other technical components for refrigerators and freezers, related trade commercial activities, and the representation of foreign firms in

Slovenia, but actually its only activity is the production of thermostats for refrigerators and freezers.

Parallel with the establishment of Biterm, on January 18, 1994, a licensing agreement was concluded between Biterm and Danfoss by which Danfoss transferred the license for the production of thermostat series 077B to Biterm. The licensing agreement stipulates that Danfoss gives Biterm the exclusive right for the assembly of the defined type of thermostats in Slovenia, provided that Biterm buys all the components for thermostat assembly from Danfoss. Danfoss can produce these components by itself or buy them from its suppliers. The licensing agreement further stipulates that Danfoss will make available to Biterm the entire know-how for the production of thermostats, and Danfoss also expressed an interest in buying a number of assembled thermostats from Biterm. The latter is carried out under a so-called *lohn arbeit* agreement.[6]

The new company became operational in February 1994. By then

• Danfoss had transferred to Biterm a technology for the production of a new, technologically more advanced type of thermostat, some new machinery, and some money for the necessary investment for the beginning of production of the new thermostat;

• Gorenje had contributed the existing machinery, equipment, and stocks of intermediates and also some new machinery.

The premises in which Biterm operates are owned by Gorenje, and Biterm pays rent to Gorenje for these premises.

The founders and owners of Biterm, that is, Gorenje GA and Danfoss, are also the major buyers and suppliers of Biterm, which resolves the marketing issue of Biterm more or less completely. The major part of Biterm's production is bought by its majority shareholder, Gorenje, while Danfoss buys thermostats from Biterm via the *lohn arbeit* arrangement.

## HISTORY

Production of thermostats in the present location of Biterm dates back to 1985, when Gorenje decided to begin with the production of capillary thermostats. Production was based on a licensing agreement with Danfoss, which then transferred know-how for the production of thermostats of series 090B for refrigerators. The actual production began in 1986. Most of the thermostats were built into Gorenje's refrigerators and freezers. The production covered the needs of nearly the entire refrigerator and freezer production of Gorenje and also of the company Bira Bihač from Bosnia for local needs as well as for export markets.

Due to changes in the legal framework—the so-called reform legislation of the then Yugoslav government in 1988 and 1989, which, among other things, enacted the first Company Law in the then Yugoslavia—in 1990 Gorenje GA decided to establish a daughter company, Emkor Rogatec. Emkor's major activity was the production of condensers and radiators, but the unit for the production of thermostats in Bistrica ob Sotli, that is, today's Biterm, also became a part of Emkor.

As a part of Emkor, the thermostat unit still produced type 090B thermostats. However, the production of these thermostats was gradually becoming unprofitable and uncompetitive. Consequently, the major buyer and user of the thermostats, Gorenje GA, began to import thermostats from other producers. The collapse of the former Yugoslav market and the loss of the buyer Bira Bihač from Bosnia brought about additional problems. To resolve the crisis of Emkor's unit for the production of thermostats in Bistrica ob Sotli, Gorenje GA and Emkor began to search for a new technology, either from Danfoss, as an already established partner, or from a new licensing partner. Finally, Danfoss was chosen, and the outcome was the establishment of a new company, Biterm,[7] as a joint venture between Gorenje GA and Danfoss.

## STRUCTURE OF THE INTERNATIONAL
## MARKET IN THERMOSTATS

The international production and marketing of thermostats is both oligopolistic, with only a few multinational enterprises producing this item, as well as oligopsonistic, with major appliance producers as the main buyers. It seems that market concentration is even increasing, since one of the major producers of thermostats, United States–based Johnson, is increasing its world market share.

The producers of thermostats are of two types: those like Electrolux and Wier Pool, who produce thermostats to be built into their own refrigerators ("final-product producers"); and those like ATEA and Ranco from Italy and Johnson from the United States, who produce thermostats for the producers of refrigerators ("component producers"). At the time of Danfoss's entrance as an equity partner, Gorenje and Danfoss were in a different position in this regard. Biterm was part of the "final-product producer" Gorenje, while Danfoss was a typical "component producer."

Such a market structure gives impetus to the internationalization of the thermostat industry and leads to the centralization of the international production of thermostats by the take-over of smaller producers by large multinational enterprises in the industry. The reasons are the following:

• Small producers are highly dependent on large producers and buyers. The best and safest choice for them is to join one of the large producers. They do not have much of a chance of joining large buyers, that is, producers of refrigerators and freezers, who, according to the lean production concept, increasingly practice outsourcing of components such as thermostats.

• An oligopolized structure of the industry increases the relevance of the so-called strategy of "defensive oligopolistic reaction" of major producers. They are constantly seeking to strengthen their global positions in the industry.

Gorenje would like Biterm to become a part of Danfoss. The oligopolistic situation in the industry also encourages Danfoss to take over Biterm, provided that it fits into Danfoss's strategic plans. Danfoss put forward such a possibility, but Slovenia is a rather small market. Therefore, much depends on the opening up of the former Yugoslav market or at least some part of it.

## GORENJE'S AND BITERM'S MOTIVATION TO SEARCH FOR A STRATEGIC FOREIGN PARTNER

In the beginning of the 1990s, the production of thermostats in today's Biterm plant, then in the framework of Emkor, faced a difficult situation. The type of thermostat (090B series) they were producing at that time became outdated and the production uncompetitive compared to other European producers of thermostats. The technological level of its competitors was much higher. Even more serious was the problem of the unsatisfactory quality of the products due to the lack of internal quality control. There were also important ecological considerations. The Copenhagen Declaration called for an end to using freon in the production of thermostats and for replacing it with propan, which necessitates the introduction of a new type of thermostat. Moreover, Emkor, for whom the thermostat plant was not the major issue, found itself in a cash-flow problem and was not able to do much to resolve the problems of the thermostat plant.

The management of Gorenje GA was fully aware that, without the modernization of production and a change in technology, prospects were rather gloomy. Therefore, the decision was made to start the production of a new type of thermostat. Gorenje, as the parent company, and Emkor were not prepared to, or capable of, investing in the development of their own new type of thermostat, in spite of the fact that they had tried to develop a new product through their own R&D. However, their human and financial resources were not sufficient for such a task, and there was also not enough time to develop their own technological solution. The quick introduction of a new thermostat was an absolute necessity and was only possible by finding a strategic foreign partner who would provide not only new technology but also some capital for the introduction of the new production.

At the same time, the overall strategy of Gorenje began to change. It started reducing costs by placing more reliance on outsourcing. Gorenje concluded that having its own company for the production of thermostats was not the best and the cheapest solution, that is, that supply from outside sources could be a better solution. In the highly oligopolized thermostat market, a small producer such as Biterm, who was threatened with being "disintegrated" from the production process of its refrigerator-producing parent company, had no other choice but to try to get a strategic partner. Since there was no such partner at home, the only possible choice was a strategic foreign partner.

## DANFOSS'S MOTIVATION

Initially, the basic intention of Danfoss was to conclude a licensing agreement with Emkor for the transfer of technology for the production of a new type of thermostat (the 077B series). The licensing agreement would require Emkor, or, more precisely, its thermostat-producing plant, to buy kits for the production of thermostats, which represented approximately 50 percent of the costs in thermostat production, from Danfoss. When Danfoss realized that the project required resources that could be obtained only by cofinancing the introduction of the production of a new thermostat, it agreed to become a minority shareholder in a newly established company for the production of thermostats, Biterm.

Although Danfoss's investment in Biterm seems to be of a "just-in-case" or a "wait-and-see" character to a certain extent, there are some indications that acquiring a stake in Biterm was a strategic choice for Danfoss. First, Danfoss is already the majority shareholder in two other companies in Slovenia, Danfoss Compressors for the production of compressors and Trata for the production of professional, measuring, controlling, and regulation equipment. Second, the fact that two other large producers of thermostats were also interested in investing in the Slovenian firm, at least with licensing agreements, indicates that, for Danfoss, a long-term arrangement with Biterm might be a part of its strategic positioning in a highly oligopolized industry. A stipulation in the letter of intent that in a couple of years Danfoss would consider acquiring a 100 percent share in Biterm indicates such a long-term strategic orientation. Third, a "strategic positioning" factor was suggested by the relatively high productivity of labor, quality, and reliability, together with Danfoss's commitment to Biterm. Therefore, Danfoss believed it would be strengthening its competitive position by investing in Biterm. Fourth, Danfoss entered into Biterm potentially to use it as a springboard for all of southeastern Europe. Danfoss's long-term idea is to cover this part of Europe from Slovenia. In this regard, much depends on the outcome of events in the rest of the former Yugoslavia.

## SELECTION OF THE STRATEGIC FOREIGN PARTNER

In principle, there were two options for Biterm: to get a strategic foreign partner who would be a "component producer" or a "final-product producer." Since Gorenje as a parent company was a "final-product producer," the search for a "component producing" strategic foreign partner who was not a competitor of Gorenje was actually the only possibility.

In selecting a strategic partner, Gorenje and Emkor not only relied on past experience but evaluated other options as well. They did a market search. Three foreign partners were considered: the Italian companies ATEA and Ranco, and Danfoss. The final choice was between Ranco's offer and Danfoss's offer. ATEA's major disadvantage was its lower technological level. The quality of its type of thermostat was not at the level of the other two potential strategic foreign partners.

After weighing the other two offers, Gorenje decided to go ahead with Danfoss. Ranco offered a good thermostat, but it was not willing to cofinance the introduction of the new product as an investor, and the price of kits to be procured by Ranco and built into thermostats was too high.

Danfoss's major advantages over Ranco were the following:
- its thermostat of the new 077B series was of superior quality;
- it offered lower priced kits;
- it charged no royalties if the kits were bought from Danfoss;
- besides the licensing agreement, it was also prepared to cofinance the introduction of a new thermostat in production, that is, to enter as an equity partner into the new company, Biterm;
- it had a stronger market position in Europe;
- it had a long history of cooperation with Gorenje and Emkor from 1981 on, which facilitated the decision since the partners knew each other well.

## RELATIONS BETWEEN BITERM AND GORENJE, BETWEEN BITERM AND DANFOSS, AND BETWEEN BITERM AND THE LOCAL COMMUNITY

Although Biterm is 75 percent owned by Gorenje, it is not treated as a totally controlled affiliation but rather has an autonomous position. Its relations with Gorenje are loose. Gorenje does not treat Biterm as a really integral part of the Gorenje corporate system.[8] Gorenje wants Biterm to be completely on its own, not taking any responsibility for it beyond guarantees on purchasing the thermostats. Such a standpoint on the part of Gorenje is confirmed by a letter of intent signed with Danfoss according to which Danfoss will consider taking over 100 percent ownership in Biterm in the next several years if the situation is appropriate. "Appropriate situation" to a considerable degree refers to the normalization of the situation in the rest of the former Yugoslavia and the opening up of markets there.[9] Gorenje obviously intends to sell its stake in Biterm and to procure thermostats on an outsourcing basis. This is in line with the latest trends in the world, where numerous multinational enterprises try to divest noncore activities and to supplement them by outsourcing. For Gorenje, the sale of Biterm would also be a kind of unbundling of its noncore business.[10] Interestingly, when a few years ago General Electric considered buying Gorenje GA, its interest was only in the core business.

Biterm is the second largest company in the local municipality of Bistrica ob Sotli and is therefore considered to be an important company for this municipality. Relations with the local authorities are good. Due to the unemployment problem in the local community, local authorities sometimes attempt to make Biterm employ more new workers than would be rational from an efficiency standpoint. These attempts, however, do not constitute real pressure.

## PRODUCTION AND PERFORMANCE

### Production

Biterm is a single-product producer that produces twenty-four models of thermostats for refrigerators and freezers. In 1994, production was 800,000 thermostat units, which was 20 percent more than in 1993. Nevertheless, the volume of production in 1994 was not yet on an optimal level. That year was the first year that Biterm was a company with Danfoss as a strategic foreign partner, and it was also the period when the production of the new type of 077B series Danfoss thermostat was introduced. The production plan for 1995 was for 1,108,000 thermostat units, but already in the first half year production had already reached 650,000 units. Keeping up such a pace would considerably increase the volume of production and would also surpass the plan for 1995. Moreover, the demand for thermostats is on the increase. At the moment, production at Biterm is taking place in two shifts, and the exploitation of production capacities is at its upper limit. The only way to increase production in the short run is to introduce a third shift, although the main problem with a third shift is the lack of an adequate workforce in the area within commuting distance of Biterm.

### Performance

Due to the trial character of the year 1994, Biterm made a "planned" loss. Trends in the first half of that year showed that a profit would be realized in 1995. To achieve a profit in the introductory period was not the primary objective. Danfoss's major objective was to supply kits to Biterm[11] and to make Biterm a reliable, price- and quality-competitive supplier. Biterm is increasingly under pressure to cut prices and consequently its profit rate per unit of production. However, increasing demand

and a higher volume of production decrease fixed costs per unit and increase total profits. Not only profits but other performance indicators as well demonstrate that Biterm's performance is improving. From the beginning of the production of the new type of thermostat, the level of productivity at Biterm increased by approximately 10 percent and the percentage of waste products decreased from 3 percent to only 1 percent in most models.[12]

Capacity utilization has also increased since the establishment of Biterm and the entrance of Danfoss. In 1994, Biterm started with 75 percent capacity utilization, while in 1995, measured in the same way as in 1994, it was 105 percent, that is, at the upper limit. As mentioned, the only short-term way to increase capacity utilization would be to introduce a third shift. Nevertheless, it seems that, for the midterm, capacity utilization at Biterm can be increased significantly by the synchronization of machinery that was provided partly by Danfoss and partly by Gorenje. The capacity of the machinery provided by Danfoss is approximately 50 percent higher than that of the machinery provided by Gorenje.[13] This creates technical problems due to the nonsynchronization of vertically interconnected machinery and also bottlenecks in production, that is, suboptimal utilization of some machinery.

### Inputs and Costs

Kits (components) supplied by Danfoss represent 50 percent of Biterm's production costs. Another 25 percent are labor costs. Kits imported from Danfoss are not available on the Slovenian market. Although Biterm is formally not forbidden to search for local suppliers for certain elements of these kits, until now no such actions have been undertaken. There are two reasons for this: first, it would be difficult or impossible to find an adequate local supplier; and, second, even more importantly, Danfoss would hardly approve such an action. After all, supplying kits is Danfoss's major source of income in its dealings with Biterm.[14]

Biterm's efforts at reducing input costs, therefore, must concentrate mostly on searching for domestic suppliers of certain auxiliary material and components, all in the framework of licensing agreement stipulations, or possibly by concluding an annex to the existing licensing agreement that would allow procurement of auxiliary material and components for the thermostats on the local market. Biterm already has local suppliers of capillaries and of tin wire and is searching for possible local suppliers of media for the filling of thermostats (gas). If Biterm is successful in finding a convenient supplier of gas, this would significantly decrease costs, because, due to strict legal restrictions on gas transport, the transport of gas is rather costly, and also the price of gas from the existing supplier is quite high.

### Quality Standards and Quality Control

Biterm is producing according to the internal quality standards of Danfoss. However, Gorenje, as Biterm's major buyer, is requesting Biterm to achieve the ISO 9001 standard certificate of quality, which defines stricter quality standards than Danfoss's internal ones.[15] The reason why Gorenje insists on the ISO 9001 certificate for Biterm is because Gorenje itself already achieved the ISO 9001 standard certificate of quality for its refrigerators and freezers. Therefore, the components built into their refrigerators and freezers should be of the same quality standard. That is why, at present, all efforts at Biterm are being made to fulfill the criteria for gaining the ISO 9001 certificate.

Quality control is the key issue at Biterm and is realized in two ways: entry quality control with Danfoss as the major supplier, and exit quality control with Gorenje and Danfoss as the major customers. Biterm's management intends to take some further steps to increase the consistency of the quality of its products through improved quality control. They intend to organize quality control in such a way that it will give an immediate warning about eventual failures in products and that it will have adequate feed-back effects on production. In short, the organization of production should change so as to further decrease the percentage of waste.

For thermostats supplied by Biterm to Danfoss within the framework of the *lohn arbeit* agreement, Danfoss conducts quality control at Biterm only occasionally, for instance, every three months. The major quality control is in Denmark upon delivery, which demonstrates Danfoss's trust in the quality of Biterm's thermostats. In the past, there have been no problems with the quality of the thermostats sent by Biterm to Danfoss.

### TECHNOLOGY TRANSFER AND R&D

The transfer of technology and know-how for the production of the new product was the very core of Gorenje's motivation in attracting a strategic foreign partner into the production of thermostats. Compared to the old type of thermostat (the 090B series) produced by the predecessors of Biterm, the new type of thermostat (the 077B) and the technology for its production transferred by Danfoss have a number of advantages:

• the 077B thermostat is of modern construction, adapted for assembly on automatic production lines, and meets all standards of quality and electrical security;

• the 077B thermostat is of higher quality, is more reliable, is more flexible (in terms of substituting individual elements), and is better suited to automatic assembly;

• the labor intensity in 077B thermostat production is lower, less than 80 hours for 1,000 thermostats, compared to 90 hours for 1,000 thermostats of the 090B type;

• the production of the 077B thermostat permits the use of cheaper inputs and fewer components;

• the 077B thermostat is superior in ecological terms and is more energy saving.

Danfoss's 077B thermostat is different in design from those of ATEA or Ranco. The types of thermostats produced by ATEA and Ranco are of a lower quality stratum than the 077B, but their designs make it easier to reduce costs, because they are more flexible in the utilization of different input materials.

In the field of thermostat production in general and in Danfoss's network specifically, one can distinguish among three levels of technology, that is, of the labor intensity of the production process: one production line producing the same volume of output employs

(a) two people at the highest level of computerized production used at Danfoss at the parent company's plant;

(b) ten people at the middle level of technology used, for instance, by Danfoss's Italian wholly owned subsidiary Climatik;[16]

(c) twenty-five people at the lowest level of technology used at the moment at Biterm.

The assembly of thermostats at Biterm is basically manual, with certain automated positions. The technology that Danfoss transferred to Biterm is obviously far from the most sophisticated in the business.[17] This is partly due to lower wages in Slovenia but may even be due more to the fact that Danfoss is presently only a minority partner in Biterm. If Danfoss became the sole owner of Biterm, it would probably introduce the middle-level technology, like the one used by Climatic. Nevertheless, the lower wage level in Slovenia remains one of the major determinants of Danfoss's engagement and of the technology used at Biterm.

As a part of Gorenje and Emkor, today's Biterm was engaged in some more ambitious R&D activities, the development of new products. Management soon realized that the plant's size, in the circumstances of a highly oligopolized industry, of risky investments in R&D, and of turbulent market and technology conditions, made R&D objectives unrealistic. Thus, creating its own development department would not be a reasonable solution for the kind of small company it is. Now Biterm is concentrated in applied research on thermostats. Biterm got the basic types of thermostats from Danfoss and has itself developed a number of derivative types. Generally speaking, Danfoss does not allow Biterm a lot of initiative in the field of technology and R&D. The contract stipulates that Danfoss and Biterm should mutually exchange, free of charge, all improvements they make in applied technology and production in general.

## MARKETING

Marketing issues are of rather low importance for Biterm. There are several reasons for this.

(a) The first, and by far the most important, is that almost the entire production of Biterm is made for known customers, that is, for its parent companies. Gorenje and Danfoss are not only the owners of Biterm in a 75 : 25 proportion, but, according to their contract, they are to buy Biterm's production in the same proportion. In 1994, 97 percent of production was bought by Gorenje and Danfoss, and only 3 percent went to "outside" customers, that is, to some smaller and specialized refrigerator producers in Slovenia and postsale servicing and repair firms.[18] Gorenje guarantees that it will not buy more than 10 percent of the thermostats it needs from other suppliers. Actually, Gorenje buys some thermostats from Ranco. In practice, Gorenje would buy more from other suppliers only if Biterm were not in a position to satisfy the needs of Gorenje. At the moment, due to limited capacities, Biterm can barely cope with Gorenje's and Danfoss's demand for thermostats. Hence, Gorenje is purchasing the missing quantities from other suppliers.

(b) The second is that Biterm is a typical licensed producer without its own development department and its own products that would require marketing. The licensing agreement provides limited scope for the licensee's own marketing efforts.

(c) The third is that, due to its small size, Biterm has very limited resources and capabilities to do any comprehensive marketing activities.

For these reasons, Biterm cannot really act in the marketing as well as in the distribution field and has no special marketing department. In the framework of the annual plan, marketing objectives and major means for their realization are defined by the manager jointly with the commercial, technological, and financial departments. The realization of these objectives is then the task of the commercial department. Marketing is just one of the activities of the commercial department, while individual marketing activities are also carried out by other departments in the company. The basic tasks and activities of the commercial department at Biterm are the procurement of material and components, the distribution of final products, and the handling of quality control and of warehousing.

According to the licensing agreement with Danfoss, Biterm is free to sell to the whole market of the former Yugoslavia, plus Albania and Romania, but not to other markets. Until now, Biterm has not made any marketing efforts on these markets. One of the reasons may be that demand for Biterm's thermostats is higher than its production capacities. Nevertheless, the opinion that Biterm should do more in the field of getting information on potential buyers and suppliers in the markets open to it is gaining ground. To this end, Biterm should know more about the prices of its competition.

To what extent Biterm will try to make some marketing efforts in the countries open to it depends mostly on two factors:

(a) future relations between Danfoss and Biterm; if Danfoss becomes a majority owner of Biterm, this would gradually lead to much more intensive marketing efforts in the former Yugoslavia, Albania, and Romania; Biterm as such does not have enough financial and human resources to enter into a marketing campaign abroad;

(b) the resolution of crises in other parts of the former Yugoslavia; marketing would acquire major importance if the former Yugoslav market opened up; at the moment, Biterm might undertake some marketing efforts in Croatia.

The mutual exchange of kits and final products between Biterm and Danfoss is effectuated as a *lohn arbeit* agreement. *Lohn arbeit* is a kind of subcontracting arrangement in which a foreign partner provides know-how and components while the local partner assembles the components and exports the final products to the foreign partner. The advantage of this type of arrangement for the partners is that no customs duties are paid for the components, since they are imported only on a temporary basis and for the assembly of products that will subsequently be exported. Production for the *lohn arbeit* agreement represents approximately 20 percent of Biterm's total production.

The sale prices that Biterm is getting for its products are basically the same in the case of Gorenje as in the case of Danfoss. Prices for Gorenje are fixed in German marks while for Danfoss in Danish krone. In 1994, the inflation rate in Slovenia was much higher than the rate of depreciation of the Slovenian tolar against foreign currencies, 18.3 percent as opposed to 6.5 percent for the German mark in 1994. This created certain problems for Biterm, whose sales prices were fixed in German marks and Danish krone.

## MANAGEMENT, ORGANIZATION, FINANCING, AND REPORTING

### *Management Structure*

Biterm is led by a supervisory board composed of three representatives from Gorenje and two from Danfoss. The supervisory board deals with strategic issues of production and finance, while management has a high degree of independence in all aspects of everyday management, including financial. The management of Biterm considers the company to be a decentralized subsidiary. Nevertheless, the fact that Gorenje and Danfoss are not just owners of Biterm but also its main customers and suppliers does not leave much doubt about the dependence of Biterm on the two parent companies.

When it was part of Emkor, which also produced condensers and radiators, today's Biterm was only a production facility without its own management; there were only workers and a foreman. The management structure of Biterm, as the company it is now, is also rather simple (see Figure 1). It is composed of a manager and two heads, one of the production-technical department and the other of the financial-commercial department. A quality-control department was also recently established. The production-technical department is further divided into the

Figure 1. **Management Structure of Biterm**

| Manager | | | |
|---|---|---|---|
| | General activities (Administrator) | | |
| Production-technical department (head) | Quality control (controller) | | Financial-commercial department (head) |
| Preparation of production<br><br>-technician | Production<br><br>-foreman<br>-head of group<br>-workers (2 shifts) | Finance/ accounting<br><br><br>-accountant | Commerce/ marketing<br><br><br>-commercialist<br>-head of warehouse |

preparation of production and the production itself, while the financial-commercial department is further divided into finance/accounting and commerce/marketing. Due to the lack of adequate staff, there is no head of the production-technical and the financial-commercial departments at the moment. In such circumstances, the people responsible for the finance/accounting, commerce/marketing, preparation of production, and quality control are directly subordinated to the manager. The manager is in direct contact with all the current activities of the company and makes all the important decisions in coordination with them.

### *Finance and Accounting*

At Biterm, the financial and accounting functions are closely connected and actually unified. In this regard, there is no problem with the flow of information between the financial and the accounting departments. Accounting comprises cost as well as financial accounting, meaning that one department monitors business results as well as financial flows. The accounting department collects and analyzes accounting and financial information and on this basis, and taking into account the existing production, supply, and sales plans, prepares the accounting and financial plans. Most important in this regard is the annual cash-flow plan, which is the crucial information for the owners in their management of the company. The opinion of management is that, for a small company such as Biterm, it is appropriate to unify the accounting and financial functions in one department. Because of the small size of the company and the lack of financial strength, management has not much possibility to influence the costs of financing. In this regard, the company is truly dependent on the owners of the company and can reduce financial costs only within the framework of choosing between the financial resources of the two owners.

Biterm is not facing any serious financial problems. The issue of current solvency is successfully managed. Gorenje provides Biterm with financial resources at a 12 percent real annual interest rate,[19] which is in any case cheaper than bank loans in Slovenia, not because of a lower interest rate but because in the case of Gorenje there are no additional costs, credit insurance, for instance, charged by the bank. Gorenje, as the major owner of the company, is a large company with a network of companies abroad and can also provide financing from abroad if needed.[20]

Not much financing is needed for buying kits from Danfoss, since this is to a considerable degree a barter trade, with Danfoss providing kits and Biterm providing final products on the basis of the *lohn arbeit* agreement. In the mutual delivery, noncash kits for thermostats payment is used as much as possible. Since Danfoss is a net supplier to Biterm, the noneffectuated payments of Biterm to Danfoss are charged an 11 percent interest rate.

### Reporting

Biterm is obligated to prepare quarterly reports for its owners. These reports are, however, more a formality, and only the annual report is a really detailed document. Since the new Slovenian accounting standards are fully harmonized with international accounting practice, there are no problems in this regard between Danfoss and Biterm, especially since a good level of mutual trust exists between Biterm and Danfoss. Additionally, relations between Gorenje and Danfoss are good. There is a high level of convergency of interests of the two parent companies. For all these reasons, reporting and communications between Biterm and Danfoss and between Biterm and Gorenje are much easier and more fruitful.

Communications between Danfoss and Biterm, which are in English and German, are organized basically through the responsible contact persons nominated by Danfoss for the major fields of cooperation with Biterm:

- the "licensing engineer" for issues of technology and production;
- "contact persons for supply" responsible for the accuracy of supplying Danfoss's kits to Biterm; and
- "contact persons for *lohn arbeit*" responsible for all issues relating to the *lohn arbeit* arrangement between Danfoss and Biterm.

Thus, the three heads of departments at Biterm, preparation of production, finance/accounting, and commerce/marketing, have direct contacts with the responsible persons in Danfoss at all times. The experience is that the "licensing engineer" in Danfoss is the most frequently contacted person even in cases when there is no technology and production in question.

## EMPLOYMENT, WAGES, AND TRAINING

### *Employment, Wages, and Labor Relations*

With the entrance of Danfoss, Biterm was formed as a new company with fifty employees. All these employees already worked in the plant before. Biterm as such has had no problems with surplus workers, since it only employs the necessary number of workers; the redundant workforce was already laid off before, by Emkor. At the moment, Biterm employs sixty-four employees, of which fourteen are white-collar workers and the rest are blue-collar workers.[21] The number of employees increased in October 1994 after the introduction of the production of the 077B thermostat and after the mastering of the first basic models of the new thermostat in the beginning of 1995. The increase in employment has been due to the fact that the production process used is to a certain extent more labor intensive than originally planned and due to the increased demand for thermostats. Wages at Biterm are slightly higher as compared to other companies in the local community.

The influence of trade unions at Biterm is weak. Since the company is small, all outstanding problems are usually resolved directly in contacts between workers and management.

## *Training*

After Danfoss's investment and the introduction of the new type of thermostat, the following training programs were initiated:

• the licensing engineer from Danfoss came to Biterm for a month to supervise and help introduce the new technology and product;

• two other engineers from Denmark spent a month each at Biterm;

• skilled employees from Biterm were trained in Danfoss, with two weekly session each.

## *Management Staff and Hiring of Employees*

Biterm is independent in hiring employees, except for the leading staff, whose engagement is to be coordinated in advance with the parent companies. Although there are many potential workers available locally, the problem of a "quality" workforce exists. There are not many workers available with the higher education and especially the relevant experience necessary for the leading posts.

Of the four managing staff at Biterm, two came from Emkor, the manager and the head of the accounting/financial department, while the other two, the head of the commercial/marketing department and the head of the production department, were selected from those submitting applications on the basis of an advertisement in the newspaper. The candidates who submitted their applications were selected by Gorenje's human-resource division. They first took several tests, which included aspects such as teamwork capabilities, communications skills, and so forth, and then those who had successfully passed the tests were interviewed. Both the head of the commercial/marketing department and the head of production who were selected had just graduated from the university, and employment at Biterm is their first job. They performed better in the selection process than some other candidates with experience.

## CONCLUSIONS: MAJOR CHANGES INTRODUCED BY THE STRATEGIC FOREIGN PARTNER

The Biterm case is a case of a company where attracting a strategic foreign investor was the only solution, not only because of the need for new technology not available at home but also because the production of thermostats is a highly oligopolized industry on the supply as well as on the demand side.

The nature and scope of the changes in the unit for the production of thermostats introduced by the establishment of the company Biterm and by the entrance of the strategic foreign partner Danfoss are determined and limited by three specific features. The first is that Danfoss is only a minority shareholder, who, at the moment, does not treat Biterm as an integral part of its corporate network and is interested mostly in a satisfactory realization of the *lohn arbeit* agreement, that is, selling kits to Biterm at a good price and buying quality thermostats from Biterm at a good price. At the same time, the option of really acquiring Biterm is open to Danfoss if the situation proves to be appropriate. The second specific feature is that Biterm is a single-product producer for known customers, which, in terms of production and marketing, is more simple. At the same time, the company is vulnerable to external market and technology changes. For example, the introduction of a new type of thermostat turned the entire company upside down. The third specific feature is the small scale of Biterm, which makes the organization and management relatively simple and straightforward.

The major change that took place at Biterm with the entrance of Danfoss has been the introduction of a new product and a new technology with closer quality control. In this regard, the entrance of Danfoss in the company was a major step forward that has given Biterm relatively good prospects. All the performance indicators have improved after the formation of Biterm as a company and the entrance of Danfoss.

Major changes in the field of management and organization are not so much the consequence of the entrance of Danfoss as of the fact that Biterm was transformed from a simple unit for the production of thermostats without its own management into a company, that is, into a legal person with its own management. The organization of Biterm has been developed under the influence of Danfoss. The management structure of Biterm is rather simple because (a) selling to known customers does not require major marketing efforts; (b) the organization of a small company producing for known customers and assured input supplies is relatively simple, and there is no room for sophisticated organization schemes; and (c) because Danfoss, due to its minority share and "subcontracting" character of cooperation, has actually not been interested in making any major organizational efforts.

The most interesting organizational aspect of Biterm's case is the communication between Danfoss and Biterm, where Danfoss nominated the responsible contact persons for all major fields of cooperation with Biterm, that is, the "licensing engineer" for issues relating to technology and production, the "contact persons for supply" responsible for the accuracy of supplying Danfoss's kits to Biterm, and the "contact persons for *lohn arbeit*" responsible for all issues relating to the *lohn arbeit* arrangement between Danfoss and Biterm. Thus, the three heads of departments at Biterm (preparation of production, finance/accounting, commerce/marketing) have direct contacts with the responsible persons at Danfoss at all times.

Achieving the ISO certificate of quality is highly regarded by companies in Slovenia, although this is less true for strategic foreign investors in Slovenian companies, at least for the well-known multi-national enterprises. The reason is that the possession of the ISO certificate is one of the rare ways in which Slovenian companies can raise the image of their products and, consequently, enter into higher-priced market segments abroad. Large multinational enterprises need this kind of legitimation much less since they base their sales abroad on their well-known trademarks.

It is difficult to indicate transition-specific aspects of Biterm's operations. The emphasis on quality started already well before the formal transition started. Gorenje, as the major owner, is a well-established multinational enterprise that adopted world market standards many years ago. In short, the transition process has not introduced so many novelties as one would have expected. There was more pressure to increase productivity, improve capacity utilization, and give more emphasis to human-resource development than before, but there were not really any dramatic overnight changes.

## NOTES

The authors would like to thank the management of Biterm for their time, readiness to cooperate, valuable information, and kindness during the preparation of this case study. The analyses "Povezava komercialne in finančne funkcije v podjetju z vidika denarnih tokov" (Linking of commercial and financial functions in the company from the cash flow point of view) of Tatjana Vračun has been used in the preparation of this paper.

1. D.o.o. stands for limited-liability company.
2. The exact address is Hrastje 2A, Bistrica ob Sotli.
3. GA stands for *gospodinjski aparati*, which means household appliances.
4. In 1994, the turnover of Gorenje GA was USD 300.5 million, assets were USD 264.1 million, and employment was 4,154. In the same year, Gorenje GA was the fifth

largest Slovenian enterprise by total turnover, the fourth largest by employment, and the eighteenth largest by assets. Gorenje GA was somehow less successful by profit realized in 1994, where it was only in eighty-eighth place, with USD 0.8 million (*Gospodarski vestnik* 44, no. 24 [June 22, 1995]).

5. After Revoz, Renault's car-producing subsidiary in Slovenia, Gorenje GA is the second largest exporter in Slovenia. According to a survey made by *Gospodarski vestnik*, the most influential Slovenian business magazine, in the first half of 1994 Gorenje GA's exports totaled USD 118.9 million and imports totaled USD 65.3 million, using the average exchange rate for the first half of 1994. The plan for 1995 is approximately USD 250 million for exports and USD 136 million for imports, using the exchange rate for the end of 1994 (*Gospodarski vestnik* 44, no. 4 [January 26, 1995]: 35, 38).

6. For more on this, see the section on marketing.

7. Emkor still exists and produces condensers and a new type of radiator.

8. One explanation is also the small size of the company.

9. Danfoss on June 1, 1995, acquired an Italian company, Climatik. This might reduce Danfoss's interest in Biterm. The depreciation of the Italian lira has made Italy a more attractive location for the manufacture of thermostats, especially in view of Italy's large and highly developed refrigerator and freezer industry.

10. Biterm occupies only half the building at that location, owned by Gorenje. The other half of the premises is empty. At the moment, Gorenje obviously has no clear idea of what to do with the empty half. Eventually, Danfoss's 100 percent engagement at Biterm, with a possible increase of production and consequent need for more premises, would be welcomed by Gorenje.

11. It thus also realized some profits.

12. In some models it is higher due to certain construction problems with one type of thermostat, which is a problem not only at Biterm but also at Danfoss.

13. On the other hand, machinery provided by Danfoss seems to be subject to breakdowns more frequently than machinery provided by Gorenje.

14. Probably also because of the use of transfer pricing.

15. Danfoss has also begun the processes of getting the ISO 9001 standard certificate of quality.

16. Before June 1995, Climatik was a licensee of Danfoss.

17. Nevertheless, technology transferred by Danfoss to Thailand and China is even more labor intensive. In this regard, the situation in the production of thermostats in Danfoss's company in Turkey is very interesting. The wage level in Turkey would suggest a rather labor-intensive technology, but the fact that there is actually no female workforce in Turkey, which is, due to its natural characteristics, far better than the male one for this type of production, puts such a consideration in question.

18. These "outside" customers and Biterm's local suppliers of smaller and auxiliary material are the only ones in regard to which Biterm can exert some "power" and marketing influence. Namely, Biterm is the only producer of thermostats in Slovenia.

19. In 1994, this interest rate was only 10 percent.

20. Interest rates in Slovenia are higher than abroad. Also, in 1994 and the first half of 1995, the inflation rate in Slovenia was much higher than the depreciation of the tolar, making borrowing in tolars additionally expensive, especially for exporters.

21. When it was a part of Emkor, what is now Biterm employed no manager or other white-collar employees. There were only workers and a foreman.

# Part II

## The Czech Republic

# 1

# Linde Technoplyn a.s.

## Maria Bohatá

## HISTORY OF THE FIRM

Industrial gas production in the Czech Republic dates to the beginning of this century, when small local production facilities as well as foreign-owned ones were founded in the Czech lands. After nationalization in 1948, the individual plants were unified, giving rise to Technoplyn, which took over the various independent production facilities for industrial gas production, although where these facilities were located near large metallurgical or chemical plants, they were integrated into them. Technoplyn was charged with producing and supplying gases and also bought excess production from the aforementioned metallurgical and chemical plants. Until 1968, Technoplyn was active on the entire territory of the former Czechoslovak Socialist Federative Republic. After 1969, the Slovak Republic was supplied by Chemika, a company created from the Slovak division of Technoplyn. Technoplyn was a state company under the concern Unichem until December 1990, when it became a state joint-stock company.

In February 1991, the state joint-stock company was transformed into a joint-stock company with majority ownership (51.7 percent) by the German firm Linde. The remainder of the shares was held on behalf of the state by the National Property Fund. Linde Technoplyn thus became part of Linde AG,[1] headquartered in Wiesbaden. The Linde conglomerate has a number of divisions. Linde Technoplyn a.s. is directly linked with the Industrial Gas Division, headquartered in Höllriegelskreuth near Munich.

During the course of careful screening, it had become clear that only affiliation with one of the largest international companies in the field of industrial gas, such as Linde, AGA (Sweden), Messer Griesheim (FRG), L'Air Liquide (France), or Air Products (United States), would lead to the preservation of Technoplyn's industrial gas production at full capacity and at international standards. After careful evaluation of the financial offers, Linde was chosen due to the fact that Linde's production structure and sales strategy most closely approached the current situation of the Technoplyn. Following the foreign partner's entry, an expansion of the market sectors in which it was possible to utilize industrial gases took place. This was made possible by the simultaneous investment of foreign capital and provision of know-how, which opened up the path to new uses for industrial gases. Production activities were further developed.

## ORGANIZATIONAL STRUCTURE[1]

The Czech firm's marketing responsibilities include the sales plan and sales strategy, prices, production policies, sales support, and advertising.

In organizational terms, the company is both a seller and a producer. It has four independent divisions:

1. economic (financial accounting, budgeting, central purchasing);
2. business (central sales, Bohemia and Moravia sales regions);
3. production (production, investment);
4. personnel, computer services, and marketing.

Company administration is concentrated in one location, which houses management for all divisions and activities in all regions of the Czech Republic. Production is concentrated in production plants, and sales activities are handled by eight sales centers, which are responsible for sales representatives and distribution points (warehouses).

The list of production and sales facilities is as follows: Prague 9—Kyje; Ústi nad Labem; České Budejovice; Pardubice; Plzen; Brno; Přeov; and Ostrava.

First to be changed following the foreign partner's entry was the organization of sales. Sales centers, each with its own sales representatives, were created. The distribution network was much enlarged, with the aim of getting the product as close as possible to the customer and his facilities. The Technology Application Department was created, thus facilitating the introduction of industrial gases into the client's production process. The Central Marketing Department was created to define sales strategy and improve the company's visibility on the market. A centralized computer system was introduced, and the role of computer services within the company was strengthened. Further, the Budgeting (controlling) Department was created, and the role of financial management was enhanced.

The Human-Resource Department was also formed. Personnel changes take place continuously. The company's aim is to train and select from among its own employees. For external hiring, a competitive selection process takes place.

The joint-stock company's management is composed mostly of Czech professionals. The company is under the leadership of its board of directors, which is in turn monitored by the supervisory board. The chairperson of the board of directors is a former manager from the state company. All departments submit regular reports throughout the year, and these reports are then regularly sent to Linde's headquarters. For this purpose, the company has installed a computer system that is fully compatible with that in Germany as well as with those of all international subsidiaries. Accounting is done according to both the German and the Czech systems.

Decisions are made by mutual agreement, and responsibility rests fully with the subsidiary's divisions. Decision-making powers in fundamental strategic issues are subject to the foreign partner's approval, while in operational activities the subsidiary's divisions have final decision-making rights.

Since its creation, the company's strategy has been influenced by the entry of its foreign partner, which occurred at the very early stages of the free-market system; prior to 1990, there was no strategy to speak of. As the dominant producer, the company aims to maintain its position and to increase its absolute market share by acquiring new market segments. Other activities, such as production and investment, are also oriented toward this goal.

The founding of the joint venture resolved most of the problems stemming from a lack of financing, outdated technological equipment, and lack of familiarity with market mechanisms. In May 1995, Linde purchased the remaining shares from the National Property Fund, thus becoming the holder of 100 percent of the outstanding shares.

## SECTOR AND MARKETS

The company occupies the dominant position on the market, sets prices, and stands out due to its high degree of reliability. It has highly diversified production sources and offers a full range of products made almost exclusively in the Czech Republic. The commodities program of supply includes:

• industrial gases: oxygen, nitrogen, hydrogen, acetylene, compressed air;
• gases for welding in protected environments: argon, helium, corgon, cromigon, varigon, mixtures containing argon, helium, carbon dioxide, oxygen, and hydrogen;
• rare gases: argon, helium, krypton, neon, zenon;
• hydrocarbons, test gases, and gas mixtures: clean hydrocarbons, propane, fluorides, forming gases, carbogen, anesthetizing gases, bananarg, synthetic air, testing gases;
• technical facilities for stocking.

Given its own production base in the CR, this dominant standing was something of a disadvantage. Full transformation to international quality standards could not be attained immediately but required a period of three to five years. The domestic market share is over 70 percent. The two major competitors have shares around 10 percent, but their aim is to acquire about a 20 percent market share each within a few years.

Industrial gases were used for the most part for welding and cutting (about 70 percent). With the entry of Linde and its know-how, the shares in the food industry, metallurgy and thermal processing, cleaning, and water treatment (environmental protection) rose sharply. While, at first, competitors were forced to rely upon production sources outside the Czech Republic, they have now completed their own domestic production facilities. Competition has intensified. The territorial structure of sales has not undergone changes, since the long-distance transport of technical gases is very expensive. Export or import is done only in case of unexpected production breakdowns in neighboring countries or domestically. The company's aim is to retain its dominant standing and to minimize losses, as well as to increase its absolute market share. The ongoing deliveries to Slovakia, where the company operated even prior to the breakup of Czechoslovakia, are now considered export. The management team wishes to meet the company's goals through the reliability and high quality of supply, an expanded distribution network, trained staff, and the application of Linde's know-how.

Any and all marketing plans following 1989 were always made in reference to the parent company.

In the field of inputs, testing and selection of suppliers were implemented. Partners who are known to Linde in Western Europe as being experienced and reliable were chosen. This practice led to changes in Linde Technoplyn suppliers, who had previously been located domestically and in the CMEA countries, to the West. The quality and reliability of suppliers must be of a Western standard.

## DECISION TO INVEST

The motive for Linde's investment was to acquire an advantageous position on Eastern markets and to increase the company's share in Europe as a whole. The decision-making process consisted of marketing studies and analyses of the business and political environment, development of valuation and offers, revision of the offer, and a final decision. Information was obtained through freely available media sources in the Czech Republic and Germany, by sending individuals to the Czech Republic, and through interviews with company management as well as with politicians. Evaluation was carried out by the market research department and other departments (production, finance) and submitted to top management. The Czech Republic was selected due to the large share of industrial production in GNP and thus the large potential market, as well as due to the quality of the workforce and the opportunity for market entry, including production bases and distribution networks. All the larger competitors expressed interest in this market. Promptness and credibility of the offer played an important role, as did the Czech management's belief in the necessity of choosing a foreign partner. From the very start, changes within the company were connected with the foreign investor.

## EXPECTATIONS AND EXPERIENCE

(a) In 1990, the company consisted of a single unit (i.e., not yet split up), all former organizational units were still unified, and the production base as well as the transport and distribution systems were out of date and insufficient. Demand exceeded supply, financial means were limited, and product prices were extremely low. Employee qualifications were on an average level and were oriented toward production and economics. The importance of the role of sales was underestimated.

(b) The company was a producer and a seller, with priority on production. The centralized management was headquartered in Prague. Six production facilities were located throughout Czechoslovakia, and two sales facilities were located in Bohemia and Moravia. The plant level also had the same activities as at headquarters: production manager, accountant, payroll accountant, planners, sales manager, inventory, and so forth.

With the foreign partner's entry, central management was strengthened, taking over all development and decision making. A large portion of the old positions at the plant level was eliminated. Sales divisions were enlarged and fully equipped for direct work with clients. The organization of the company as a whole is the same as that for all subsidiaries. Exceptions depend only upon size. Given the nature of company management, record keeping was modified according to company standards and was developed in great detail.

(c) Total capacity remained on approximately the same level. However, changes did take place in capacity for production of various items, such as liquefied and gaseous products. Production inputs now fully meet the required quality standards. Sales meetings are attended by production representatives, and production management is helpful in solving problems, but some shortcomings remain. Productivity has increased thanks to new technology, better utilization of time, outsourcing of inefficient activities such as maintenance and security, and improved organization (see Table 1).

An internal management system has been created, allowing exact monitoring of costs and records. Energy consumption has significantly decreased due to new production technologies and has reached a level comparable to that in the West.

Gas production in itself does not have problems related to environmental protection, and it is compatible with West European standards.

(d) Sales plans were created for the Czech Republic and Slovakia at the sales representative level, and these are being fulfilled. The main strategy is to promote the use of industrial gases in new fields. Product innovation is on a very low level, and it is necessary to develop and implement complex technical solutions using company products. Less than 1 percent of sales is spent on advertising and promotion. This sum is approximately stable and is spent on trade fairs and exhibits, advertisements in trade journals, external advertising, client training, demonstrations, and press materials (brochures, gifts). Marketing activities

Table 1

**Main Indicators**

|  | 1990 | 1991 | 1992 | 1993 | 1994 |
|---|---|---|---|---|---|
| Sales (CSK million) | 589 | 1,077 | 1,360 | 1,698 | 1,980 |
| Employment: | | | | | |
| Blue collar | 564 | 549 | 540 | 464 | 408 |
| White collar | 352 | 337 | 335 | 333 | 332 |
| Profits (gross, CSK million) | — | 5 | 137 | 221 | 183 |
| Profits (net, CSK million) | — | 5 | 136 | 150 | 91 |
| Value added (CSK million) | — | 279 | 365 | 498 | 511 |
| Investment (CSK million) | 17 | 496 | 1,186 | 840 | 774 |

are integrated into the company's computer network. The basic monitoring and analysis systems are the same and thus are fully comparable. Foreign management provides professional support.

Expansion of this area will be ongoing; the use structure for the product will come to match that in Western Europe. The major competitors remain firms with a production base in the Czech Republic.

(e) The number of foreign staff is very small. They come to the Czech Republic for short periods of two to five years and are selected according to their importance for the company's development in management, sales, application of technology, and know-how. Ninety percent of managers are local. They are selected as much as possible from existing employees or through open competitions. A selection system exists for middle management and higher levels. Those with language abilities are sent for a short training program abroad, but local courses and training programs are also available. The workforce is on a good professional level. Workers are highly flexible, to an extent that is sometimes excessive for a centralized firm with unified management. The employment level continues to drop due to the departure of those staff whose positions represented overemployment. In agreement with the labor union, a plan for staff reduction has been prepared that is linked with financial support and assistance to departing employees in finding new employment. This staffing reduction has been successful, with no negative impact on morale. The company retains good employees and offers them alternative work opportunities. Employment levels will continue to fall, although at a slower rate.

Thematic plans have been developed for employee training. Individual initiatives that are consistent with the company's aims are also supported. Both lectures and practical session are utilized. Although practical training is more time intensive, it is more effective in conveying the necessary information and takes priority, particularly for sales representatives.

Wages are subject to negotiations between management and labor. The union's standing within the company is analogous to its position in the country. Wages are differentiated according to qualifications, and overall wage levels and working conditions are above average. The firm guarantees prosperity and reliability as related to payroll issues and working conditions. The tariff wage rate is most widely used, with modifications according to individual performance. For blue-collar jobs, a system of performance-related bonuses has helped to increase productivity.

(f) Finances are planned by the subsidiary, and efficiency of their use is calculated and documented. Funds are allocated within and by the parent company in accordance with established priorities. External as well as local sources are used. The parent company makes financial decisions. When money is allocated to it, the subsidiary bears full responsibility. The financial plan is included in the business plan and includes investment, profits, credit, and liquidity. The plan has been negatively affected by the ongoing high level of customers' debts, which tends to delay their payments to Technoplyn. The plan is evaluated on a monthly basis, with a comprehensive evaluation and proposals for modification taking place twice a year. Foreign management is responsive to positive as well as to undesirable deviations from plan. The subsidiary is implementing accounting methods consistent with those used in other affiliated companies. Changes are implemented on a continuous basis. The first reaction is chaos, as the old system is disturbed, followed by a stabilization period and then routine operations. Overall, these changes have been successful. They do, however, place extra demands on staff during the transition period.

The subsidiary does not sell its own securities. Following a period of heavy investments, profits are gradually growing.

(g) As of May 1995, the company was a fully owned subsidiary of Linde. This single-owner structure simplified management and decision making.

(h) Negotiations in the project planning stage were highly demanding given the political situation in 1990 as well as the fact that there was no practical experience with similar projects. In the early phase of operations, state agencies did not cause any difficulties. Negotiations took place in a positive atmosphere, and both partners showed mutual respect and a willingness to work together. Investment has not met with any grave problems of a political or legal nature.

(i) Equipment was on the technological level of the 1950s. Following the foreign partner's entry, some of the technological base was completely eliminated, while part was modernized through further investment in such a manner as to meet European standards for product quality and safety.

Equipment used is fully comparable with production in the parent company's other subsidiaries. It does, however, place heavier professional demands on the employees.

Since the foreign partner's entry, the subsidiary has ceased to do its own research and development. These activities are carried out by the Technical Applications Center and a modern laboratory in Höllriegelskreuth near Munich on a centralized basis to avoid fragmentation of efforts and means. This facility handles requests from all over the world and also develops special formulas for gas mixtures. Results are applicable throughout the entire conglomerate.

The technology employed in gas production has a direct impact on productivity, on the quality of final products, and on competitiveness. Without new technology, it is not possible to ensure the required quality or competitiveness. On the subsidiary level, there are no links between marketing and research.

(j) Technoplyn owned several recreational facilities and a number of company apartments. Some of the recreational facilities were eliminated, leaving only the two best ones. Their future depends on their profitability. The company is trying to reduce social activities to a minimum and instead to have employees arrange these activities themselves via a third party.

(k) The main achievements, which were planned from the very beginning, were modernization and improved safety standards for production equipment, improvement of transport and storage facilities, widening of the distribution network, increased product quality, guaranteed reliability of delivery, increased quality of sales personnel.

The production plan has been retained almost completely, but production of new, high-quality products, made possible by new technologies, was added. The absolute volume of production, in physical units of measurement, is not growing. A transition to new products is occurring, and the mix of old products structure also changes due in part to a transition from gaseous media to liquefied products.

Production quality has not yet been fully attained. Improvement is expected in connection with the introduction of ISO 9001 certification. Infrastructure problems continue to hamper development of the firm's business. Some access routes are not appropriate for the latest transport technology, telephone lines are unreliable, making data transfer difficult, and so forth. With time, language problems have been solved, and staff have the opportunity to attend language classes, depending upon their position. Overall results are positive. The company has stabilized, with an almost completely rebuilt and modernized production base, a developed distribution and sales network, and a trained labor force.

**NOTE**

1. Linde Technické Plyny s.r.o. (Ltd.) is the subsidiary operating in the Slovak Republic.

# 2

# Pražské Pivovary a.s.

## Marie Bohatá

The joint-stock company Pražské pivovary (Prague breweries) was created through the transformation of the state company of the same name on May 5, 1992, when it was registered at the District Court for Prague 1 in accordance with its privatization project. Until April 30, 1992, Pražské pivovary was a state company. The joint-stock company was founded by the National Property Fund, the sole founder, on the basis of a Founder's Certificate in the form of a notarized registration. Following the first two stockholders' meetings, in July 1992 and March 1993, when the National Property Fund of the Czech Republic was the sole stockholder, the first regular stockholders' meeting of real stockholders, resulting from the first wave of voucher privatization, was held in October 1993.

### DESCRIPTION OF THE FIRM

The company runs three breweries: Bránik, Holešovice, and Smichov, as well as a malt house in Vinohrady and a bottling plant in Kladno that was closed in December 1994.

The company's economic activity consists of a wide range of activities besides the brewing of beer:

- production and sale of beer and malts;
- production and sale of syrups and nonalcoholic and other specialized beverages;
- production and sale of dry ice and carbon dioxide;
- production of concentrates, additives, and other products derived from the main production activity;
- manufacture of advertising and promotional materials and objects;

- purchase of malt barley and other raw materials and inputs for production;
- integration with producers of basic raw materials for production activities;
- production, repair, and installation of single-purpose machines, equipment, production lines, and spare parts for food production;
- provision of computer and other services;
- maintenance of records and statistical information for the information system;
- marketing and distribution activities;
- private road transport (freight and passenger) as per special permission;
- specialized museum;
- administration of apartments and of social, cultural, accommodation, and dining facilities;
- provision of services to local agencies, social organizations, and citizens.

## HISTORY OF THE COMPANY

Beer brewing in Bohemia and Moravia dates back hundreds of years. In the mid-nineteenth century, most Prague breweries were still situated among residential buildings and thus were not able to increase production capacities to meet the growing demand for beer.

In 1869, a new brewery, Akcionářský pivovar na Smichove, was founded. This was a time when the entrepreneurs in the Austro-Hungarian Empire were expanding the use of share capital. Following the example of Měšťanský pivovar in Plzen, whose founder-stockholders and partners had grown wealthy since its creation in 1842, the registration of shares of the Smichov brewery was begun. The new firm was to brew 22,500 hectoliters of beer. However, with only small building additions, production was soon doubled.

Malting began in February 1871, and the first beer was brewed on May 1. The brewery's restaurant was completed, and the construction of tap rooms commenced. Its location close to the train station was a great advantage for the brewery. From the start, the brewery was a uniquely Czech company. In 1889, beer production reached the 100,000 hectoliter mark.

As old breweries in central Prague were closed, modern industrial breweries began to be built. In 1897, První Měšťanský pivovar in Holešovice opened, and in 1900 production commenced in Hostinský pivovar in Bránik; both these breweries are currently part of the joint-stock company.

The brand name Staropramen was created in 1913 for the company's beer and was registered as a trademark. Staropramen's share capital grew continuously, as did dividend payments even though heavy competition with Občanský akciový pivovar persisted until 1939, when Staropramen bought out its rival.

Prior to World War I, technology for production had been modernized gradually. For example, refrigeration was introduced, and a new, steam-driven brewing house was built. In 1912, the brewery bought its first truck, although it continued to use horses for deliveries for a long time thereafter. During World War I, beer production declined significantly. As there was a shortage of high-quality inputs, only four- to six-degree beer was brewed. After the war, as industrial and residential building was renewed, partial reconstruction of the brewery took place. During the great depression, beer production fell again, to increase only after 1934.

After 1935, a general reconstruction of the brewery was implemented, leading to simplification, increased efficiency, and more hygienic production. The first steel tanks were installed, replacing wooden barrels. In this period, annual beer production was already 820,000 hectoliters. Keeping to its tradition, the Smichov brewery focused on producing the popular 10 and 12 percent lager. The breweries in Bránik and Holešovice took over the production of 8 and 11 percent beer.

The brewery was among the first companies to be nationalized, in 1945, and the replacement of old equipment took place in the years following. In 1950, production attained prewar levels. In 1960, annual production passed the 1,000,000 hectoliter mark, and seven years later, production stabilized at 1.3 million hectoliters. Staropramen pioneered the transition from wooden to aluminum transport barrels and implemented the cistern transport of beer. It developed the first mobile cellars in locations with high sales of beer in barrels. Two bottling plants were built at other locations.

From the start, the brewery was meant to supply Prague and its surroundings with beer in barrels and, later, with bottled beer as well. Export of beer was done more for status, with only a small amount of beer being exported to Vienna, to some German and Swiss towns, and even to the United States.

In 1953, the brewery became an official export company, and, in 1967, the state quality inspector awarded it the title of "Model Quality Plant" for the consistently high quality of its beer.

The brewery lost a significant part of its land in 1979 due to the construction of the Prague metro system. The very land that was lost had been the intended site for new facilities, meant to resolve the brewery's most pressing technological bottlenecks.

Pivovar Bránik, a plant belonging to Pražské pivovary, was founded in 1898 by a group of Prague maltsters as the joint-stock company Společenský pivovar pražských sladků. Its construction took fourteen months, and the first beer was brewed on September 5, 1900. In the first season, production was almost 80,000 hectoliters. At the end of the 1920s, at a time of economic prosperity, the brewery was renovated. New brewing facilities and other equipment increased production capacity by a factor of two. During World War II, production dropped. In 1948, the brewery was nationalized, and the Research Institute of Brewing and Malting was opened on its property. The brewery was given a new name, Testing and Development Brewery. Since 1958, the Bránik brewery has been part of Pražské pivovary. Its production capacity in 1990 was 220,000 hectoliters. In the same year, a far-reaching renovation of the brewery was begun. After a new brewing house was completed, the fermenting and postfermentation stage was transferred in 1992 to twenty new cylindroconic tanks. Also in 1992, new equipment for beer-can filling was installed to meet the needs of Pražské pivovary as well as of its partners. In 1994, a water-treatment facility was built. At the same time, equipment for filling kegs was installed. The aim of this modernization was to increase production capacity to 600,000 hectoliters.

První pražský mestanský pivovar was founded in the Holešovice District of Prague in 1895. Starting from 80,000 hectoliters, annual production gradually increased to a record level of 500,000 hectoliters in 1992. In 1993, 60,000 hectoliters of Staropramen was brewed under license. Priority is given to quality and overall commercial position. The "Beer of the Year" award was retained for the eleven-degree dark beer "Mestan."

The brewery is eleventh among the seventy breweries in the Czech Republic in terms of sales on the domestic market. Pražské pivovary's production had always concentrated on beer, and its domestic market did not extend into regions beyond Prague. Prior to privatization, Pražské pivovary was significantly out of date compared to the technology in large foreign breweries.

In 1992 and 1993, the company's administrative bodies were consolidated, and discussions were held regarding the participation of a foreign partner. The main reasons for interest in a foreign partner were the significant capital needs for reconstruction and the desire to increase current export activities and to enter new export markets with the foreign partner's help.

The British company Bass was finally selected from among a number of foreign investors. Bass is a joint-stock company concentrating on the production of beer and nonalcoholic beverages, food products, distribution, hotels, and entertainment. With ten breweries and sixty brands, Bass is the leader on the British beer market. It also owns the Holiday Inn hotel chain. At present it owns 34 percent of Pražské pivovary shares.

**ORGANIZATIONAL STRUCTURE**

As of December 31, 1994, the company's administrative bodies consisted of the following:

(a) stockholders' assembly;

(b) supervisory board, a six-member board headed by a chairperson, who is not employed by the company; two members of the board are elected by employees, and another two represent Bass; an additional two members are elected by shareholders;

(c) board of directors, composed of twelve members; its chairman is the chief executive officer of the company; the vice-chair is an employee of Bass, which also selects three other members, so that its representation on the board of directors is roughly equivalent to its ownership shares. The board also contains four representatives of the largest shareholders and four of the company's directors.

The composition of administrative bodies has remained essentially unchanged since the foreign partner's entry. Members of the top management team are the chief executive officer; the finance director, responsible for strategic planning, the financial division, and computing;

the logistics and technology director, responsible for distribution and logistics, as well as production; and the sales and marketing director, responsible for domestic sales, foreign sales, and marketing.

Following the foreign partner's entry, changes were instituted in the names of certain divisions. For example, the economic director became the finance director, the technological director became the technology and logistics director, and so forth. The sales director's responsibilities were expanded to include new foreign sales and marketing departments, and the position of finance director gained increased influence. Bass's entry did not have a significant impact on personnel filling these positions.

The current chief executive officer and chairman of the board has worked for the company since 1964 in various positions including deputy director in charge of production. In 1968–69, he was abroad on a study stay. He graduated from two departments of the Chemistry and Technology Polytechnic University and received a diploma from the European Business School in Prague in 1991. In 1993 he was elected to the post of vice-chair of the Czech Association for Brand Products.

The finance director graduated from the Chemistry and Technology Polytechnic University and ENPC, Paris, where he obtained an MBA. He has been working for the company since 1985.

The logistics and technology director came to Pražské pivovary in 1978 from Plzeňské pivovary, where he played a significant role in that brewery's modernization as the deputy director for production. He graduated from the Chemical and Technological Polytechnic University and has completed a number of postgraduate programs in food technology, economics, and marketing. He has experience working at the Holsten Brewery in Germany.

The foreign partner is represented on Pražské pivovary's executive board by the director of Bass Beers Worldwide Ltd. He has worked for Bass since 1970 and is a certified accountant and a member of the Institute of Certified Public Accountants in England and Wales. Another Bass representative on the executive board is the director of financial auditing for Bass Brewers. He began working for Bass in 1979. He is a certified public accountant, holds a Bachelor of Science degree from Queens University, Belfast, and an MBA.

There is no special advisory committee. The professional qualifications of the two foreign members of the executive board indicate the form of

Bass's monitoring of Pražské pivovary's activity. Bass draws on Pražské pivovary's accounting records, which are kept according to both Czech and international accounting standards. The company is not a Bass subsidiary and has no subsidiaries itself. The breweries in Holešovice and Bránik are managed as production facilities.

Even prior to the selection of a foreign partner, Pražské pivovary's sales strategy was focused above all on increasing sales both on the domestic market, above all in Prague, as well as on the export market. In order to compete successfully against other well-known Czech breweries such as Prazdroj and Gambrinus in Plzen, Budvar in České Budejovice, Kozel in Velké Popovice, Radegast from North Moravia, and numerous other companies trying to increase their share of beer sales in Prague as well as abroad, high production quality was essential.

The foreign partner's arrival enabled a more ambitious implementation of plans for strategic increased exports, particularly to Great Britain. Bass has opened important foreign markets for Pražské pivovary that would otherwise have been inaccessible. Doing business in these markets yields higher profits, as well as raising the firm's managerial and technical know-how.

Foreign participation did not lead to any fundamental changes in this strategy, but it provided greater focus for the export strategy.

Bass was selected as a partner following an extensive evaluation of interested parties that included contacts with a number of internationally renowned breweries. Bass best met Pražské pivovary's expectations in the following spheres:

• access to well-developed foreign managerial know-how in fields such as marketing, distribution, information systems, and finance;

• access to export markets, such as Great Britain, targeted by Pražské pivovary as attractive;

• support for the company's growth targets on the Czech market;

• a desire to carry out employee training programs, particularly in management, and to implement a system of performance-based compensation.

Bass's appeal is due above all to the following:

• it is the leading brewing company in Great Britain and also has the largest beer distribution network in that country;

• it has no prominent label that would be in direct competition with the high-quality lager produced by Pražské pivovary;

• it has a similar corporate culture, management style, and strategic aims;

Table 1

**Pražské Pivovary's Ten Largest Shareholders** (as of May 16, 1995)

| Name | Value of shares in CZK 1,000 |
| --- | --- |
| Bass International Holdings | 369,054 |
| National Property Fund | 157,830 |
| Investment Fund of Creditanstalt | 86,708 |
| Spořitelní privatizační fond | 79,026 |
| 1. Fond Živnobanky | 68,829 |
| Komerční banka | 48,769 |
| Kristalový investiční fond | 30,742 |
| Restituční investiční fond | 23,063 |
| 1. Czech Coupon Invest-fond | 21,128 |
| IPF Komerční banky | 19,757 |

*Source*: Shareholders' database.

- it has experience consolidating one of the largest European beer markets; and
- it is a vertically integrated brewing corporation with a long tradition.

Pražské pivovary stock is held by a number of investment funds and banks that participated in the first and second wave of voucher privatization, by numerous private shareholders, and also by the state's National Property Fund. The number of shares issued and fully paid for at a price of CZK (Czech koruny) 1,000 each constituted a sum of CZK 683.4 million in 1993 and CZK 1,164.9 million in 1994.

Following Bass's accession, Pražské pivovary issued an additional 481,478 shares priced at CZK 1,000 each in January 1994. This offer was fully subscribed.

Table 1 shows the ten largest shareholders as of May 16, 1995, according to the shareholders' database.

Pražské pivovary owns 60 percent of a joint venture founded in Germany in November 1992 under the name Staropramen Prager Bier, Vertriebsgesellschaft mbH. The net assets of this joint venture as of December 31, 1995, were CZK 12.6 million, as opposed to a mere CZK 3.5 million in 1993. This company was registered on September 2, 1993, in Germany, with founding capital of DEM 200,000.

## SECTOR AND MARKETS

Pražské pivovary is among the four largest brewing companies in the Czech Republic. Its products are comparable in quality and price to those of its competitors. The year 1994 was one of great changes in the brewing industry. Excess capacity led to increased competition on the domestic market, because nationally distributed brands, such as Prazdroj, Budvar, Radegast, and others, continued to expand their sales in the markets of regional breweries such as Pražské pivovary. It is surprising, given this pressure and apparent switching by consumers to more popular brands, that none of the smaller breweries has gone bankrupt as yet.[1]

While the long-term trend for beer sales is declining, the long, hot summer of 1994 led to a 4 percent growth in consumption per inhabitant as compared to 1993. Beer consumption per individual reached 161 liters in 1994. Consumption is shifting toward ten-degree beer, while demand for special beers is low. Retail beer sales from store outlets grew with the sale of bottled beer. Beer in cans is becoming increasingly popular.

Despite a slow start in 1994 and the continuing trend toward a decreasing market share for Pražské pivovary, a reorganization of sales activities and increased marketing successfully halted the decrease in market share and led to a gradual return to the previous market position from mid-1994 on.

Pražské pivovary finished out 1994 with a market share of 10.5 percent. The main competing breweries have the following market shares for this period: Plzenský prazdroj, 17 percent; Radegast, 9 percent; Velkopopovický Kozel, 5 percent. Naturally, all of the competitors are trying to attain the highest possible sales and to increase their market share.

The structure of beer sales in the Czech Republic and of exports has not changed substantially since 1990.

Pražské pivovary's marketing aims can be classified into two general categories:

• to increase the domestic market share slightly, to between 11.0 percent and 11.5 percent;

• to increase export markets as a share of total beer production significantly from 6 percent to 15 percent. With Bass's support, the main target country for exports is to be Great Britain.

Marketing strategy consists of a number of activities that are continuously supplemented or modified as the need arises. Marketing aims are expected to be achieved within a few years. Constant monitoring of the competition's marketing activities makes possible a more precise definition of Pražské pivovary's own marketing efforts.

Following the foreign partner's accession, the number of marketing staff approximately doubled; the organizational structure of the marketing department was also modified. The department's methods are similar to those used by Bass, in that more emphasis is being placed on the consumer and on improved sales services.

The situation as far as raw-materials supply has not changed since 1990, even after the foreign partner's entry. Only part of the malt is imported, and input quality and the reliability of suppliers remain good.

## DECISION TO INVEST

Bass's decision to invest in Pražské pivovary was motivated by the following factors:

• The beer market in the Czech Republic not only is stable but also, together with the stabilization of the economy, provides opportunities for future growth. Pražské pivovary is well established on the market, with a high likelihood of not only standing up to the competition but also increasing its market share, above all in the Prague region. The popularity of its brand also contributes to this likelihood.

• The costs of beer brewing are very advantageous.

• Bass's support for Staropramen sales on the British market will further strengthen its position there.

The process leading up to Bass's capital participation was not simple. In addition to other owners who were directly involved, the decision-making process also involved professional consultants for negotiating contracts regarding future joint activities. These complex negotiations lasted over a year. From Bass's point of view, the decision to invest was a very serious one, since privatization was still taking place, and it was not clear what the final ownership structure of Pražské pivovary would be. Ownership relations were additionally complicated by the fact that the major investment funds who were owners were also part owners of other breweries. Bass obtained information about investment opportunities in the Czech Republic and in the brewery industry from consulting firms and banks. Consulting firms also evaluated the attractiveness of possible investment levels.

Prague is an attractive market, and Pražské pivovary has a dominant standing there. No less important factors are the more than one hundred–year tradition of beer brewing, quality, very positive wages, and a trained labor force.

At the time of discussion regarding Bass's capital participation, competitive interests were only of very minor importance. A general factor was the government's interest in the entry of foreign capital into privatized companies that needed to reconstruct and to modernize their production facilities and to gain progressive production and sales know-how. The government stipulated essentially the same conditions for all foreign investors, and these conditions proved to be acceptable to Bass.

The changes in production and business strategies as well as in finance that occurred following Bass's entry were equally the result of Bass's participation in company management and half due to the development of the Czech market economy.

## EXPECTATIONS AND EXPERIENCE

### General Situation

In 1990, Pražské pivovary was in a good position as far as product quality and beer sales on the domestic market were concerned. The technical condition of production facilities was poor.

Within the given financial and other opportunities that resulted from Bass's participation in the firm, a number of partial investments were made in new technology. Measures were also implemented to ensure further training of employees and to reduce production and other costs.

The volume of production remained more or less the same, but many changes took place in sales.

As far as domestic sales are concerned, the company still had three independent sales divisions at the start of 1994. These divisions competed among themselves and were not especially successful in protecting Pražské pivovary's position on the beer market in the Czech Republic. During the first half of the year, there were gradual declines in the volume of beer sold, particularly in the greater Prague region. The executive committee confirmed a decision by management that the domestic sales division would be reorganized in a way that reflected working under Bass's experience and practices.

• Sales teams responsible for sales in specific regions of the Czech Republic were created.

• The orders department, Telesales, was concentrated into one location and began to develop more active contacts with customers.

• A service team of staff who install tap-room equipment and ensure its maintenance and cleaning was created.

• Sales representatives as well as service technicians were equipped with vehicles and materials for sales support.

Together with the institution of sales support activities such as "scratch and win" tickets, anniversary celebrations, and so on, these innovations in marketing led to a turnaround in sales during the second half of the year. The drop in the volume of sales in Prague and its surroundings was arrested, and new customers were gained in other regions. The new sales team characterized its mission with the motto "Our customers pay our salaries." This motto describes the fundamental aim of the company, to become a company that is fully focused on its customers.

In 1994, Pražské pivovary exported beer to ten countries. The most important markets were Germany, Slovakia, Russia, Ukraine, Sweden, Finland, and Great Britain. Thanks to its German subsidiary, Staropramen retained its position in Germany despite negative conditions on the German beer market. In 1995, it was the second most imported label in Germany, after Plzenský prazdroj. The former Soviet Union, especially Russia and Ukraine, accounted for a significant share of exports. These markets are promising but presently commercially and politically unstable.

A large decrease occurred in exports to Slovakia due to protectionist measures taken by the Slovak government. At the end of 1994, a representative office was opened in Bratislava, making possible a gradual stabilization of the situation. If there are no further restrictions on imports in the future, exports to Slovakia should increase.

In 1994, exports through Bass's distribution system in Great Britain and the United States began, and exports to other countries where Bass operates were under active consideration. These exports should become an important part of Pražské pivovary's foreign activities and would also fulfill one of the goals of Bass's investment. With Bass's assistance, the company began testing markets in Great Britain in October 1994 and in the United States and Italy in January 1995. The result of these steps was a large increase in exports, which in June 1995 exceeded the annual export plan by 50 percent.

Twenty-two middle managers underwent a very demanding and long-lasting training program. Six three-week modules were developed for domestic training, followed by a two-week training program at Bass in Great Britain. Training programs also aim at improving the English-language ability of middle managers.

## Management Structure and
## Organizational Structure

The management structure of Pražské pivovary has undergone almost no changes, except for the aforementioned increased emphasis on the marketing and finance divisions. The structure has, however, been supplemented by an executive committee, a level between the board of directors and company management. Bass has proportional representation on the board of directors and on the executive committee. Because relations are not those of a corporate headquarters with its subsidiary, there can be no question of division of rights or of monitoring. The foreign partner's interests are handled by its representatives on the board of directors and on the supervisory board. Decision making is centralized, above all in relation to the two other breweries, Bránik and Holešovice, which are categorized as plants, each with its own director.

Records are prepared according to Czech regulations as well as to international standards. They provide sufficient information to make possible the evaluation of the business by Czech shareholders as well as by Bass. The Czech office of an international accounting firm, Coopers and Lybrand Praha s.r.o., prepares the financial statement at the close of each fiscal year.

## Production

After Bass's investment in the firm, beer production increased. Growth of output is expected to be about 20 percent per year at first. The ingredients remain the same, and production depends in essence on domestic raw materials. Since Bass's entry, labor productivity has increased as well, due to the installation of new production technologies and equipment. Production waste was reduced. This reduction was not, however, related to Bass's participation but rather to changes in general production conditions and above all to the modernization of production technologies. A company program for the reduction of production losses has been delineated. This is a long-term issue closely connected with the implementation of new technologies, with the training of employees in the use of such technologies, and with necessary changes in work procedures. Small savings in electricity consumption have been achieved, although again as a result of the installation of new technology. It is difficult to compare energy consumption in this brewery with that of foreign breweries. According to available information, the level of energy consumption in West European breweries is lower only in those cases where production facilities are equipped with special energy-saving equipment.

The impact of production on the environment has not changed for a long period, nor has it changed since Bass's arrival. The installation of special cleaning equipment at the end of the production process would reduce pollution, but, given the high cost of such an investment, it is not now under consideration. It is more advantageous for the company to pay fines from time to time.

In 1994, CZK 290 million were invested into technological modernization. The decisive investments were above all a new bottling line for kegs in the Bránik brewery, the purchase of kegs with a value of CZK 70 million, and the purchase of new trucks for CZK 20 million.

### Sales and Marketing

In 1994, the sales plan for the domestic market was met, with 1.6 million hectoliters of beer being sold. The export plan was also met, with 100,000 hectoliters of beer being exported. Detailed information regarding sales and measures implemented for the stabilization and growth of both domestic and foreign sales have already been explained. Differences between domestic and foreign markets are insignificant. In both cases, the markets demand high quality. Beer with higher alcohol content sells well on foreign markets, while on the domestic market demand for ten-degree beer predominates.

The marketing department has initiated new work methods drawing upon foreign experience. At present, the department performs quite well thanks to the application of the experience and direct participation of well-known foreign companies. Marketing efforts are thus approximately on the same level as those at Bass. The success of new marketing strategies is difficult to evaluate at present due to the short time period in question. Sums spent on advertising and promotion are high in relation to the average for Czech companies and have increased recently in each area. Total spending is about 5 percent of sales.

Given that the competition is continuously gaining strength, Pražské pivovary has focused most of its activities on its main brand, Staropramen.

There were many firsts in 1994:

• Staropramen's first television advertising campaign;
• the first promotion in tap rooms, in the form of "scratch and win" tickets;
• the first series of annual "party nights" festivities;
• the first national sponsorship of an ice-hockey team.

All of these initiatives were supported by a number of other activities, such as the open house at the Smichov brewery commemorating the one hundred twenty-fifth anniversary of its founding. Celebrations continued with a gala evening for special guests at the National Theater. A number of smaller sponsorship events took place for the Bránik brand and for the Mestán brand of the Holešovice brewery.

In addition, Staropramen became the main sponsor of the Velká Pardubická horse race, on the occasion of which Bass invited important clients from Great Britain and thus promoted Staropramen in this key export market.

Pražské pivovary is moving away from direct advertising toward various media activities aimed at increasing its visibility, as well as toward participation in a variety of important celebrations and meetings. The lower costs and higher efficiency of this new marketing strategy were confirmed by an extensive evaluation of activities in 1994. The main conclusions of this evaluation are the following:

• Staropramen achieved above average exposure in the media as the main sponsor of major-league ice hockey (EHL) in the 1994–95 season: 13.5 hours of television exposure during fifteen live broadcasts and seven recorded matches on Czech television; 454 articles or photographs clearly presenting the Staropramen label in words or images, with a total of over 63 million copies sold; 23.5 minutes of verbal presentation of the Staropramen brand on the hockey show "S mikrofonem za hokejem" ["On the Air After the Hockey Game"][2] on Czech radio; 1,317,000 viewers of 304 matches of the EHL, who saw Staropramen promotional materials on the rink barriers.

• Staropramen carried out a number of activities as part of the EHL sponsorship, including a successful guessing game for beer drinkers.

Table 2

**Average Employment**

| Year | Administration | Blue collar | Support staff | Total |
|------|----------------|-------------|---------------|-------|
| 1990 | 217 | 1,010 | 75 | 1,302 |
| 1991 | 219 | 995 | 82 | 1,296 |
| 1992 | 260 | 957 | 72 | 1,289 |
| 1993 | 297 | 920 | 64 | 1,281 |
| 1994 | 336 | 919 | 50 | 1,305 |

The greater cost-effectiveness of sponsorship as opposed to the forms of advertising used previously is evident from the fact that advertising on television in the same time slots as the hockey games would have been CZK 157.4 million, while the sponsorship costs were only CZK 31.5 million. Cost savings for sponsorship versus advertising in print and broadcast media were of the same order.

*Employment, Wages, Training*

Average employment figures are given in Table 2. The growth in administrative staff is related to increases in sales and marketing personnel.

All managers are Czech citizens. Most are long-term employees of Pražské pivovary, in some cases professionals who came from other breweries. Managers are selected through a competitive process, and this principle will continue to be applied in the future. Many top managers have already completed the company's management training programs. Middle managers followed, participating in the aforementioned programs. Professional enhancement programs are expected to include study visits at Bass. Intracompany training is an ongoing means for increasing the skills of professional staff. External specialized organizations are also engaged for this purpose.

The previously mentioned problems with the organization and management of sales were resolved through organizational changes, resulting in a significant increase in sales. Top management has no significant problems that cannot be resolved by operational measures.

In general, employees are of good quality. Key staff in production or administration are highly qualified professionals, an advantage that is further enhanced by low turnover. The only disadvantage is seen to be lower flexibility, but the training programs are aimed at rectifying this situation. Only supplemental operations have a relatively high turnover, which is clearly related to wage levels. Total employment over the past five years has been relatively stable (see Table 2) but with larger changes among the three basic categories of staff.

Some "downsizing" occurred among production support workers as a result of changes in production technology and more efficient equipping of these workplaces. Part-time workers are insignificant in number. The reasons for the growth of the administrative staff were mentioned above. "Lean management" will increasingly be instituted in the coming years. The level of employment, in management's opinion, is at present roughly appropriate for production and sales conditions. Considering the out-of-date production system and its technology, productivity is surprisingly high.

Wages and salaries are paid according to generally approved wage regulations, under temporary government-imposed wage controls, and keep in step with inflation. Although the labor union's role in the company is smaller than it was under the socialist system, the union does play a role with regard to wages, as is the case in larger companies throughout the country. Wages are adjusted annually through collective agreements that are negotiated and signed by management and union representatives, the heads of the Independent Labor Union for Staropramen, Holešovice, and Bránik. An addendum to the collective agreement is the "Principles for Wage Payments," which set specific monthly and hourly wage rates for the given year for individual employment categories, as well as the level of bonuses and the conditions under which bonuses will be paid. Generally, bonuses are linked to performance standards set by the objectives for each month. Wage and salary payments are made strictly in accordance with conditions set by the collective agreement. The company strategy in this field is and shall remain to link wages directly to the amount and quality of work in all sectors.

Bonuses and special premiums for managers are tied to the fulfillment of stipulated criteria and have been successful in motivating managers. The same applies to production employees.

### Finance

The company itself determines the sums to be invested through annual and medium-term plans, linking production and modernization plans and financial plans. Funding sources for these purposes are local, internal to the company. Stock offerings are not used as a source of income. One exception is the January 1994 supplementary offer of shares, which raised a total of CZK 481,478,000. Bass International Holdings N.V. purchased 396,054 shares from this offering. Concurrently, it accepted a certain level of responsibility for the company's management. Company management makes investment decisions for all plants. The directors of each plant also bear partial responsibility for the implementation of approved investments.

At the time the company was founded, as well as when Bass joined it, financial resources and needs were balanced and debt ranged up to 25 percent of founding capital.

Financial plans are always closely monitored and have always been met. The company has strict decision-making limitations for fulfillment of the financial plan for given management levels.

The company's relations with local banks are good, and no great problems exist. Short-term loans are most common, but long-term loans, beyond one year, are also used. Decisions regarding loans are made by the executive committee.

In 1993 and 1994, the company operated at a loss. In 1993, this pretax loss was CZK 238.7 million and in 1994, CZK 77.2 million. These losses were due to several causes. Above all, they were the result of costs for modernizing production; further, they were the result of a marked increase in marketing and sales support expenses, as well as of relatively low beer prices in the highly competitive Czech market and in the Prague market in particular.

### Ownership

The ownership situation of Pražské pivovary is a result of the voucher privatization program and is influenced by Bass's 34 percent ownership stake. Compared to other large companies privatized through voucher privatization, the company has the advantage that its ownership structure is not excessively fragmented. Five main owners are represented in the firm's administrative bodies.

Changes in ownership structure may occur through the sale of shares held by the National Property Fund on the capital market. Problems with the current ownership structure are of a general nature, as with other privatized Czech companies. Conflicts among owners' interests are not evident to the degree that they are in some other companies where top management has a weak and unstable position.

### Dealing with the Government

Discussions with relevant state agencies during the preparation of the privatization project and its implementation were efficient and satisfactory to the company. The liberalization of the economy precluded the need for more fundamental negotiations with government agencies subsequent to the founding of the joint-stock company. Relations with the local government are also trouble free.

During negotiations with Bass and during the entire selection process of a foreign investor and its evaluation, no grave barriers arose on the part of the National Property Fund, the government's representative in the company, which attests to the fact that the Czech legal code and political system do not present barriers to foreign investment in the Czech economy.

### Technology

Prior to Bass's investment in the company, most of the equipment was very out-of-date. Since the company's creation in 1992, new equipment has gradually been installed, but this is a longer-term process and is very demanding financially. No direct transfer of technology from Bass to Pražské pivovary took place after Bass's entry.

Pražské pivovary does not conduct its own research and development. These activities are done on a contractual basis by the Brewery and Maltster's Association. The company does, however, have its own laboratory to monitor product quality. Links between external R&D and marketing are indirect only; the results of R&D activities are integrated into marketing activities. The importance of technology for labor-productivity growth and for increased production capacity is great. To a large degree, it also determines competitiveness of the firm relative to other beer producers. Technological backwardness is evident among the competition as well. The technological skills of Pražské pivovary's employees are on a very good level; the only shortcoming is the lack of financial means for technological modernization.

### Unbundling and Social Assets

While still a state company, Pražské pivovary had numerous social facilities, such as company cafeterias in each production facility and large recreational and rehabilitation centers in the Krkonoše Mountains. Several dozen company apartments were also provided for employees. Following the conversion of the firm into a privatized joint-stock company, there has been a tendency to eliminate these facilities. Bass did not play any role in this decision.

Social services for employees do not rely solely on company facilities. Social costs and services for employees are paid from a social fund, the statute, creation, means, and use of which forms a separate addendum to the collective agreement between management and the labor unions.

The social fund is administered by the firm but deposited in a separate bank account. Money for the social fund is derived from a base allocation from the company, expressed as a percentage of the payroll or a set amount per permanent employee. Further funds are based on a negotiated allocation, subject to business performance or tied to agreed-upon activities. Payments on loans to employees issued during previous periods also are deposited in the social fund.

The social fund is used for

• camps and other activities for employees' children;
• interest-free loans to employees;
• subsidies for cafeterias in the workplace;
• subsidies for group rehabilitation stays in Karlovy Vary for employees;
• awards and gifts on the occasion of work and personal anniversaries;
• activities of the pensioners' club;
• tours and sports activities;
• special grants for social support, up to CZK 10,000.

Some smaller, less frequented social buildings have already been sold off, while the sale of others is under consideration. The reason is that a commonly held conviction exists, not just at Pražské pivovary, that these "socialist" institutions were often misused, that they were highly inefficient, and that services to employees should be of a different nature, such as those of the aforementioned social fund. The company also is considering supplemental retirement insurance for employees.

Table 3

**Main Indicators**

|                                    | 1990  | 1991  | 1992  | 1993  | 1994  |
|------------------------------------|-------|-------|-------|-------|-------|
| Sales (thousand hectoliters)       | 1,630 | 1,650 | 1,620 | 1,598 | 1,600 |
| Exports (thousand hectoliters)     | 60    | 85    | 85    | 100   | 105   |
| Employment:                        |       |       |       |       |       |
|   Blue collar            | 950   | 940   | 950   | 935   | 920   |
|   White collar           | 210   | 210   | 240   | 290   | 330   |
| Profits (net, million CZK)         | 25    | 30    | −100  | −250  | −150  |
| Investment (million CZK)           | 85    | 50    | 120   | 200   | 220   |
| Fixed Assets (million CZK)         | 1,080 | 1,110 | 1,100 | 1,135 | 1,353 |
| Gross wages (CZK/month)            | 3,800 | 5,600 | 6,100 | 8,000 | 8,300 |

*Performance*

The retention of a stable position on the domestic beer market, despite increasing competition and a slight decline in beer consumption per inhabitant, can be considered a success. An additional success is the marked growth in exports (see Table 3) and the commencement of activities, with Bass's support, that will further promote exports. These aims were an integral part of the business plan when the firm was privatized. The plan also calls for the gradual modernization of production, although only to the extent made possible by available financial means. These partial technological changes have been made, even at the price of economic losses.

The restructuring of sales, financing, and marketing is a further success. A new finance system and monitoring of expenditures was implemented. This system makes use of new methods that have been successfully applied in breweries abroad.

It is too soon to pass judgment on the overall success of these measures, but even now it is practically certain that there will not be a deterioration of the firm's long-term prospects. Pražské pivovary's sales and output results (Table 3) are comparable to those of competing breweries in the Czech Republic but are not above average.

## NOTES

1. The Czech parliament recently passed a lower taxation level for small breweries as opposed to larger ones.

2. A show where fans call in after the game and offer their opinions.

# 3

# Škoda Automobilová a.s.

## Marie Bohatá

Škoda Automobilová a.s. (hereinafter referred to as Škoda) is one of the oldest automobile manufacturers in the world—the third oldest, celebrating its hundredth year in 1995. Its official logo says "Tradition for the future." As the second largest Czech company, following the Czech energy monopoly CEZ, Škoda is a company of great importance for the Czech economy. It employs more about 4 percent of the Czech labor force both in the production factory itself and in its supply and sales networks. The company's contribution to Czech exports is more than 4 percent and is expected to increase over time.

### HISTORY OF THE FIRM

In 1895, the bookseller Václav Klement (1868–1938) and the mechanic Václav Laurin (1865–1930) opened a workshop in Mladá Boleslav to make bicycles. The first bicycle's name was Slavia. Later the program was extended to include motorcycles. The Slavia motorcycle, which began to be produced at the start of 1899, was the most advanced one among all those produced within what was then the Austro-Hungarian Empire.

The first Laurin and Klement automobile, which was given the name "Voituretta," left the factory gate in 1905, marking the onset of an important stage in the production of excellent vehicles in Mladá Boleslav. In 1907, the family firm was changed to a joint-stock company (a.s.). By that time, the L&K motorcycles and automobiles were well known in the world, and their successes in a number of races and competitions were well reflected in commercial successes.

In 1929, the L&K Company produced a whole range of cars and trucks, buses, aircraft engines, and powered plows. However, the factory needed huge investments for further development. The L&K Company was unable to gather such funds by itself, so it began to seek a suitable partner. In 1925, it merged with the European engineering giant Škoda Works of Plzeň. In 1930, a Joint-Stock Company for the Development of the Automobile Industry (ASAP) emerged within the Škoda Concern. Late in 1933, the first new car, referred to as "Type 420," left the factory gate. Type 420 marked a substantial turning point in the design and construction of the automobiles made in Mladá Boleslav. The key feature of the design was an engine with the coupling in the front and the gear box and the differential gear in the back. The continuous development of passenger automobiles was broken by World War II, when production was completely refocused to military use.

After the war, in 1946, the company was separated from the Škoda Works of Plzeň; it was nationalized and renamed Automobile Works, National Enterprise (AZNP Mladá Boleslav). In 1947, the factory began to make cars of the S 1101/1102 Tudor series. A new type, denoted as S 1200, started to be produced in 1952. Later, in the 1950s, two smaller firms were associated with AZNP: these were the Repair Works at Kvašiny and the Petera and Sons firm of Vrchlabí, which had produced aircraft, automobile bodies, and vehicles. The new car, Škoda 440 (Sparták), was introduced to customers in 1954. Several other types were derived from Sparták, including the Škoda 445 (Octavia), 450 (Felicia), and the 1202, which continued to be produced until 1964.

In 1964, production was started in the newly built modern plant. The first car type made in the new plant was the S 1000 MB, to which the S 1100 MB was later added. Škoda 100 and Škoda 110 were successors to those first types. They began to be produced in 1969.

The series production of the entirely new model series of Škoda 105, 120, and 130 was started in 1976. The Škoda 130 type was particularly successful in various automobile competitions, and these sports successes were reflected in good sales results in European markets.

Following the world trend of moving the engine from the back axle to the front, AZNP started developing a new Škoda car in 1982. The body was designed by the Italian company Bertone. The result of this effort was the new basic type of the Škoda 781 Favorit development series. Favorits continued to be produced over the period from 1987 to

1994. On the whole, more than a million cars of the successful Favorit/ Forman/Pickup series were produced.

Early in the 1990s, the Mladá Boleslav car company sought a financially strong partner who would have the adequate know-how and experience in development, planning, and product innovation needed to secure the company's competitiveness at an international level for a long time to come. In December 1990, the Czech government decided to cooperate with Volkswagen. Škoda Automobilová a.s. as a Škoda–VW joint venture started operating on April 16, 1991, and became the fourth brand of the transnational Volkswagen Company, alongside VW, Audi, and Seat.

## ORGANIZATIONAL STRUCTURE

Škoda has three plants: the basic plant with about 14,000 employees in Mladá Boleslav, two branch plants in Vrchlabí, with 1,000 employees, where special Felicia and Felicia-Combi models are produced, and a plant in Kvašiny, with around 1,200 employees, where consumer versions of the pickup and the Felicia one-plus are made.

Upon the creation of the joint venture, fundamental changes in the entire organization were introduced. The company uses the German organizational model, that is, a board of directors that is the executive body. There are no directors, chief executive officers, or presidents, and work relations are very direct. The executive committee, composed of four VW representatives and four Czech representatives, supervises this board of directors. In addition, there are three representatives of trade unions, and over that is the stockholders' assembly.

Quality, price, and service determine the new company strategy. VW's quality management system has been adopted, which means that not only does Škoda do an audit every day but there is extensive monitoring of flaws found in Škoda cars, after three months and twelve months of operation. Cars that brake down in the Czech Republic and in foreign countries are both included in this audit. Precisely what the flaws are is determined, then measures are taken to prevent similar problems in newly made cares, and a constant evaluation is made of the number of flaws. Customer satisfaction is also taken into account. Research on flaws in the Felicia after three months for Germany or the Czech Republic shows a 50 percent drop in the number of flaws per 1,000 cars.

Cooperation with suppliers has changed substantially. The concept of supplier integration has been introduced, probably for the first time in the Czech Republic, but also among the first times in the VW conglomerate. The reason is that some parts are large and difficult to transport, so suppliers are becoming integrated with Škoda. At present, there are six integrated suppliers. The parts are transported to Škoda facilities and installed there, so the company saves on transportation costs. The supplier benefits as well: he knows every single day exactly what his quality situation is. This type of cooperation has a very positive influence on quality, and at the same time it is responsive to certain operational changes that are implemented. For the Felicia model, there are 174 suppliers from the Czech Republic who deliver goods valued at CZK 14 billion and 19 suppliers from Slovakia at CZK 2.1 billion; the remaining 22 percent are foreign suppliers. For details, see Figures 1–3.

Ten percent of Škoda's foreign investments go to suppliers. Thirty-three joint ventures connected to Škoda have been founded in the Czech Republic and eight in Slovakia; sixteen completely new ones have been created. Among them are not only German but also French, Italian, American, and British companies. Simply put, Škoda is trying to attract the best there is in the auto industry. Furthermore, as part of global sourcing, the best suppliers with the best quality and the best prices also cooperate with the conglomerate, so that the goods are not just for Škoda but also to a much greater extent for VW. Some integrated suppliers have contracts up to the year 2000 and some even beyond that.

Within the general efforts related to the start of the production of the new model, an integration program was organized for all employees in order to enhance their identification with the product and the company. The new car was shown and introduced at 800 events held for some 14,000 employees. Each department and unit of the company demonstrated their contributions to the production of the new car and to the prosperity of the firm at those events.

Last but not least, Škoda is eliminating all sorts of activities that are not directly related to its core business, for example, cafeteria services, cleaning, and energy production. These employees are not being put out of work but are transferred to other specialized companies if they wish.

## SECTOR AND MARKETS

Škoda's output was increasing at a time when the plants of other Czech firms producing transport equipment were operating with

Figure 1. **Supplier Industry—Production Material, End of 1994**

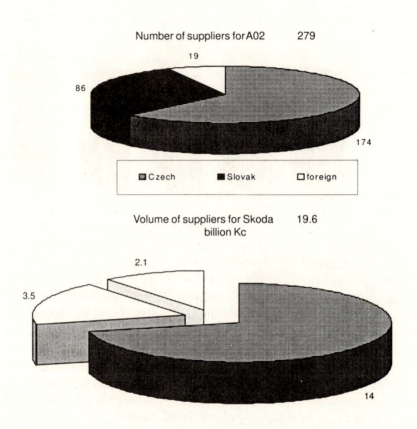

Number of suppliers for A02      279

Volume of suppliers for Skoda      19.6
billion Kc

increasingly underutilized capacities. This increase in output and sales
was due mainly to the rapid growth of exports to the West. Škoda
succeeded in this at a time when the automotive industry was in a deep
crisis worldwide, which caused most other European car producers to
experience a strong decline in capacity utilization. This increase in
exports to the West, together with a near stagnation of its exports to the
East, caused a dramatic shift in the territorial structure of exports in the
first three years of the existence of this joint venture. This development
is depicted in Table 1.

In most other Czech engineering firms, such a change in the export
orientation was accompanied by a decrease in the volume of their
exports.

Figure 2. **Production of Škoda Automobiles**

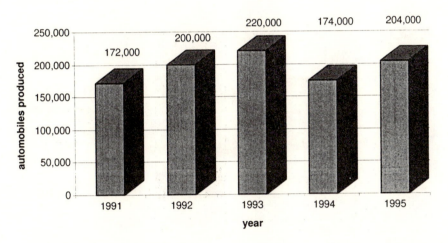

The export earnings of Škoda increased from CZK 8.2 billion in 1991 to CZK 17.6 billion in 1993. In the course of these two years, the share of exports in overall sales of this firm also increased from 40 percent to more than 50 percent. These data suggest that Škoda succeeded in increasing its competitiveness on Western markets far beyond all expectations. This increase in competitiveness was achieved with far less investment than originally had been considered necessary for this purpose, mainly because of the implementation of organizational changes in administration and production that increased the productivity of labor by about 7–10 percent yearly. Increased competitiveness was achieved also thanks to the reorganization and extension of the foreign distribution network, as well as by the fact that VW's good image enabled this joint venture to surmount some of the psychological barriers that hampered the sales of Škoda cars when Škoda was on its own.

This spectacular increase in exports of Škoda cars was partly due also to improvements in their quality. In all, 900 quality improvements had been effected between 1990 and the middle of 1991. These were the result of implementing foreign technological innovations at Škoda, as well as by other forms of technology transfer, such as training programs, quality monitoring schemes, and so forth, which were targeted not only at individual plants of this firm but also at some of its local suppliers. This led to the implementation of numerous quality improvements,

Figure 3. **Sales of Škoda Automobiles**

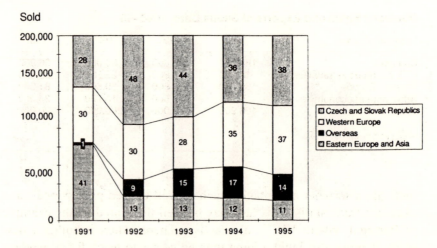

enabling Škoda to rely heavily on the local market as a source of parts and components. All these efforts have resulted in a 30 percent increase in quality so far.

The implemented integration scheme also has had a positive influence on the capacity utilization of numerous enterprises situated not only in the Czech engineering industry but also in the production of steel plate, of plastics, of technical textiles, and so forth. Taking into account that even these suppliers have a wide range of local subcontractors, Škoda directly or indirectly influences more than a tenth of Czech manufacturing industry. Here we have to note that new development concepts implemented by Volkswagen may have caused a marked deceleration of most of the positive trends described above.

## DECISION TO INVEST

It is often assumed that there is in fact only one reason to invest in the Czech Republic: low labor costs. In the course of daily contact with Volkswagen, the Czech members of the top management team have realized that the reason is, above all, the political stability of the country and only secondarily the relatively low level of production costs, mainly labor costs. Another motivating factor is the nature of the supplier industry. Furthermore, there is a great logistical advantage: the Czech Republic's location in the middle of Europe. Last but not least,

Table 1

**Domestic Sales and Exports of Škoda Cars, 1990–93**

| Location of sales | 1990 | 1991 | 1992 | 1993 |
|---|---|---|---|---|
| Domestic | 123,000 | 42,000 | 96,000 | 96,000 |
| CEE countries in transition | 18,700 | 70,600 | 26,600 | 29,000 |
| Western Europe | 39,700 | 52,500 | 59,500 | 61,000 |
| Other market economies | 5,500 | 6,500 | 18,500 | 34,000 |
| Total | 186,900 | 172,000 | 200,000 | 220,000 |

*Source*: Škoda database.

there are also other advantages, such as well-trained professionals and excellent trade skills. This fact may be well illustrated on the example of Portugal, where VW is also active. There, when it builds a new plant, it must also build a large training center to teach future workers absolute basics, such as measurement and so forth.

On the Czech side, the main motive for attracting a strategic foreign partner was the need for investment, know-how, especially managerial know-how, and quality improvement.

## EXPECTATIONS AND EXPERIENCE

### *Overall*

Competition in the automobile industry is intense. Thanks to successful rationalization programs and continuous enhancement of product quality, Škoda has been able to maintain its positions in its current markets and, at the same time, to enter new territories.

One of the main worries of the company has been quality, although many improvements have been made in this field. The company never suspected that problems regarding pricing would subsequently become a major issue. Both Škoda and its supplier industry have the same advantages related to labor costs. However, the moment the supplier industry attains world price standards, it can be endangered, for example, by a devaluation in Spain, which makes Spanish suppliers more attractive. This is not just a short-term issue or a problem of quality; it is a problem of competitiveness affecting not only Škoda but the whole VW family of firms.

### *Management Structure, Organizational Structure*

As mentioned above, the company uses the German governance model, that is, a board of directors as the executive body. There are no directors, chief executive officers, or presidents, and work relations are very direct. The executive committee, composed of four VW representatives and four Czech representatives, supervises this board of directors. The vice-chair of this committee is Vladimír Dlouhy, the minister of industry and trade of the Czech Republic. In addition, there are three trade-union representatives. Above that structure is the stockholders' assembly, which for now is very simple because there is one representative from the Czech side, represented by Minister of Finance Ivan Kočárník, and the German side also has one representative from VW.

Škoda's board of directors has five members, two Czechs and three VW employees. Each member has his own departments directly beneath him. Many departments in the present organizational structure were in fact part of the old structure, and no fundamental changes were made there. Some were created from scratch or were radically changed. For example, in the case of the audit and inspection department, such a department existed in the old Škoda, but it played a completely different role. Today, audit and inspection is, of course, a very strict department, divided into technical and financial activities. Its job is not only to carry out inspection but also to help the company, and it must always conclude with measures for rectifying shortcomings. This is an absolutely different philosophy from what the company had before, not to mention the political aspect that was present before.

Trade unions play an important role in Škoda. Unlike in other companies in the Czech Republic, they are quite strong and active. There are problems in reaching a consensus between the management and the trade unions and in harmonizing the vision of Škoda's management and that of the trade unionists. This situation is often criticized by the VW representatives.

### *Production*

In the late 1980s, the output of Škoda reached about 170,000 automobiles per year. In 1989, 183,000 of these cars were produced. The impact of the collapse of CMEA trade, together with the dramatic decrease in the purchasing power of the population of the former Czechoslovakia, resulting mainly from restrictive macroeconomic policy and price liberalization, thus caused a rapid decline of sales, which showed up also in increasing underutilization of capacity.

In spite of the dramatic decrease in sales in the countries in transition, the output of Škoda cars has increased steadily since 1991. It increased by nearly 20 percent in 1992 and by another 10 percent in 1993, while the total industrial output of the former Czechoslovakia was still plummeting.

On the whole, 173,586 cars were produced in 1994, including 10,602 Felicias. Compared with 1993, production had declined by 46,026 car units (–21 percent). This was due to the introduction of the new car type.

Increases in production in 1995 faced further technical obstacles due to the need to vary production to include right-hand drive for England and other countries, air conditioning, a stronger 1.6 motor, a 1.9 diesel motor, and, at the end of the year, power steering.

## Sales and Marketing

In 1989, 183,000 Škoda cars were produced; 120,000 of these were sold on the domestic market. Most of the remaining cars were exported to former CMEA countries. A few thousand Škoda cars were sold in the United Kingdom and in some other West European and Scandinavian countries, but efforts to increase sales in North America, mainly in Canada, proved to be unsuccessful, in spite of the costly discounts that had been made on Škoda automobiles offered on these markets. The aforementioned impact of the collapse of CMEA trade, together with the dramatic decrease in the purchasing power of the local population, thus caused sales to fall.

Due to these and other influences, Škoda's losses reached nearly CZK 800 million in 1990. Under these conditions, it was impossible to obtain loans, which were at that time regarded as necessary for modernizing its plants and, thus, also for improving the competitiveness of Škoda automobiles on Western markets.

The effort to obtain financing for these investments and simultaneously to achieve better access to Western markets was certainly among the main reasons why the government of the former CSFR began seeking at that time a strong strategic Western investor in this branch of the Czech engineering industry.

Table 2

**Sales and Marketing Expenditures** (CZK million)

|  | 1994 |
|---|---|
| Czech Republic | 14,266 |
| Export | 16,758 |
| Total | 31,024 |

During the first months of the existence of the joint venture, its sales possibilities deteriorated further, not only because of the above-mentioned influences but also because of the local population's preferences for used cares from Western Europe. Also, sales possibilities on Eastern markets were decreasing further. Total sales in transition countries, which had reached 80,300 Škoda cars in 1990, decreased to only 13,260 in 1992. Sales in all of Central and Eastern Europe improved partially in 1993 but remain low.

In 1991, for example, Škoda exported almost 40,000 cars to Yugoslavia; due to the war there, today it exports far fewer, although it does export to Slovenia, Croatia, and Macedonia. The main reason is not just the lower purchasing power in Central and Eastern Europe but customs barriers. As an example, formerly Škoda exported 30,000–35,000 cars to Poland, not all of which remained in Poland. Then customs barriers were imposed. These include a 35 percent customs fee plus a supplemental tax of 6 percent for a total of 41 percent in 1993. Škoda exports fell to insignificant levels. As a reaction, the company opened an assembly plant in Poznań. Since then, Škoda assembles there and sells more than 7,000 cars, which seems to be the only way to deal with the problem of customs barriers.

Another, perhaps much greater, problem is China, as well as the countries of the former Soviet Union, where both low purchasing power and customs barriers are a problem. Yet one more big problem is getting payment for the cars. In some countries, Škoda's policy is to ask for the money first and then to deliver the cars.

The domestic market is of course very important, but it is only about one-third of total sales.

Exports to Western Europe have progressed very well and continue to do so, in part due to aggressive marketing (see Table 2). In fact, today Škoda is actually having problems supplying enough vehicles.

Table 3

**Škoda Sales Network**

| Dealers | 1991 | 1992 | 1993 | 1994 |
|---|---|---|---|---|
| Western Europe | 1,092 | 1,307 | 1,526 | 1,631 |
| Overseas | 68 | 133 | 165 | 211 |
| Czech and Slovak Republics | 137 | 228 | 272 | 264 |
| Central and Eastern Europe, Asia | 22 | 134 | 142 | 181 |
| Total | 1,319 | 1,802 | 2,105 | 2,287 |

In most of the markets outside Europe, the company has to compete on price, because Škoda is not a well-known make. The financial results are nevertheless viewed as relatively good.

Although in 1994 the company reduced production of the Škoda Favorit/Forman series, replacing it with the new Škoda Felicia, the number of cars supplied to customers declined by only 8.6 percent, to 183,624 cars. The supply of 53,384 cars to the local sales network was well below the 1993 level, but the actual number of cars sold to domestic customers, 63,756, was just slightly lower than in 1993, which was due to the large number of cars in stock at the beginning of 1994.

Škoda is increasingly recognized as a car maker committed to quality and to a high standard of customer service. This general perception has been reflected in export successes, especially in Western Europe, which is a marketplace characterized by aggressive competition. Škoda currently exports about two-thirds of its total output to more than sixty countries. In important markets such as the United Kingdom, France, Spain, and Italy, in the early 1990s it achieved sales increases of around 10 percent or more per year. In addition, it has successfully entered new marketplaces, including Syria, Colombia, and Egypt.

Originally, all domestic sales were conducted through the state organization Mototechna, and abroad everything was done through Motokov, a state-owned foreign trade company. During a very short period following the liberalization of foreign trade in Czechoslovakia, this strategy had to be changed. Škoda now sells only through private organizations, with a few exceptions, specifically in Germany, France, England, and Italy, where it has its own import and distribution companies, sometimes even connected with the Volkswagen parent company. As Table 3 suggests, the sales network has developed quite substantially. In the Czech Republic, there are already as many as 200 dealers for Škoda cars. Outside the country, the company exceeded the level of 2,000 sales points in 1994.

### Employment, Wages, Training

At the end of 1994, Škoda had 15,985 employees, including 13,855 people in Mladá Boleslav, 951 in the Vrchlabí Plant, and 1,179 in Kvašiny. This is 1,063 fewer than in 1993. This number includes 175 employees who had to leave because of a breach of work discipline and 436 for organizational reasons. Another 99 people were transferred to other jobs within the program of supplier integration, and 353 left because of retirement, military service, or expiry of a fixed-term contract. The decrease in the number of employees not directly engaged in car production is a significant source of increased labor productivity. During 1994, the company wanted to reduce the number of employees in auxiliary services. While doing so, the management team took the social implications into account, as well as the fact that the labor market was able to absorb more of the labor force; for example, as of December 31, 1994, the unemployment level in the Mladá Boleslav District was as low as 1.6 percent. There are still some problems in the structure of employment. The company wants to reduce the proportion of white-collar workers in the total number of employees below 50 percent.

Profiles of requirements for specific target groups of employees were developed as the basis for the Personnel Development Project. The project was focused on those target groups that were likely to exert the greatest influence on the change process at Škoda. A labor profile in the form of assessments organized for workers, foremen, candidate (prospective) foremen, candidate managers, and managers served as a basis for skill-development programs.

In the area of economic education, a number of training courses and workshops were organized. Managers, prospective managers, and officers with specific responsibilities whose education and prior experience partly failed to meet the requirements of a market economy acquired extensive professional knowledge in their respective areas in the training courses. In addition, Škoda was the first in the Czech Republic to establish a two-year private secondary school for industrial traders and managers.

Wishing to attract the best university graduates, Škoda has developed a program called "Škoda in Dialogue with the Young," which targets students and offers them benefits such as scholarships, internships, subjects for theses, and so forth. In doing this, the company introduces itself as an attractive employer. Škoda works with key universities in the Czech Republic in providing these benefits.

## Finance

In 1994, the company's revenue was CZK 31.024 billion, 10.4 percent less than in the previous year, when revenue had been CZK 34.610 billion. The lower revenue is the result of lower sales, which were down by 21 percent. The high inventory level, which had been created to bridge the period of transition to the new model, was reduced to 4,248 cars before the end of December 1994. The annual loss was reduced compared with its 1993 level: in 1993, the loss was CZK 4.261 billion; in 1994, only CZK 2.371 billion. However, when comparing results, it must be taken into account that the 1993 financial statements were affected by the extraordinary charge of CZK 4.157 billion caused by the need to adapt to the new Czech commercial law. The loss was due mainly to the low volume of production. In this an important role was played by the gradual reduction and removal of the Favorit type series, involving the reconstruction of production facilities and a shut-down period and also by advance expenditures relating to the extension of the range of the models of cars to be produced.

Shareholder equity as at December 31, 1994, was CZK 34.638 billion. This figure was 20.3 percent up from the 1993 figure. This increase was largely represented by increases in liquid assets and tangible fixed assets. The sources of funds included, first of all, the increase in capital and a substantial improvement in internal cash flow. With the capital increase, the company's net liquidity amounted to CZK 1.4 billion. The balance indicators of Škoda are favorable. The company's fixed assets are covered at 116 percent by its own capital and by long-term outside capital. In 1994, this total was well above 100 percent. Short-term liquidity, the ratio of liquid funds, short-term receivables, and loans to short-term outside capital, amounted to 99 percent. The total-resources proportion represented by own capital was 62 percent.

In order to ensure compatibility, Škoda uses both the international system of accounting as well as the Czech system.

## Ownership

At the starting point in 1991, when the joint-stock company Škoda was created, the Czech side held 69 percent and VW held 31 percent. In December 1994, the shareholders adopted an annex to the 1991 contract amending and detailing the key points of the original contract to reflect the changed framework conditions. As of December 31, 1994, VW's interest in the company was 60.3 percent. By the end of 1995, there was to be another investment, so that the ratio would be VW 70 percent to 30 percent for the Czech side.

## Dealing with the Government

There is a certain conflict between the hands-off policy of the government and the need for the state to exercise, even if temporarily, the role of a responsible owner. Thus, without abandoning laissez-faire principles, the government now follows a pragmatic policy of intervening in cases where it is seen as desirable to do so. Despite the government's proclaimed principle of equal treatment for all foreigners investing in Czechoslovakia, the government did negotiate special entry conditions for foreign investors into some ventures with state-owned firms. The Volkswagen–Škoda arrangement, which waived antimonopoly provisions, provided a number of trade barriers against imports of competing cars, and involved the government in business negotiations, is the most visible example of such an arrangement. Besides, two ministers of the present government are members of Škoda's boards.

Due to both its large size and good performance, the prosperity of the Škoda–VW joint venture had acquired major importance for the host country from a macroeconomic point of view as well. This can be regarded as the main reason why the authorities of the Czech Republic accepted the change in attitude that Volkswagen adopted toward this joint venture in the middle of 1994, why they agreed to the reduction of investments that had originally been envisaged in its various plants, and why they accepted the numerous changes in the development concepts to be implemented at Škoda.

Tough discussions took place reflecting a changed situation on both sides: VW's economic problems, including an operating loss of around DEM 2 billion, stagnation of demand on the German car market, the need to reduce employment, and so forth, required VW to reduce the

Table 4

**Spending on Education in the Czech Republic** (CZK million)

|  | 1991 | 1994 |
|---|---|---|
| Elementary school | 5,224 | 2,703 |
| Vocational school | 7,401 | 7,880 |
| High school | 3,652 | 4,183 |
| University | 706 | 1,219 |
| Total | 16,983 | 15,985 |

ambitious investment and development program it had promised for Škoda. On the Czech side, the government of Václav Klaus was more promarket in its approach to negotiating with VW.

Despite some rumors signaling hesitations or even unwillingness of both partners to continue the relationship, a consensus was reached. This debate illustrated a gradual subordination of development concepts planned for Škoda to the broader interests of the VW group to which it now belongs, that is, a process that was to be expected. With regard to this fact, friendly government attitudes toward this joint venture during the first three years of its existence can be regarded as unique and exceptional. Nevertheless, it was mainly this attitude that largely contributed to bringing all the favorable preconditions for developing a successful automobile industry in the Czech Republic to fruition.

*Technology*

Škoda is investing very intensively in technology. Today, at the development stage, it invests 23 percent of turnover, whereas the usual figure for car producers is 6–8 percent. Presently, this means that on average CZK 20 million per day are invested. As Table 4 indicates, total capital expenditures in 1994 amounted to CZK 7.617 billion, which is 2.821 billion more than in 1993. The 1994 capital expenditures went mainly to the gradual replacement and refurbishment of production facilities, the introduction of the Felicia model, preparation of the new variations of the Felicia, and the development of production facilities for the next type series.

The new Felicia model marked a jump forward in Škoda's brand quality. Having this model, the company could enter the second century of its existence with confidence.

The first half of 1994 was a period of all-round preparation for the launching of the Felicia. The following data may be used to illustrate how challenging this task was. To start making the Felicia, it was necessary to introduce 1,187 new automobile parts, and, as new additional features were to be added to the car in 1995, another 896 or so parts had to be developed or modified. The total number of parts in the base model of the Felicia is 2,139.

Besides preparing the variants of the Felicia, the company's development capacity was fully committed to work on the new type series. The same applies to the newly built designer center.

Škoda Automobilová a.s. is ready to play the role of a model in environmental conservation activities. Air pollution has already been successfully reduced. Emissions of sulfur dioxide from the heating plant fell by 80 percent in 1994, and emissions of organic solvents from the paint shops were reduced by 20 percent. A new paint shop was opened in 1995. The new technology produces specific emissions that fully comply with the strictest European limits, and some of the indicators are far below those limits. The waste incineration plant, which failed to comply with emission limits, was closed in 1994. The recycling of wastes has increased considerably. In 1993, about 39 percent of wastes produced were used again, but this proportion increased to as much as 88 percent in 1994. The total quantity of wastes was reduced by 8.5 percent over the same period.

The new car, the Felicia, meets all requirements for future recycling: it is easy to dismantle, and the materials are suitable for recycled use. Furthermore, the company is preparing its own plan for recycling its cars after they are put out of use.

There are positive trends in improvement and innovation. Over 2,000 employees, that is, 12 percent of all people working for the company, submitted 4,000 improvement proposals in 1994, which is 51 percent more than in 1993. Of these proposals, 42 percent were successful, and the authors received remuneration totaling CZK 9.1 million. The benefits from the improvement proposals were in excess of CZK 100 million. With these results, Škoda ranks among the best companies in the Czech Republic.

### Unbundling and Social Assets

As mentioned earlier, Škoda eliminated many activities that were not directly related to its main interest, that is, the production of cars.

Social assets are a typical example. Employees who are affected by this policy are not being put out of work but are transferred to new, specialized companies.

## OUTLOOK

As the production of the Felicia model increases, sales volume is expected to grow to more than 200,000 cars. The production capacity will be limited to some extent because of the need to start up production of other new products, such as the Felicia-Combi, Pickup, Van Plus, the 1.6-liter spark-ignition VW engine, the 1.9-liter Diesel VW engine, driver and passenger-side air bags, an antilock brake system, air conditioning, and power-assisted steering. In addition to the positive effects of the large volume of production and sales, financial results will also reflect the measures taken to cut costs. On the other hand, costs relating to the new products, the construction and refurbishing of production facilities, and preparation of the new model series will also grow, so that profits in the short run cannot be expected to be much higher than in 1994.

Major returns will only be realized when the company finishes the restructuring and modernization programs, the expansion of production capacity, and a widening of the product range. It is assumed that Škoda's results will stay within the range of the original plans and assumptions.

# 4

# Temac a.s.

## Maria Bothatá

**COMPANY HISTORY**

Asbestos production by this company began on May 5, 1919, when Josef Daník from Prague started producing sealing and related asbestos materials in a former brick-making plant in Zvěřínek. Production was interrupted for one year in 1926 and was restarted on February 17, 1928. At that time, a new company was established, Asbestos and Rubber Works, Ltd. During the years 1930 to 1938, other developments occurred in asbestos and rubber production. Because of these, the firm had to respond quickly to the needs of the rapidly developing industrial sector in Czechoslovakia: in 1932, the firm started producing brake and clutch linings; in 1934, asphalt roof coatings and cork asphalt boards; and, in 1935, bicycle tires and rubber and bakelite-pressed products. During the period of the Nazi occupation, the company was declared Jewish property and entrusted to an administrator. Subsequently, it was sold to Danko Wetzel, a German company from Dortmund. During this period, the production program was modified in favor of asbestos production, but production volume did not increase due to the lack of basic raw materials, asbestos and natural rubber, which had to be imported. The company was nationalized on October 27, 1945, and subsequently became part of the national company Eternitové závody Praha. In 1949, the company was integrated into the Czechoslovak Leather and Rubber Processing Company as part of the concentration of production. During these years, several experts from the Bata company joined the firm. They introduced a new organization within the company and were responsible for the present profile of production. The production of friction materials was transferred to the Osinek plant in Kostelec nad Orlicí, and, later, the production of standard asbestos products was transferred to the Karna plant in Marianské Lázně. During subsequent years, the company was gradually expanded, old buildings were reconstructed, and machinery was modernized, and, during the 1950s, the company was one of the most modern ones in all of Czechoslovakia.

In December 1990, the company was transformed into a state joint-stock company that was privatized with the participation of foreign investors on November 17, 1993. At that time, DNI Holding b.v. of Rotterdam became the majority owner. The ownership structure was as follows: DNI Holding b.v., 93 percent; National Property Fund, 3 percent; and the towns of Písty, Zvěřínek, and Sadská, 4 percent. The current ownership structure is as follows: DNI Holding b.v., 98 percent; and the city of Sadská, 2 percent. The company's name was changed to Temac a.s., mainly because the Asbestos name was too reminiscent of the asbestos products that, during the current period, are being phased out due to increased sensitivity about the ecological hazards they pose.

Production consists mainly of compressed asbestos gaskets, compressed synthetic gaskets, industrial gaskets, automotive gaskets, braided packings, die-formed packing rings, industrial textiles, rubber molded seals, and engineering plastics.

Hofland Deltaflex is a group of industrial enterprises in which the specific production of each plant makes a substantial contribution to the activities of the group as a whole. It has production plants in the Netherlands, Belgium, Great Britain, the Czech Republic, South Africa, and Singapore. Its products include metallic gaskets, jointing material, stuffing box packings, composite hoses, couplings, technical rubber, and engineering plastics for the petrochemical industry, shipping, and industry at large.

Within a few decades, Hofland Deltaflex has grown into one of the major industrial suppliers of seals. The twofold basis for this rapid development remains attention to quality and, above all, to the needs of the customer, together with an open eye for rapid technical development and the added value of its own production facilities.

## *Organization*

The worldwide activities of Hofland Deltaflex are controlled from the head office in Rotterdam, where DNI Holding is also located. All the autonomously operating plants are allowed to adapt their market approach to the local situation. The core of the organization consists of a team of product managers assisted by specialists and a large group of internal and external advisers.

DNI Holding b.v. was selected for investing in the Czech firm on the basis of a selection process whose criteria were access to Western markets, access to asbestos-free technologies, and a promise to retain most of the production program. In view of the fact that DNI Holding b.v. fulfilled these prerequisites, both the consulting company advising on the privatization process as well as the National Property Fund recommended that the sale should be made specifically to this company. The takeover created a partnership that is mutually advantageous for both sides, because the Czech company provided its partner access to Eastern markets, and because the new company could sell under the DNI name, thus gaining access to Western markets.

### Quality and Training

By qualifying for ISO 9002 certification, Hofland Deltaflex has taken a further step toward total quality management. Naturally the company sees this certificate as a confirmation of the success of its efforts to achieve high quality levels. Deltaflex regularly organizes extensive training programs for the production staff and product seminars for its customers.

### New Forms of Supplier–Customer Cooperation

Hofland Deltaflex offers customers extensive cooperation in purchasing and supply, and the old-fashioned way of doing business by selling from inventories against orders has been eliminated. Using schemes such as integrated supply and key supplier, the customer and Hofland Deltaflex come to solid agreements that allow both parties to concentrate on their core business.

### THE COMPANY'S ORGANIZATIONAL STRUCTURE

The company is managed by the general director, who was appointed by DNI Holding b.v. and is its employee. The directors of the individual sections answer directly to him. The activity of the sections is checked once a month through a "board meeting" with the participation of the chairman of the board of directors and two Czech deputy chairmen.

Reports on the individual sections, sales, quality control, production, finance, and so forth, are presented in writing.

The company is divided into individual production centers according to type of production, which have their economic management monitored independently, and nonproduction centers, that is, administration, development, quality control, and supplies. An economic management report is made out once a month and contains detailed information about the economic situation within the centers and their overhead costs, all compared with the plan for the period in question and based on Western-style "management accounts."

The company's organizational scheme can be found in Figures 1–3.

Following privatization, several members of top management who were not in favor of the company's privatization through foreign capital participation left the company. After Deltaflex took control, several minor changes were made in the organization in order to strengthen control over the individual sections. Special emphasis was placed on raising the quality of the sales department, expanding the services provided to customers and having a more flexible reaction to their requirements. The original marketing department as such was eliminated, and its activity was to a great extent taken over by headquarters in Rotterdam. In the financial department, emphasis was placed on raising the quality of financial reports and monitoring economic results in accordance with Western standards.

The privatization agreement for the Asbestos company also included an obligation to maintain the preprivatization level of employment. For that reason, the company is attempting to develop personnel from among its own employees. When there is a job opening, an open competition is organized in which emphasis is placed primarily on the employee's expertise.

The company is managed by a board of directors, and its activity is controlled by a supervisory council that includes some trade-union representatives and the owners of DNI Holding b.v. On a monthly basis, headquarters receive minutes from the board of directors' meetings, a management report, and a balance sheet developed in accordance with Western standards. Accounts are also prepared on the basis of the Czech system. Strategic decisions are subject to approval by Rotterdam headquarters. Other matters are fully within the authority of the local general director.

The company's business strategy was strongly influenced by the

Figure 1. **Temac—Factory Organization Scheme**

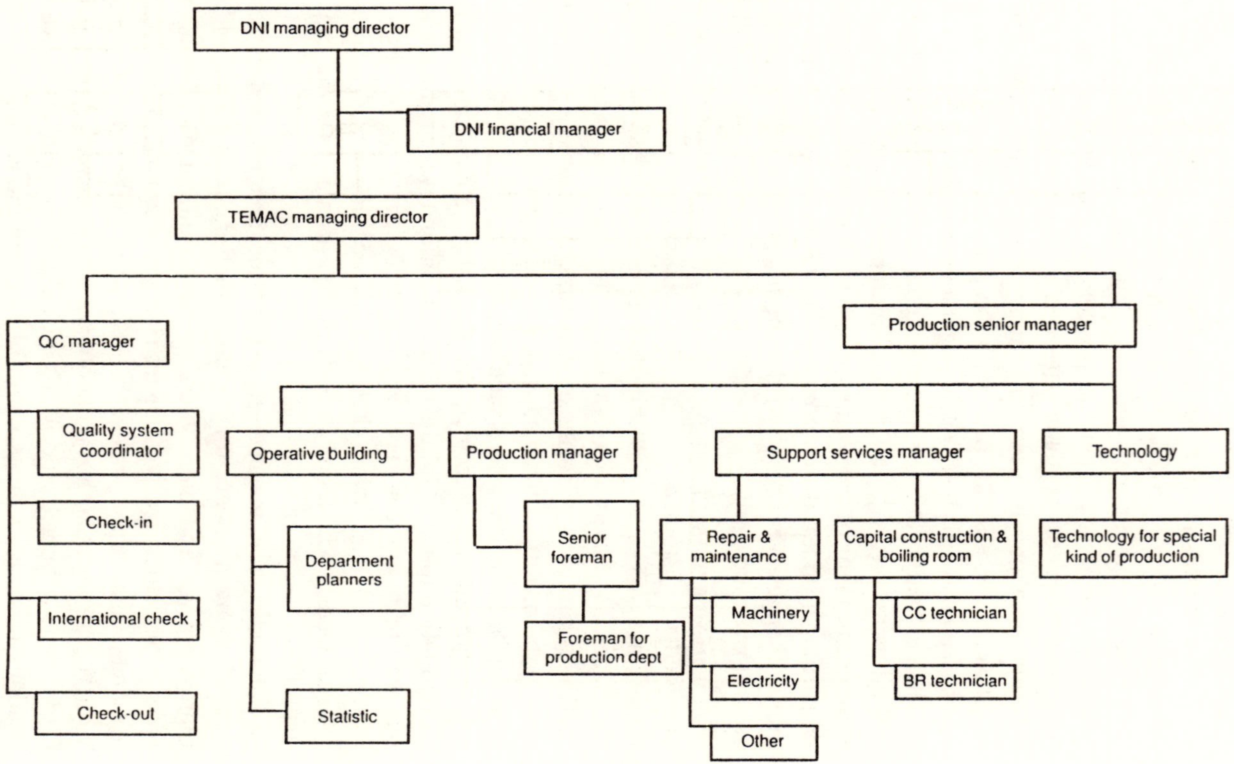

Figure 2. **Temac—Factory Organization Scheme**

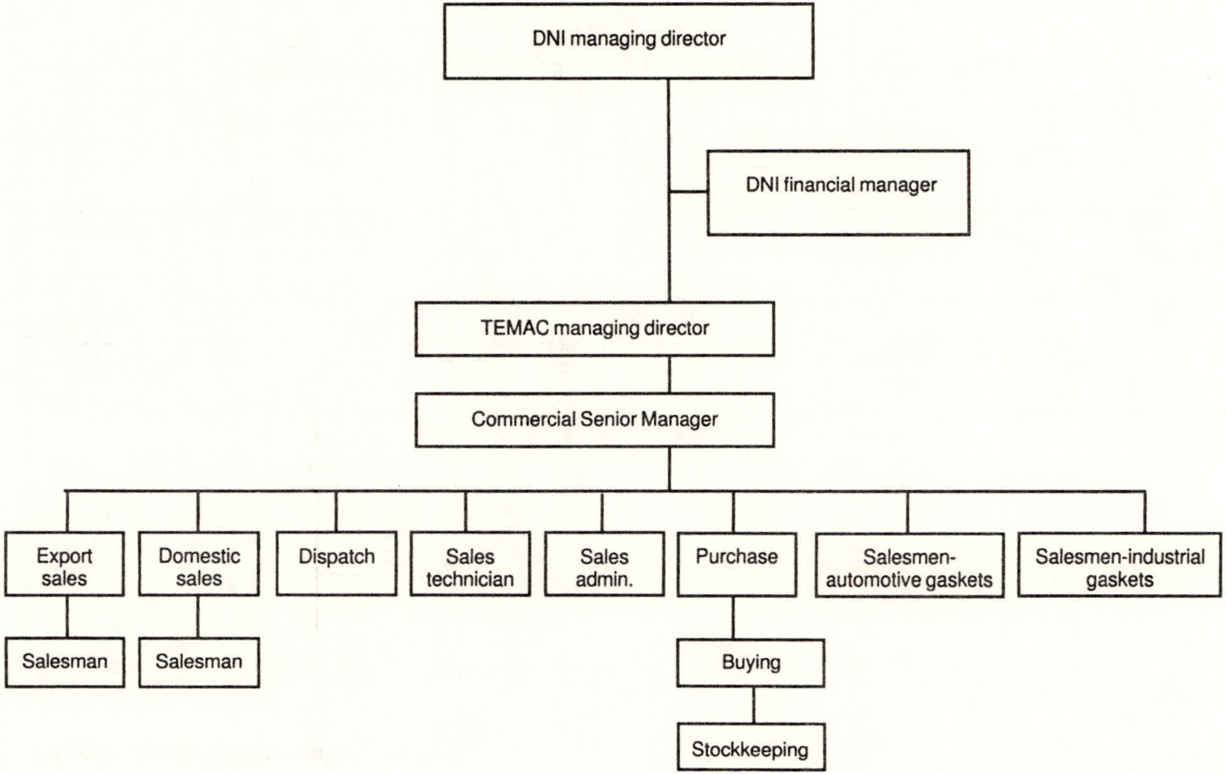

Figure 3. **Temac—Factory Organization Scheme**

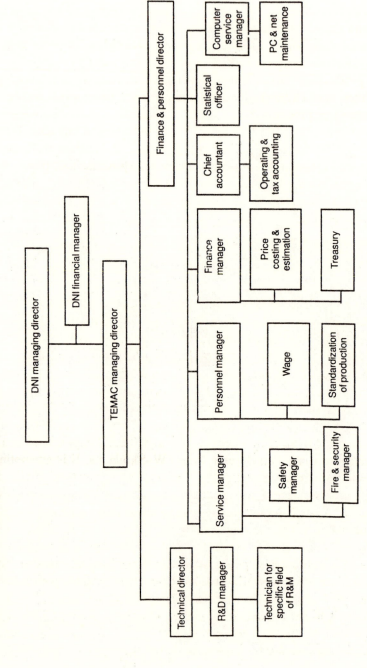

takeover by the Dutch company. Temac became the holding company's main production plant and the distributor of all its products in Central and Eastern Europe. The company's organizational structure was changed to reflect this strategy by strengthening the foreign sales department. Another change was the transition to asbestos-free production. As part of this task, the development laboratory in Zvěřínek was expanded and oriented toward developing and testing asbestos-free products.

The sale of the company to a foreign partner was intended to bring access to asbestos-free technologies, access to Western markets, and the overall modernization of production. It is possible that these objectives could have been attained without a foreign partner but only at the price of a long-term restructuring that would have been financially very demanding.

## SECTOR AND MARKETS

The Temac company has a significant share of the market in the former Eastern bloc countries. After the entry of DNI Holding, it also became possible to sell its products under the well-known Hofland trademark. Consequently, it managed to gain access to very demanding markets, but it has to fight constantly for its position against ever-increasing competition. Temac seeks to compete on the basis of price, expanded customer service, strong advertizing by a team of DNI experts, and the development of new sealing-material applications.

Temac's share of the domestic market is high despite competition from a number of smaller companies providing the same or a similar assortment of products. Temac is a significant supplier of sealing materials to Liaz, Tatra, Zetor, and VW–Škoda a.s. It is attempting to become the major supplier to the entire VW conglomerate. The competition's objective is to acquire as large a market share as possible, primarily in the production of sealing materials involving extensive manual labor and nonasbestos materials.

During the past few years, the use of asbestos fiber sealings has declined, and there has been a rise in the use of plastics, ceramic fibers, and so forth; in this regard, there has been a visible shift, particularly in the Eastern market. The number of competing companies that are attempting to get a foothold in the traditional markets of Asbestos is, of course, also rising. The loss of certain East European markets was offset by the possibility, for example, of exporting to the Republic of

South Africa and to the United States. It is therefore apparent that the sales structure is being changed in favor of exports to developed markets. The company has also become the exclusive Central and East European distributor of products manufactured by other companies in the DNI group. A special issue is the market in Slovakia. After the division of Czechoslovakia, the sales volume significantly decreased due to customs, financial, and other barriers introduced by the Slovak government, but the company, of course, is attempting to maintain its position on this market.

Cooperation with suppliers changed following Temac's implementation of the ISO and VDA quality standards for automobile-industry suppliers. The quality of supplied materials is evaluated on a regular basis, and only reliable suppliers who provide a guaranteed quality are retained. As a result, quality has improved significantly. There is also pressure from the foreign partner to use quality raw materials.

## DECISION TO INVEST

Deltaflex viewed its investment in the Czech Republic as an opportunity to acquire a functioning production facility with a significant market share in the former CMEA region. Another reason was the advantage of low costs. At present, certain manufacturing technologies are being transferred to Zvěžínek. The quality of the workforce also played a significant role. In general, an important factor in favor of the decision to invest in the Czech Republic was the long-term expectation of a stable political and economic situation.

As for the decision-making process, there were two competing plans for the company's privatization: one, worked out by the company's director, was the sale to a foreign partner. The second one, worked out by other top managers, involved the participation of domestic capital. Both alternatives were discussed at the Ministry of Economy. Due to the anticipated phasing out of asbestos production and the lack of a quality domestic substitute, the plan calling for a foreign investor was recommended. Several possible investors were selected, and a feasibility study was worked out with the assistance of a consulting firm. Following comprehensive negotiations with the ministry, DNI Holding b.v. was finally chosen because it provided the most extensive guarantees to maintain employment at the 1993 level, to eliminate asbestos dust, and to invest in new technologies. Today, the privatization decision through the entry of foreign capital can be seen as very important because it provided access to asbestos-free technologies, the lack of which would have led to Temac's demise.

## EXPECTATIONS AND EXPERIENCE

### *Overall Perspective*

The company became independent in 1990; prior to that, it had been managed by the general directorate of its parent firm in Gottwaldov. The situation on the market had changed significantly because by then regular customers, Řempo (Czech Republic) and Rempo (Slovakia), who had traditionally purchased a majority of the production, had gradually ceased to make purchases. In the socialist economy, due to a permanent shortage of everything, the main goal of companies was maximizing production, and sales on the domestic market took the form of organized distribution. In the drastically changing environment caused by marketization, the previously underestimated importance of generating sales caused severe problems because firms no longer had guaranteed sales for their products. This situation characterized Asbestos, too; moreover, many customers could not, or would not, pay.

### *Management Structure*

The company had functioned as a manufacturing organization, and it sold very little of its output on an open market. Most of the sales were made through the Řempo network in Bohemia and through the Rempo network in Slovakia. Export were handled by the foreign trade organization Motokov. Until 1990, Temac was managed by the general directorate in Gottwaldov, which had to approve all the strategic decisions, such as plan, investments, and so forth. Essentially, the company's organizational structure was the same as the present one, with one difference: the sales department. Following the entry of Deltaflex, there was a change in the emphasis on developing a strong sales department, bringing the middle technical staff closer to the manufacturing process, strengthening the financial department, and changing financial reporting with an emphasis on the best possible overview of the company's economic management.

Table 1

**Basic Indicators for Temac, 1990–94** (in thousand CZK)

|  | 1990 | 1991 | 1992 | 1993 | 1994 |
|---|---|---|---|---|---|
| Total sales | 179,631 | 220,197 | 183,213 | 223,200 | 180,737 |
| Exports | 11,650 | 29,833 | 56,620 | 44,640 | 61,145 |
| Employment: | 590 | 481 | 366 | 360 | 357 |
| Blue collar | 444 | 354 | 257 | 245 | 249 |
| White collar | 146 | 127 | 109 | 115 | 108 |
| Net profits | 26,046 | 57,523 | 15,214 | 7,428 | 0 |
| Investment | 11,008 | 17,356 | 22,723 | 13,850 | 19,128 |
| Fixed assets | 143,274 | 139,953 | 145,937 | 150,691 | 144,731 |
| Gross wages | 24,470 | 22,947 | 20,533 | 29,751 | 32,940 |
| Value added | 81,424 | 111,295 | 64,797 | 97,946 | 66,760 |
| Capital employed | 202,622 | 223,991 | 223,571 | 251,024 | 250,034 |

## *Production*

The company's overall capacity remained almost unchanged, with some production areas being reduced while some were expanded (Table 1). The quality of production inputs is constantly improving, due both to the introduction of the ISO 9000 standard, in which quality is regularly checked at the supplier, as well as to higher-quality raw materials.

The role of headquarters with respect to the production department is limited to strategic decisions. It becomes familiar with the production situation and potential problems from regular monthly reports from board of directors' meetings. Productivity has increased partially due to the introduction of new technologies and partially as the result of a stricter adherence to working hours as certain "socialist" habits of slack work discipline were eliminated. The introduction of total quality management has brought about a detailed monitoring of losses, and these have also become more visible. One of management's first tasks was to monitor, evaluate, and, finally, lower potential losses.

Significant savings in energy were not achieved because the changes in technology have not been such as to permit such savings, and the substitution of coal for gas is only anticipated. In comparison to a Western company equipped with a similar technology, the level of energy consumption is somewhat higher due to the outdated equipment. One of the reasons why this particular foreign investor was chosen was to gain access to asbestos-free technologies. The share of the asbestos-based products is decreasing, with a positive impact on the environment.

## Sales and Marketing

The sales plan is formulated for individual territories and individual product types. At present, the plans are usually exceeded. The company's present strategy is to offer the same high level of services to all customers, regardless of the territory. The former Eastern-bloc countries typically have a greater demand for asbestos products, even though this has also been changing gradually.

As mentioned, Temac is a distributor of DNI Holding products for Eastern and Central Europe.

Approximately 0.7 percent of the company's turnover is allocated for advertising. Out of this amount, the largest portion is allocated to producing high-quality marketing literature. Other sums are allocated to participating in various expositions, publicity, and the introduction of the Temac name to the market. The company's marketing is managed and coordinated from headquarters in Rotterdam, although certain publicity events and expositions are organized jointly.

At present, the market is developing in favor of a transition to asbestos-free production. The main competitors will be the West European companies that have their manufacturing plants in countries with low costs.

## Employment, Wages, Training

Temac has only one foreign manager, the company's general director. All other employees are Czech. Lower-level managers are recruited on the basis of newspaper advertising. Upper-level managers are hired only through open competitions. The basic prerequisites for these positions are management skills and capabilities and knowledge of foreign languages.

The company's objective is to raise the living standards of all its employees. As of 1995, no comprehensive training program for managers had been developed. Managers are able to attend training sessions that they themselves select. In 1994, all the middle- and higher-level managers completed management training sessions on communications, time management, personnel management, and assigning tasks. These were provided on site. Because Temac's managers have experience working in a foreign-owned company, their chances of getting a good job outside the company are quite high. The only training for workers that was centrally planned and organized was for the ISO 9000 quality system.

The quality of the labor force, and primarily blue-collar workers, is very high. A high work ethic and flexibility were not understood initially, but over time the situation improved. Management seeks to persuade all employees that they should work and treat the company the way they want the company to treat them. Employment has remained more or less constant. By signing the privatization agreement, DNI had pledged to maintain the employment level as it had been at the time of the sale. Only a few employees were terminated. These were employees not fulfilling their work duties. Management's objective for the future is to change the currently unfavorable proportion between blue-collar workers and white-collar workers in favor of the former.

Wages are negotiated regularly with the trade unions. Each year a collective agreement is worked out. The trade unions do not play an important role; in too many cases they only observe instead of actively participating in affairs. Wages are paid out on the basis of the employee's qualifications based on a simple tariff system. Managers are motivated through a system of bonuses based on economic results. Blue-collar workers are motivated primarily through bonuses based on the quality of production. In view of the technology used and the technical condition of the equipment, productivity is at a good level, and it will gradually be increased on the basis of a modernization program.

### Finance

It is necessary to emphasize at the outset that Temac is the largest manufacturer within the DNI Holding b.v. group, but from the point of view of profits, it is one of the smallest. Accordingly, the company is also viewed by its owners from this perspective.

Temac develops a plan of financial needs. Headquarters only issues instructions concerning the holding company's overall strategy for Temac. Most financial resources are local, and Temac has a policy of using only internal resources if the situation allows. Financing is determined on the basis of the following scheme: strategic investments, headquarters; smaller, operating needs, local management. Some examples follow:

1. transferring technology from the plant in Belgium to Temac—the decision was made by headquarters in Rotterdam with financing from the holding company's resources;

2. reconstruction of the manufacturing halls in Zvěřínek with financing from Temac's internally generated funds.

The company's goal after the entry of the foreign partner was for a specified amount of money to be invested in subsequent years, primarily to modernize production. This objective was included in the purchase agreement and is being fulfilled. Obviously, Temac also has to provide profits to its owners, and it has to generate resources for its own modernization.

At the beginning, headquarters only monitored the company's economic activity. Gradually, it has attempted to exercise some control over costs. The company's overall results are reported to headquarters on a monthly basis, and headquarters reacts to them as part of its management of all the companies within the group.

The relationship between Temac and its banks is good; Temac has always been considered to be the best client in the region. The company takes out credit loans only in extreme situations, sometimes refraining from borrowing even to the detriment of its ability to resolve pressing problems. The majority of loans has lately been short term. The decision to finance through a loan is made by the local management, with the approval of headquarters. It was assumed that, following the takeover, there would be a significant decrease in short-term debts to suppliers and in overdue receivables. This objective was achieved for outstanding debts, and currently the situation is considered to be very good. As for receivables, improvement is still needed. This inability to reduce overdue receivables due to inadequate legislation regarding payment claims, different tax regulations, and so forth, was a surprise to headquarters.

Temac is maintaining its accounts only on the Czech standard. The results, however, are reported in a modified form to headquarters. The consolidation of the results of all the companies within the group is carried out in accordance with Dutch standards.

Starting from a low base, Temac's profits have increased, and, in view of its connection with a strong partner, it is expected that they will continue to do so in the future as well.

## Ownership

Temac's shares are registered and are not publicly traded. The future plan of headquarters is to buy out the remaining shares and thereby obtain 100 percent of the company.

A great advantage of the existing ownership structure is the majority owner's total control over decision making, which results from its ownership of controlling interest in the firm.

As of now, there has not been any consideration given to increasing the basic capital, and Temac does not sell its own securities.

## Dealing with the Government

Negotiations with government authorities were without any major problems during all phases of privatization. Temac would like to cooperate with the local municipalities of Zvěřínek, Písty, and Sadská. Cooperation with the Zvěřínek municipality has been particularly positive: the company provides the municipality with assistance in matters such as the construction of a sewer, lighting, and so forth.

## Technology

Prior to Deltaflex's investment, Temac's technology was outdated and corresponded approximately to the 1950s and 1960s. One of the reasons why the sale to the foreign partner was made was to facilitate the company's modernization and the adoption of asbestos-free technology. Work was being done on the latter's development by Asbestos, but its pace did not meet market demands. Technology to manufacture composite hoses and certain types of industrial sealing materials has been transferred to the company; the gala opening of the production facility for these products took place on September 23, 1995. In the case of composite hoses, the machinery and equipment were transferred from abroad to Temac. After this technology is modernized, it should ensure for Temac an increase in productivity and profits and offer better-quality products, and thereby also permanent competitiveness on all markets. The importation of the used machinery brought up a problem concerning the customs duty because the customs legislation did not fully cover this specific issue.

Temac has its own research and development facility. The objective is to create a research and development base for all the group's companies. It is obvious that the main task will be to develop products on the basis of customers' demands. Following the entry of the foreign partner, a new central laboratory was constructed. The research and development center is directly subordinated to the technical director.

## Unbundling and Social Assets

In the past, the company owned a whole series of social assets, such as apartment buildings for its employees, an accommodation facility, a nursery, and a recreational facility. It has sold some of these, without any pressure from the foreign partner, reconstructed others, and leased some. Today, due to high maintenance costs, the company is attempting to own as few of these buildings as possible. It is attempting to sell a majority of the apartments to individuals and to lease the remaining buildings.

## Performance

The most significant results are the development of a strong sales department, an increase in production quality, the introduction of the ISO 9000 quality standard, and the attainment of level A as a supplier to Škoda a.s. These achievements were all included in the business plan. The original manufacturing program was maintained and has been expanded with the technologies transferred from abroad. The sales department was expanded. It aims to provide the customer with the broadest services, such as the previously mentioned company literature, rapid reaction to customers' orders, technical service for customers, and so forth. Problems with the infrastructure apply in general in the Czech Republic. The most severe are telecommunications. The language problems within the company are gradually being eliminated, but the general language skills of both managers and workers are still low.

In comparison with other Czech companies, the overall results appear to be positive, especially the sales increase and the successful transition to a new style of work.

# Part III

## **Bulgaria**

# 1

# Berg—Montana Fittings Ltd.

## Malinka S. Koparanova

### COMPANY PROFILE

Branch: Iron and steel products
Co-investor: Berg AG, Basel, Switzerland
Output: 5,000 tons (1994)

### PRODUCTION CHARACTERISTICS

- Fittings;
- Castings of malleable cast iron;
- Parts cast from iron alloys;
- Alloy steel.

The company produces over 100 types of fittings, galvanized and black, with dimensions from one-half inch to two inches, made of white core malleable cast iron Kx 35–4 as per BDS 4867–75 (corresponding to DIN 1692–GTW 35–04 and ISO 5922–W 35–04).

The fittings are suitable for working pressures up to 25 bar and working temperatures up to $300^0$C when transmitting different liquids and gases.

### HISTORY OF FIRM

Montana Fittings was founded in 1960 in the town of Mihailovgrad, the previous name of Montana, and it has been the biggest supplier of fittings, malleable castings, both black and galvanized, and castings in gray iron in recent years, not only in Bulgaria but in the Balkans as well. The firm went through several organizational stages: First, it existed as a small part of a bigger plant, but then, for five or six years, it was turned into a firm. It was in the 1970s, however, that the company began to function as a separate enterprise for household types of fittings.

In 1978, a decision was made to build a new plant for fittings in the location where the company is now situated. Soon after that, the new factory was built, without, however, interrupting the work of the old one. Step by step, the main activities, such as mechanical processing, galvanizing, and so forth, and part of the firm's equipment were removed and transferred to the new building, and only some melting furnaces remained in the old plant.

In 1988, the fittings plant was transformed into a firm according to the Commercial Law. The new firm included both the old and the new plants and produced fittings and two types of special iron and steel. Production was mainly for the domestic market and only small volumes of fittings were exported to Iraq and Iran.

During 1989–90, the company experienced difficulties in adapting to the new economic environment and the emerging economic crises in the country. The firm went through a number of changes, including changes in managerial staff. The structural organization began to change at this time also.

Montana Fittings had maintained a good relationship with the Swiss firm Berg AG for more than ten years. Berg AG was among the main suppliers of technical equipment for the new plant. The relationship was renewed soon after 1992 when the president of Berg AG visited Montana. This visit led to a series of personnel exchanges between the companies, first to Montana followed by visits to Switzerland. Negotiations with the foreign partner moved from a kind of cooperation for the supply of technical equipment to the Bulgarian firm to a consideration of an investment by the Swiss firm in Montana. The first ideas for cooperation were for buying equipment for the new firm that would allow it to increase the quality of the fittings produced to bring them up to international standards. This first stage took one year to work out.

In September 1993, Montana Fittings began negotiations for foreign participation in the enterprise after working out some preliminary offers and schemes. The proposal for an investment in Montana Fittings by Berg AG came from the latter and was sent forward to the Ministry of Industry. It was there that the investment was accepted as being suitable for both sides. From September 1993 to May 1994, the two partners negotiated with the Bulgarian authorities, and the offer was sent to all the necessary commissions to obtain their permission. In May 1994, the new firm was established, with 50.4 percent of the ownership going to Berg AG and 40.6 percent to the Ministry of Industry. Since then, the joint venture has been developing according to a business program worked out by Berg AG and by Montana Fittings for the next five years.

## ORGANIZATIONAL STRUCTURE OF THE FIRM

Changes in the organizational structure of the company began in 1992. However, new a structure was introduced in the middle of 1995. The proposal for these changes was provided by the general manager and the managerial staff, all Bulgarians. These changes were related to the new business program and flowed from it.

Berg–Montana Fittings has begun to work according to the business plan worked out by the two partners. It identifies the main priorities of the joint venture. These are:
- introducing a system of quality control;
- improving working conditions;
- improving marketing activities;
- developing new technologies and improving existing ones;
- introducing an innovation program to expand the range of produced fittings.

The company therefore created an appropriate organizational structure consisting of:
- board of directors as representatives of shareholders—first level;
- general manager—second level;
- third level—directors of the following divisions:
—human-resources division;
—trade division;
—production division;
—mechanical processing division;
—material control;
—technologies and innovations;
—general engineer;
- fourth level—working places, or departments, depending on the division.

The company reports to Berg AG through meetings of the board of directors and reports on them, as well as by providing current financial information.

Control on the part of the foreign partner is through the board of directors, but Berg AG relies greatly on the general manager. He is the one who makes decisions on operational management and defines the company's investments, although the latter are subject to approval by headquarters. However, there have been no cases when the general managers' decision has been rejected. All the managerial staff comes from Montana Fittings, including the general manager, who started his professional career in the factory.

## SECTOR AND MARKETS

Berg–Montana has over 80 percent of the Bulgarian market for fittings, selling around 100–120 tons monthly. The company is the biggest producer of fittings in Bulgaria and has domestic no competitors among producers in the country. Competition from foreign producers has appeared recently, and the company is anxious about the quality and variety of its fittings and castings. The import of some types of castings from Russia started to create problems in 1994. Although the prices of imported products are at least 10 percent lower than those of Berg–Montana, and, although their quality is not comparable, they are suitable for many applications. The demand on the domestic market is low due to the financial situation of Bulgarian enterprises, and their choice of product is often dictated by price. Fortunately, the range of the fittings and castings imported from Russia is not wide.

There are also imports from Italy and Turkey, but they are small in volume and variety.

The marketing strategy of Berg–Montana is to keep its leading position on the domestic market and to expand exports.

In the 1990s, the company began to export its production to a number of countries, mainly in the Balkans, as well as to Algeria, Morocco, Lebanon, and some European countries, such as Hungary, Poland, the Czech Republic, the Netherlands, Belgium, and Spain. By 1992, exports were around 300 tons annually, and they have been expanding. The targeted countries are Balkan countries, European countries, and Arab countries. The company has become a member of the International

Association for Fittings (EMFIT), which helps the firm to increase its access to international markets.

Supplies of inputs are of both domestic and foreign origin, the latter comprising most of the materials and all the spare parts for the equipment. Since the end of the 1980s, both of these two kinds of inputs have changed, as has the way of obtaining them. Quality of inputs has improved, and the company had no problem in buying the necessary quantity of inputs at the requisite quality after the Swiss investment. The Swiss parent is entirely responsible for providing imported inputs, and no financial problems, if they exist, at Berg–Montana can hamper the supply of imports. As for inputs from the domestic market, there are no problems because the firm has already set up relations with local producers.

## DECISION TO INVEST

There is a general tendency to close down melting furnaces in Western countries and to move them elsewhere. Romania, India, and Mexico are the other countries where Berg AG has subsidiaries. The key motives behind the decision to invest in Bulgaria were the good relations that already existed between the foreign partner and the Bulgarian firm. Additional factors, such as cost advantages, both labor and material, and location, also contributed to the decision.

Berg AG made its choice based on personal contacts with an engineer at the Bulgarian company. This individual later became the general director of the new joint venture. He admits that "Berg AG has invested in me first of all and later, when they saw the firm, in the company and its development prospects." They evaluated Montana's position on the domestic market, the capacities of the enterprise, and the labor skills. Berg AG had been acquainted with the firm for more than ten years and was very well acquainted with the traditions there and with the managerial and working staff.

The general director of the company was involved in the preparations for the investment and in the development of the business plan for the joint venture's first five years. The negotiations with all the relevant commissions in the Ministry of Industry went smoothly.

The general director's opinion of the changes taking place in the firm recently is that they are the result of both the transition process and of the opportunity for free choice on the market on the one hand

and of the involvement of the foreign partner on the other. The latter could be viewed as a result of the transition as well.

## EXPECTATIONS AND EXPERIENCE

### *Overall*

At the end of the 1980s and the beginning of the 1990s, Montana lacked the funds to use its equipment fully. There was a shortage of working capital, there was no money to invest in technological changes, there were debts to the banking system of around BGL 40 million, and the firm could barely meet the interest payments on its debt.

As a result of the involvement of Berg AG, some of the financial problems were resolved. As part of the investment contract, Berg AG paid off most of the debt the company had accumulated. The foreign partner invested in new equipment, and the company gained access to international markets. As a result, the firm has increased the volume of production and sales, especially for export, and the output produced is of better quality.

### *Management Structure*

The firm's organization is based on the firm's strategy as determined by the business program. This program was determined jointly by the Bulgarian firm and the foreign investor.

As an enterprise of the Ministry of Industry, Montana used to be run as a part of the centrally planned economy. With the liberalization at the beginning of the 1990s, organizational changes began to be instituted and the firm's organization changed. New functions, such as sales and marketing, appeared; the activities of each of the departments changed, that is, although they retained the same functions, the content of these functions changed.

From the beginning, the Swiss parent gave the Bulgarian affiliate considerable autonomy to make and implement business decisions. The parent does require that there be reporting through formal and informal channels but has not intervened in day-to-day operations. In practice, there is one expert from the mother company, the former trade director of Fisher, another big company belonging to Berg AG, who advises the joint venture on technological problems. Being aware of the transition period, Berg AG did not seek profits in the first three years of the joint venture, and this is reflected in the management strategy. Reaching high quality standards and meeting the technical requirements of international markets is the top priority. The operational arrangements between Berg–Montana and the head office are the same as with all of Berg AG's subsidiaries. At the same time, this relationship must reflect the requirements of the Commercial Law in Bulgaria, whereby the annual general assembly is responsible for control and management of the firm. However, if there are opportunities due to some potential sales contracts of great importance for the subsidiary, representatives of Berg AG visit the company.

The monitoring of current business is done by the mother company monthly using the financial statements of expenditures and revenues and the balance sheets prepared by the subsidiary. All the accounts follow the requirements of Bulgarian standards. The conversion to another type of accounting system relevant to the mother company's requirements is carried out at the head office. The head office has also taken on the obligation of supplying the subsidiary with the necessary imports. Most of the material for the products of Berg AG Montana are imported. The parent company covers the cost of all imported materials and spare parts for the company's equipment. They also make payments to suppliers without insisting on being immediately compensated by the subsidiary, and, if the latter has some financial problems, it can delay making payments without any penalties. Contracts for purchases of supplies are made by the subsidiary. Arrangements for imports and spare-parts supply are an advantage of having a foreign owner. Montana had experienced serious problems in obtaining imported inputs due to its lack of financial resources required for import transactions and due to delays in making foreign exchange payments, which took about three to six months. At the moment, there no delays and no failures, and the system is working within deadlines. Payments to Berg AG for imported materials are made every three months, six months, or annually, according to contracts, but always taking into consideration the subsidiary's financial situation.

## Production

The company has a medium-sized capacity on an international scale. However, it operates at 65 percent of capacity. The production process is fully automated; it is computerized, and all the parameters are computer determined and controlled. The only constraint on output was, and is, the lack of markets. The domestic market has been shrinking since the end of the 1980s; at the moment, it is one-third of what it was before the economic crisis of 1985–88. The company used to produce 3,600 tons of output, while at the moment it produces 1,200–1,400 tons.

The structure of output has changed since the involvement of a foreign partner. Before, 1,200 tons were destined for the domestic market and 300 tons for exports; now, 1,200 tons are sold on the domestic market and 4,800 tons are exported.

Productivity has increased since the start of the joint venture. The company is producing more because markets have improved, its financial position has improved, and the number of employees remains almost the same.

Since the involvement of a foreign partner, environmental effects from operations have been reduced. The new pollution-abatement program seeks to protect the environment, and improvement is already observed in this area. There is a program for making the company's production even more environmentally friendly, and new improvements lie ahead.

### Sales and Marketing

On the domestic market, sales in Berg–Montana are handled through a network of distributors. Some of the stores and warehouses are their own property, and others are supplied by the company with payments following sales. Prices are determined by the company everywhere. This system, used for the past two or three years, has not shown any shortcomings. The company also offers discounts to retail outlets, which differ depending on sales volumes. On international markets, the company usually works through direct contacts with final consumers.

The marketing strategy of the firm is to expand both domestic output and products for export by improving quality using new techniques and by increasing the variety of products. Berg AG supplies the necessary equipment and provides the training for the workers operating the new machines. With the participation of a foreign partner who provides access to international markets and with the Bulgarian economy showing signs of survival, the demand for the firm's products will grow.

The foreign partner provides access to information about the industry. On this basis, the company can formulate its own marketing strategy.

The company does almost no advertising, except for advertising done at different trade fairs jointly with clients or distributors. As for international marketing, the company is included in the advertisements of Berg AG. The firm has contracts for export to Lebanon, Slovakia, the Czech Republic, Belgium, and the Netherlands and will work on increasing the number of countries to which it exports regularly.

### Employment, Wages, and Training

There are no expatriate managers at the subsidiary. All the employees are local people, and most have worked in the firm since before the involvement of the foreign investor. New hires are recruited through an interview with a commission consisting of the personnel director, the department director, and a specialist from the department. The candidate must then be approved by the general director. A career in the company usually starts at a lower level, and the tendency is to promote specialists from within the company to senior positions. The same applies to the general director as well.

The personnel director and the general director have a strategy for recruiting staff and evaluating them that is based on the development of the company over the next five years, and the need for personnel is based on this strategy. Their system aims at achieving a certain quality level of employees at the subsidiary and at improving the corporate culture of the firm. They have set up an information system on human resources in the firm. Although this strategy was conceived long ago, it has been applied only since the beginning of 1995. It has been worked out and implemented entirely locally.

The company operates on two to three shifts, with working time largely dependent on demand for its products. In instances when orders cannot be met by the regular workers, the company hires temporary workers for additional time at night or on Saturdays and Sundays. Such hiring occurs during the summer months as well, and temporarily recruitment for about two to three months is usually the norm. The number of employees in the company is about 1,050–1,100, of whom 1,000 are permanent employees.

Wages in the company are set by evaluating the capability, responsibility, and intellectual and physical capabilities of the employees and the position they have in the firm. The system consists of categories that measure the relevant characteristics of employees by points. The sum of this evaluation is used to define, within certain boundaries, the exact wage for any position. Depending on the performance of the worker, the department director, together with the personnel director, could approve an increase in the initial wage after six months of work or more if necessary.

Wages at the firm are higher than wages in the region due to the character of the work in the company and the fact that the firm is the only one specializing in this sector in the region. However, wages are higher than the average sectoral wage due to the firm's business potential and labor policy. The region suffers from high unemployment, and enterprises that could provide workers with comparable salaries are not to be found in the area.

All employees go through different training courses, the design and frequency of which are entirely within the competence of the subsidiary.

Around 30–40 percent of the workers are members of trade unions in the company. The managerial staff negotiates salaries with the unions, managers inform union leaders regularly of current business developments, and they regularly adjust wages to inflation. As a result, there have been no problems with the trade unions.

## Finance

The subsidiary identifies the need for investments, restructuring, and further development by analyzing markets and the position of the firm. It is very decentralized in making decisions on investments and development, which form the first step. If these investments are within the framework of the five-year business plan, which has already been accepted by the head office, then the final decision is made locally.

The second step in defining investment development is to report to the head office about what is needed and to identify the resources that will be used: either these will be internal, or there will be a need for outside funding. It is the subsidiary that determines the use of local funds. However, decisions regarding external funding for investments are done jointly with Berg AG, since they provide the investments. However, there is no limit on investments financed and made locally. In practice, it is the responsibility of the general director to make a decision in this area.

Responsibility for the financial management of the company is shared by the general director and the finance manager, who is also the chief accountant of the subsidiary. The subsidiary uses a local branch of a Bulgarian bank. It is difficult to find a bank that will make financial transfers without a delay.

The firm takes out short-term loans for working capital only. The decisions to do so are made locally, and there is no need for coordination with the head office. The company often uses credit lines because sometimes it experiences delays in payments. Because a substantial part of the company's revenues, more than 60 percent, come from abroad and meanwhile the company needs the money for buying inputs, 30–40 percent of which are cash outlays, the credit line is used to fill the gaps.

Long-term borrowing, however, is different and rather complicated. The company does not take out long-term credits, and they are not included in the business plan either.

The subsidiary's balance sheets have improved since the foreign partner's involvement. The firm's debt has mostly been paid off, and the company's financial stance has improved. Payables are resolved on a regular basis. Receivables have also generally improved in the past months, which is due to growing demand on the domestic market. International payments are also duly made, and the company has experienced no more financial problems.

### Ownership

The structure of ownership of the subsidiary is the following:
- 50.4 percent for Berg AG;
- 40.6 percent for the Ministry of Industry.

The general director's view on the evolution of ownership is that this is not a problem on the agenda at the moment, and the company has not yet thought it over.

### Dealing with the Government

There are difficulties in dealing with government authorities, one of which is delays in government decisions and their implementation. The second is the bureaucratic red tape of going through a whole set of commissions, meetings, and councils for getting government approvals for routine decisions.

However, the company has no problems in its relationship with the department of the Ministry of Industry responsible directly for the firm.

Since the establishment of the joint venture, the general director has had no contacts concerning operational management with the Ministry of Industry. The only obligation on the company's part is to inform the Ministry about the general meeting of the board of directors only in instances when the agenda includes items concerning the state-owned participation in the company.

Berg–Montana has problems locally, on the regional level, most of which, however, are not caused by economic reasons. Regional authorities provide no help for the firm, but there are also no harmful interventions.

The company has raised the problem of "unfair" competition related to the import of fittings that do not meet Bulgarian standards but that are very cheap. It has contacted the Committee for Standardization and other committees, but there has been no response whatsoever.

### Technology

The firm renewed its production equipment by creating the second plant even before the foreign partner's involvement, and the technological level was good. The changes since the joint venture was established are in the technology of melting. The new equipment is used for the processing of zinc, and the process is automatic and not manual as it was before. This will allow for savings in materials and energy. Some additional projects for improving the gas system and the furnaces for warming the metal have been worked out and are in the process of implementation. The technology for this conforms to the latest standards. All the projects for improving the technologies were not included in the plan for the first year. The following year, investment focused on the introduction of a new melting furnace.

### Unbundling and Social Assets

There has been no unbundling of any parts of the company. The firm is retaining the social assets that had been acquired, but there are not many of them.

The company has some social benefits that have not been changed since the foreign partner became involved. It provides food free for a certain class of workers and at a 50 percent discount for the rest of the workforce. The workers receive working clothes free, and transportation to work is free of charge as well.

## *Performance*

The big success of the investment lies in improving the performance of the firm through an increase in output and sales and access to international markets. The improvement of product quality is an advantage that is observable only recently. Most of the indicators of improved performance have been incorporated into the business plan, and their scope has been extended to exports and sales. The freezing of profits has been also planned from the very beginning of the joint venture.

The main problems remain in collecting payments both from abroad and domestically. For example, there was a problem in receivables from the Czech Republic, where the company had increased its market share and is planning to go ahead due to the closure of the local firm for fittings and castings. The company has tried to shift to another bank, but the same problems have recurred .

In terms of long-term restructuring, the firm is following the five-year program set up in the business plan. The first measures have already been introduced. Another technological line from a nearby town is being awaited that will contribute to product quality. As long as the foreign partner supplies the equipment, and this equipment conforms to world standards, technological restructuring is proceeding.

The firm is the biggest of its type in the country and has become a leading supplier of fittings and castings in the Balkan region recently. Although the firm is trying to get better output quality, the general manager evaluates the performance so far as successful.

# 2

# Danone–Serdika J.S. Co.

## Malinka S. Koparanova

### COMPANY PROFILE

Branch: Milk production and dairy products;

Shareholders: Danone Group (BSN before July 7, 1994); Serdika, a state-owned Bulgarian dairy-product company; European Bank for Reconstruction and Development (EBRD)

Established: May 1993

### HISTORY OF THE FIRM

A joint venture was set up between the Danone Group, the world's largest producer of fresh dairy products, and Serdika–Sofia, the most popular Bulgarian state-owned firm for milk and dairy products with the biggest market share. The new company specializes in yogurt production.

Dairy products form the greatest share of products in the range of the output variety of the BSN, or from July 1994, the Danone Group, totaling a 28.8 percent share; followed by grocery products, 18.7 percent; biscuits, 16.3 percent; international, 10.0 percent; beer, 9.2 percent; mineral water, 8.9 percent; and containers, 8.1 percent, as of the end of 1994.

Danone Group's 1994 consolidated sales totaled up to FF 76.8 billion and those of dairy products, FF 24.2 billion. The sales structure of dairy products is the following:

- fresh cheese, 32.4 percent;
- yogurt, 31.0 percent;
- desserts, 14.3 percent;

- aged Italian cheeses, 10.9 percent;
- others, 11.4 percent.

The production of yogurt and white cheese in Bulgaria is a traditional activity. These products have good quality and a considerable share of the output of the food-processing industry. It is characterized by high consumption rates domestically and relatively high exports all over the world. However, the loss of markets since the start of reforms have substantially affected milk and dairy production. Lower domestic demand as a result of falling consumers' purchasing power has been reflected in a drastic decrease in the sale of milk and dairy products. The decline in the output of agriculture, on the other hand, has worsened the conditions of suppliers, and, in 1992 and 1993, this sector experienced both shortages of inputs and financial problems.

The state-owned company Serdika–Sofia is among the market leaders in this sector on the Bulgarian market. However, with the more than fourfold decrease in milk consumption since 1989, the prereform year, and severe problems both in the supply of milk and in maintaining sales, the company fell into financial difficulties. The relationship with the foreign investor was established at the beginning of the 1990s, when representatives of Danone first visited Serdika–Sofia. In 1992–93, the Berov government initiated a policy to promote FDI and to encourage joint ventures as a step toward the privatization of the whole economy. Soon after that, a series of joint ventures were set up in different sectors. In the case of the joint venture between Serdika and Danone, the Bulgarian shareholder is the Ministry of Agriculture, which is represented by the general manager of Serdika on the board of directors.

A strategy of entering into new markets, and especially the emerging markets of Eastern Europe and Russia, was adopted by the Danone Group in 1990–94. They established a series of subsidiaries in Poland, the Czech Republic, Hungary, and Bulgaria. "In strategic terms, we pursued a very active acquisition policy throughout the year [1994], targeting markets outside Western Europe," states the chairman's message to shareholders in the annual report of the Danone Group.

## ORGANIZATIONAL STRUCTURE

Danone–Serdika has an organization that is similar to all the other subsidiaries in the Danone Group. It includes the following levels:

- board of directors;
- general manager;
- departments with heads of departments.

The board of directors, called the board of the administrative council, consists of shareholders: three people represent the Danone Group; two represent Serdika–Sofia; and one represents the EBRD. The president of the board is from the Danone Group; he is also the general manager of the East European Division at headquarters.

The following departments were introduced with the establishment of the joint venture:

- marketing, integrating the functions of sales and distribution;
- the finance department, which splits the two functions of chief accountant and planning (cost) controller;
- production department;
- purchasing department;
- milk-purchasing department, which is split to adapt to the market characteristics of the company's activities;
- human-resources department.

Experts from headquarters are assigned to every department of the subsidiary. They come regularly to advise on different topics related to current work. All the managers and employees are Bulgarians, with the exception of one permanent expatriate, the general manager, who comes from the Danone Group. The managers were recruited after an interview with the general manager of the joint venture, and most of them come from the emerging private sector in Bulgaria. The workers were taken from the Bulgarian firm Serdika. Both blue- and white-collar workers have gone through a number of training courses and seminars both in Bulgaria and abroad.

The chain of reporting follows the generally accepted path: the general manager reports to the president of the board of directors of Danone–Serdika, and the latter reports to the general manager of the Division for Fresh Products–Europe. In the beginning, the general manager for Eastern Europe used to come every six weeks for up to two days during which the general manager of the joint venture would report on all operational matters. The financial report is continuously updated and sent to Paris, where the headquarters for Europe–Fresh Products of the Danone Group are located. The financial report includes budgets, plans, the strategic plan for upcoming years, and so forth. Every year the firm draws up a detailed plan on an annual basis within a three-year framework, projecting variances and their consequences. There are three reporting standards that the joint venture has to meet: the criteria of the Danone Group, those of the EBRD, and Bulgarian standards. The three parties have the right to impose their own criteria when the subsidiary prepares reports for the shareholders of the joint venture. The company prepares a strategic plan for three years for the Danone Group that is continuously updated as well as a strategic plan for the EBRD, which is for a ten-year time horizon. The accounting in the strategic plan follows a double principle, according to Bulgarian standards and according to Western criteria.

The business strategy of the subsidiary is to become a market leader on the Bulgarian market, that is, to have at least a 25 percent share of the domestic market. However, it does not intend to achieve this objective at any price. Market share and volume must be linked to profitability, and this indicator is the one the company monitors most closely. In the long term, however, the subsidiary may be interested in exporting fresh dairy products on the one hand and in diversifying its portfolio of products on the other. According to the general manager, the joint venture may try to take advantage of its capacity and market possibilities abroad to begin exporting. By linking this potential to the Danone brand and know-how in milk and fresh products, positive results could soon follow.

If the part of Serdika that is not part of the joint venture is put up for sale, the company will try to buy it. It is situated close by, and its output is in the same sector. The company has already thought it over and has a plan ready. However, the deal will depend to a great extent on the price.

There has been no change in the ownership of Serdika–Sofia; it was and is a state-owned company. The ownership of the joint venture reflects the shares of the capital of the shareholders. It is evolving over time through increases in its capital brought about by additional purchases of shares by the Danone Group.

## SECTOR AND MARKETS

Danone–Serdika is improving its position in the domestic market for yogurt. Its market share has increased recently, but the general manager pointed out that the company's strategy is to become a market leader rapidly by obtaining a market share around 25 percent or more. He was very unwilling to give an exact figure, but judging from the strategy, this goal had not been achieved yet. According to the general manager, the market in Bulgaria is unique, and competition in milk and dairy products is a special case. The state-owned companies in the sector have special prices to buy the main input, milk. When selling output, they do not care about their profit margin. It is primarily for these reasons that competition in dairy production becomes a "special case."

There are three kinds of players on the Bulgarian market that the joint venture considers when evaluating its competition:

- imported milk and dairy products;
- small domestic private businesses;
- state-owned firms.

The first player is not a serious competitor for the firm. The general manager considers the high prices of imported milk and dairy products and their orientation toward different consumers' tastes as the main reasons for the low probability of attaching any importance to this group as a competitor. The second participant on the market, private business, is still too weak. Many private businesses are founded merely to make a quick profit, and, often, the owners do not have the requisite technical and business know-how. In many cases, they will not be on the market for a long time.

The third player, state-owned firms, is the most important because these companies have the biggest market share. However, the current unfavorable financial situation on the one hand and the current managerial situation, in which employees cannot be fired or hired according to the needs of the company, on the other, make their participation on the domestic market problematic in a market environment. However, their ability to keep prices low has kept them in business. As long as they can afford to produce at low prices, there will always be a market for them. Their product costs around 40 percent less than that of Danone–Serdika.

## DECISIONS TO INVEST

The previous executive director of Serdika had presented an investment offer by the Danone Group to the Bulgarian government about a year before the joint venture was established. One of the reasons for the Bulgarian rejection of the first offer was the special situation of the sector: Bulgaria is considered to be the homeland of yogurt, and the French offer proposed to bring new packaging and French yogurt recipes, which would require the venture to pay royalties for the yogurt technology. Two days after the rejection of this proposal, negotiations were re-opened, initiated by the Danone Group. The second time, representatives of the EBRD were introduced into the talks, and the joint venture was established legally in May 1993, with capital shares divided 50 percent for Serdika and 50 percent for the Danone Group.

The general manager was involved in the talks, and he describes them as difficult and delicate. The basic purpose of the joint venture was to improve the financial situation of the Bulgarian company, or at least part of it, since the joint venture applies only to the yogurt-production part of the business.

Negotiations with the Bulgarian government lasted more than one year. The difficulties in the talks were due to the fact that the joint venture is in a delicate and sensitive sector for the Bulgarian economy. Yogurt is considered to be very important for the economy and for the national identity as well. For the representatives of Danone, "it was very difficult and delicate to explain to them that Danone is a world market leader and can bring something to the yogurt in Bulgaria," according to the general manager. The problems were not related to the financial part of the deal.

In the joint venture, Serdika was bringing its material assets and the Danone Group cash for new investments, which were very necessary at the time. There was a preliminary agreement that the EBRD would become a shareholder as well, but it was only later, after the initial establishment of the joint venture and in the first capital increase in March 1994, that the EBRD became a shareholder by taking 15 percent of the capital. Shares were redistributed to the other two holders in the following way: the Danone Group got 53 percent and Serdika got 32 percent.

Danone is a world market leader in fresh milk and dairy products, and the group wanted to be represented on the Bulgarian market, since Bulgaria is known as the homeland of yogurt. Bulgaria has a high level of consumption of yogurt; on a per capita basis, consumption is among the highest in Europe. The Danone Group made a business plan and determined that a Bulgarian subsidiary would be profitable.

Some other factors were taken into account when considering the possibility of the joint venture, such as low labor costs, but "buying the market and saying that Danone is a good yogurt" was the main reason.

A second evaluation of the transaction was conducted for the Danone Group by Price Waterhouse. On the Bulgarian side, an evaluation was done by appointees from the Agency for Privatization and ministry agencies.

For Danone, the policies and attitudes of the general manager of Serdika were the ones that were important, because it is the daily transactions that he oversees that affected and affects the activities of the joint venture. He was a representative on the board of directors, but he has recently been fired and has not yet been replaced. There is no direct influence on the joint venture's operations by government authorities. However, the indirect effects are felt very much. The government and the Ministry of Agriculture are concerned about the problems of the joint venture, but they have never showed any interest in trying to solve them, as the general manager admitted. For example, for the new capital increase of the joint venture, an authorization on their part was required. The general manager asked for it and waited for six months. Bureaucracy, lack of interest, and absence of responsibility are the main negative effects emanating from local authorities.

## EXPECTATIONS AND EXPERIENCE

### General Characteristics

The Bulgarian part of the joint venture, Serdika, was a state-owned company whose financial situation had been deteriorating since the start of the reform. Before the establishment of the joint venture, it had experienced unprofitable performance for the third year in a row, and lacked working capital. The involvement of a foreign partner solved these problems. After the joint venture was established, production and sales increased.

### Management Structure

The joint venture established a completely new organization in terms of structure, functions, and decision making. The main idea was to give people greater autonomy in making decisions about the activities for which they were responsible. Decision making within the whole company split operational activities and strategic decisions. Operational functions are managed by the subsidiary, while decisions on capital outlays are approved by headquarters. These arrangements are the same in all of Danone's subsidiaries.

The reporting mechanism follows the general organizational scheme. The report to headquarters from the subsidiary is made on a regular basis, and the president of the East European Division of the Danone Group initially came every six weeks to advise and control the setting-up process. The other channel is regular contact with the experts attached to every department of the subsidiary. In practice, they engage in an active exchange of information.

## *Production*

Danone–Serdika was established in May 1993. The joint venture has increased the capacity of Serdika, and the company has the potential to increase this capacity yet more, and the subsidiary will be able to utilize this as well. Employment has increased from 90 in 1993 to over 200 in the course of two years.

The firm has experienced difficulties in obtaining inputs of the quality necessary for production. In the winter of 1993, agriculture suffered a sever crisis, and milk production dropped. The company decided to pay more for milk, although prices of milk at that time were very low, and to pay suppliers regularly, making payments to cover deliveries promptly every fifteen days. Danone–Serdika preferred to seek inputs far from Sofia, because around Sofia there were only small farms. The quality of milk purchased, as well as control over it, is considered to be very important, and the company covered transport costs to obtain these inputs from larger but more distant suppliers.

The manager used to go far from Sofia in the beginning, to Belene and surrounding regions "and everywhere," he admits. Small private farms could not be used for reasons of quality standards. In practice, such farms prevail in milk production in Bulgaria. The second interesting fact is that the company prefers to buy milk from fewer suppliers because of concerns about the reliability of supply. The contacts with large suppliers are more reliable.

Productivity has increased, but the most important consequences for the manager are in the qualitative changes in the organization of production, in the environment of the workers, in their attitude toward work, and in the quality of output. The joint venture has also introduced new techniques and technological lines that are less energy consuming and that have fewer adverse environmental effects. Productivity has increased both as a number and as a quality. The yogurt produced in the subsidiary is of good quality, but it is necessary to achieve such quality on a regular basis.

### Sales and Marketing

The marketing objectives and promotional materials of the subsidiary are partly related to those of headquarters. The marketing strategy of the subsidiary is focused on expanding its market share in Bulgaria, which coincides with that of Danone. Danone–Serdika is targeting the segment of the market that can afford to pay a premium of around 30 percent for better-quality yogurt. With the Bulgarian economy coming out of its crisis in the middle of the 1990s, increasing consumer purchasing power should help the production of Danone–Serdika to increase.

In the long run, the range of products may diversify with more dairy products. Then the company will seek to export fresh dairy products. This strategy is related to the development of the subsidiary in the near future. If the rest of the state-owned firm Serdika–Sofia is put up for privatization, the subsidiary is interested in buying it, depending on the price. Danone–Serdika already has a business plan for including this part of the company in the subsidiary, but the final decision will depend on the privatization evaluation and procedures.

### Employment, Wages, and Training

The only expatriate manager in the subsidiary is the general manager. He has been entirely involved in recruiting the employees of the joint venture. All of them are Bulgarians and are recruited by the general manager through an interview. The managers come mostly from private business and are highly self-motivated.

"I am very enthusiastic about the intellectual level of Bulgarians," admits the general manager. Some of the workers have come from the state-owned firm Serdika, but they have adapted very quickly to the new organization and attitude. There is a lot to learn, and they acquire the knowledge quickly because they are highly educated. The qualifications of all the employees are very high. The workers have good technical experience, and all of them have diplomas from special schools. The managerial staff is highly qualified; they all have higher education, and some even have two specialties. All the staff members working at the joint venture have been highly evaluated by the general manager, who points to their contribution as part of the success of the joint venture.

The personnel director is the one who conducts the first interviews with potential employees and makes the preliminary selection. Those who have passed this interview are considered for employment by the general manager.

There has been a great deal of support for training. Specialists come from headquarters every six weeks to train people. Sometimes people are sent for seminars or for courses as well, but 90 percent of the training is local, in Sofia. The results were very good; even the workers from Serdika have adapted, and they now meet the new criteria. There are several programs in the subsidiary for training employees. First, workers were trained to adapt to the new technological conditions. Second, the managerial staff is undergoing training specific to their departments. If they are in the marketing department, they go to marketing courses; if they are in the finance department, they go for finance and accounting courses. Third, there are courses for the managers of departments to develop managerial skills. In these courses, the variety of the techniques applied is greater, from conservative methods to situation games. There are fewer managerial responsibilities than would be the case in an independent firm, however, and management in the subsidiary is still very different from that in a Western company.

These programs are planned by the subsidiary in its annual budget. The personnel director works out the details of the programs and the budgets for them. The next step is to include this part of the budget in the subsidiary's budget and to get it approved by headquarters. Once done, the financing of the courses is included in the subsidiary's budget. The training budget is managed and controlled by the personnel director.

There are additional training programs that are centralized for all Europe and distributed by headquarters in Paris. For example, all the personnel directors of Danone Group's subsidiaries are gathered to exchange experience and be trained in some new strategies in human-resource management. Such meetings are used to establish the objectives for certain divisions and to spread the adopted strategies throughout the whole structure of Danone. There is a third type of training that is performed in the subsidiaries but organized centrally.

These seminars, or courses, depend on the needs of the employees and the situation of the affiliate.

In addition, courses are organized locally depending on the managers and their needs. The managerial staff is highly qualified. All of them have university degrees, and some even have two different university degrees. The personnel director of the joint venture has a Ph.D. in sociology. Most of the training is provided locally with the help of the personnel director. She is responsible for modifying the programs according to people's needs. This is a necessary condition since the qualifications of both blue- and white-collar workers is very high, and there are points in the program that are useless while others need detailed study.

The employees have good skills, but some problems with employee relations appeared with the introduction of the foreign partner. The personnel director's assessment is that "Bulgarians are rather conservative in moving from one place to another, as was the case with the people coming from Serdika." The employees are motivated by a different attitude toward the company and the business as a whole and the changes in the conditions as a direct effect of the foreign partner's involvements. New machines were bought, and there are far better working conditions because the building is completely renovated, and, in particular, there is air conditioning in the production facility, the workers are supplied with new clothes every three months, and so forth. As a result, the employees of Danone–Serdika have changed their attitudes very quickly.

The motivation by salary is also applied to the employees of the subsidiary. Salaries are adapted to inflation in Bulgaria by indexation. An additional increase to blue-collar workers is given to some departments along with the general indexation. The managers receive bonuses related to the operational results of the company.

The subsidiary has a wage-setting policy consisting of two main elements:
- the ratio among the company levels;
- labor-market specificity in the country.

The strategy of the subsidiary is to set wages at least at the average for the local market. Wage motivation works for some employees only. Others began their careers in Serdika and will remain until they retire regardless of the fact that they could go to a different place and be paid higher wages than in this company. They have just gotten used to working in the factory, and they are fond of their work. Workers are paid a premium that is not related to the volume of work but is used as motivation for the whole period and is traditional for the group: bonuses are given for Easter and Christmas. Managers are also granted a bonus once a year.

In regard to the managerial staff, the strategy is to maintain a level that is competitive for the local market to ensure good managers. The subsidiary does not provide the highest salaries in Bulgaria but tries to keep them on an above-average level.

The changes in the number of employees are due to hiring more people during the summer months to cover the seasonal vacations of the workers and to maintain the continuous dairy-production process. The human-resources director maintains the size of the workforce at a uniform level, and sometimes more workers are hired during the winter season due to absences for health reasons. The company's strategy is to hire students who may eventually come back after graduation, and the period worked is used to get them acquainted with the company. There is a general tendency toward an increase in the number of employees of Danone–Serdika. The number was initially 90, and in October 1995 it was 213. The subsidiary has a trade union, Podkrepa, which includes around 30 percent of the employees. Negotiations are traditionally carried out and indexation is provided by the director. There have been no problems with them so far.

There were problems in human-resources management in 1994 when the management team was in the process of being formed and at the same time the subsidiary experienced problems due to the poor economic environment.

### Finance

Investment strategy is worked out by headquarters taking into consideration the business opportunities of the subsidiary.

Financing investments and restructuring are discussed by the subsidiary with headquarters. The subsidiary initiates a program for investments or restructuring and develops its costs in the budget. The next step is to receive approval on it or corrections to it. Then, within the already approved numbers, the distribution for investments could change, and this kind of decision is made by the subsidiary. Such changes must, however, be supported by serious arguments and could include shifts to other items if necessary for the company. Business opportunities are also considered by the subsidiary, and some changes could be made in the investment program as a result. Local initiatives are greater for the functions of marketing, sales organization, salary policy, and operating losses and profits.

The company was established with a capital of BGL 178 million, followed by an increase of BGL 250 million. Presently the company is waiting for another capital increase.

### Performance

Since May 1993, there has been a great improvement in the performance of the joint venture. The subsidiary has exceeded the targets set out in its plan. The general manager believes this success to stem from the joint effect of the work of the Bulgarian team and the new techniques and organization provided by Danone.

In the beginning, a rather pessimistic evaluation of the work of the joint venture prevailed on the foreign investor's part. This resulted in a lowering of the planned figures. In such circumstances, it was not very difficult to exceed the targets. The pessimism came, above all, from the macroeconomic environment in 1993 and 1994. The acceleration of inflation rate at the end of 1993 and the high level of price increases in 1994, coupled with the poor performance of agriculture, which affected the raw-material supply of the company in its first year of establishment, were both viewed as detrimental to the joint venture's profitability and ability to increase production.

In 1995, the joint venture stabilized, and the price premium for the Danone–Serdika product was higher than expected. Raw materials are less of a priority among the problems of the company as a result of its policy to find reliable suppliers for the time being on the Bulgarian market.

Headquarters does not make any concessions to the Bulgarian subsidiary or to any other East European subsidiary. The Danone Group has standards and applies them everywhere: it determines the target profit and the market share. The only exception may be made for deadlines: instead of reaching the targeted figures in two years, it may be necessary to do it in, say, four years. The same refers to accounting principles, because the balances must be consolidated at the leave of the parent firm. From the point of view of quality, the standards are rather flexible, because the subsidiaries have to be the best in their country. The objectives of the subsidiaries therefore depend on consumer taste, which is market specific. Products undergo an analysis in which they must meet quality criteria, and the last test is a consumer test. This test is a blind test, where the product is compared with the competition's products.

## Most Important Problems

The general manager's overall view of the setup of a joint venture in Bulgaria is that "The atmosphere is difficult. You must be very brave and tough to invest in Bulgaria. You must fight to be able to put your money in."

Working on the domestic market for nearly two and a half years, the subsidiary's main obstacle is the population's low purchasing power, which limits the volume of sales and the markup over local products' prices.

Being the only foreign investor specializing in yogurt production in Bulgaria is pointed as being another factor creating problems. There are legislative, political, and competition constraints for the subsidiary in Bulgaria. For example, yogurt prices are limited by price controls on private businesses. Political stability is an important issue for the foreign investor as well.

The biggest problem for Bulgaria, as pointed out by the general manager of Danone–Serdika, is that the government authorities do nothing to attract foreign investors, and this is not only on the administrative side but on the legal level as well. An example is the import tax on investments for a joint venture, which can be as high as 15–20 percent.

Legislation is considered to be unfavorable to business, and some accounting problems are appearing as a result of the high inflation rates in 1993 and 1994. For example, the revaluation of balances is impossible after a year of 125 percent inflation. Although this is a technical problem, it is difficult to explain to shareholders.

The experience of the joint venture, however, is providing positive results, and the final words of the manager stressed the good qualification of the managers and workers and the possibilities for becoming a successful business in Bulgaria.

## *Main Success*

The evaluation of success always has two parts: (a) the quantitative part, when figures talk; and (b) the qualitative part, the personal satisfaction of the managers.[1] As for the qualitative part, the general manager was proud to share his satisfaction at taking a moribund business and turning it into a vital organization that provides a living for 213 people. The image of Danone–Serdika is now becoming established on the Bulgarian market. The company is becoming known and appreciated by consumers on the domestic market.

## NOTE

1. Managers of the subsidiary are cautious about providing any detailed information on the company's development. Even financial information that is considered public according to both Bulgarian and Western law is considered confidential. The general manager is the one who determines the degree of openness to the public. It is his view that there should be a strict organization of who will be provided what type of information to whom and when.

# 3

# Vidima–Ideal Ltd.

## Malinka S. Koparanova

## GENERAL INFORMATION

Vidima–Ideal Ltd. is a Bulgarian–American joint venture (JV) founded in April 1992 between a Bulgarian state-owned company and American Standard Inc. from the United States. The company is situated in Sevlievo.

## COMPANY PROFILE

- Manufacturing of sanitary and industrial fittings;
- Sales of sanitary and industrial fittings;
- Manufacturing and sales of soft-drink vending machines;
- Servicing and maintenance of its own products;
- Products include the following:
—All types of sanitary and household fittings of the following types:
    —dual-control sink, bath, bidet, and basin mixers supplied
       with rubber seals;
    —single-lever sink, bath, bidet, and basin mixers supplied
       with ceramic seals;
    —bathroom accessories;
    —water-supply pipe valves;
    —water-drainage fittings; plastic and brass sink traps;
    —wash-out equipment;
    —safety valves and electric water-heater mixers;
—Industrial fittings:
    —half inch, three-quarter inch, and one inch brass;
    —from one and one-quarter inch to two and a half inch cast iron;
    —soft-drink vending machines.

The company is developing its economic activities, which include manufacturing and marketing in Europe together with Ideal–Standard, a German subsidiary of the American parent company.

## *Capital*

The company's capital is USD 12,533,000, with the following structure:
• the American share is USD 6,395,000, of which 90 percent is in cash and 10 percent is in material and nonmaterial contributions;
• the Bulgarian share consists entirely of the real estate that the firm possesses.

## HISTORY OF THE FIRM

The history of the Bulgarian company involved in the JV goes far back into the 1930s, when a partnership for manufacturing cans was founded by a group of seven manufacturers in the region. Twenty years later, in 1952, the enterprise merged with a plant in Sofia, and it began its specialization in water-supply fittings. In 1968–70, after a reconstruction, Italian technology was introduced for the production of a whole range of sanitary and household fittings. Some of this equipment is still functioning.

At the beginning of the 1980s, a comprehensive program for reconstruction and modernization of the enterprise was undertaken, without interrupting the production process. Also, the company's name was changed from Stoyan Buchvarov to Vidima. The modernization introduced new products and production technologies and enabled Vidima to introduce its own design for single-lever and dual-control mixers as well as some other products.

At the beginning of the 1990s, with the start of the reform in Bulgaria, different proposals were put forward for different forms of cooperation, mainly for working under license from foreign manufacturers. There was a proposal from a firm in Germany, but the offer of American Standards Inc. was the only one for a joint venture. The American offer was accepted by the Council of Ministers as the best one, and in April 1992, Vidima–Ideal was set up.

The American partner, American Standard Inc., was established in

Delaware more than 100 years ago. Today the company operates in 27 countries and has 89 enterprises, specialized in three main products groups:

- air-conditioning;
- sanitary wares and fittings;
- truck brake systems.

American Standard Inc. has a turnover of about USD 4 billion per year. The sales of air-conditioning systems under the Trane trademark provides 55 percent of the turnover, while sales of sanitary ware and fittings under the Standard, Ideal–Standard, and American Standard trademarks provides a further 30 percent. The sales of Wabco brake systems form the last 15 percent of the company's sales.

The role of Vidima–Ideal is to develop its technology, production, and sales within the framework of American Standard's worldwide structure through direct cooperation with Ideal–Standard of Germany, which is a leading sanitary-fitting manufacturer in Europe established in 1970 by American Standard.

American investments in the joint venture total USD 6,395,000 and are split among the following items (accordingly to the contract):

- USD 150,000 for training;
- USD 612,000 as imported equipment;
- USD 380,000 for market access;
- cash investments in the assets of the JV.

Soon after the setting up of the JV, the cash was used to purchase machines, technology, and inputs to start the production process in such a way as to meet the requirements of markets different from those known previously.

## ORGANIZATIONAL STRUCTURE

### Vidima–Ideal within the Structure of American Standard Inc.

Within the organization of American Standard Inc., the company belongs to the division for construction products. Construction products are divided into six groups, with sanitary fittings being the smallest one. The group consists of four companies located in Germany, Bulgaria, Mexico, and the United States. The plants supply all the other twenty-seven American Standard business units for sanitary products with fittings and thus complete the production circle.

The relationship between Vidima–Ideal and the German firm is close due to the close technological cooperation. The technical levels are more or less the same, the only exception being the German firm's marketing organization, which is responsible for all the German production of fittings but only sells part of the Bulgarian firm's products for the moment.

### The Structure of Vidima–Ideal

The scheme, frequency, and requirements of reporting to headquarters follows a general approach and is the same for all the subsidiaries. Some exceptions were made during the first two years after the setting up of the joint venture, but they concerned the deadlines of the reports only. Since 1994, companywide reporting practice has been applied on a regular basis. The firm maintains a system of accounts based on Bulgarian standards and one based on international (USGNP) standards. Reporting procedures include regular reports of monthly balances, reports on economic activity, and the cash flow of the company.

The joint venture follows a unique system of reporting to headquarters. There is a computer center at the company that is responsible for keeping track of all expenditures and revenues. The balances are finalized on the third day of the month using the computer system. After that, a transformation of all the primary accounts is estimated by the financial director for the official account, including the management account, and so forth. This set of accounts is sent to headquarters on the fourth day through a computer network. On the sixth day, a forecast for the next month through the end of the current year is given, taking into considerations the changes in the company and the environment.

The joint venture is fully responsible for the business strategy, both in its design and in its implementation. It is consolidated in American Standards Inc. due to the latter's share of 51 percent. The same rule is followed in all the subsidiaries of the American firm. Headquarters is regularly informed about the current situation in the company, including all the details and results that are observed by the firm.

The joint venture is responsible for the short-run forecast and the operational plan of its activities as well. In July they provide the company strategy for the next five years and correct the current plan. In November they do the operational plan for the next three years, which is used for the forthcoming short-run forecast. The firm is responsible for the annual plan as well. In practice, it has different parts providing different aspects of the company's activities.

It is the financial plan that includes the balance sheets, the statements on expenditures and revenues, and all the means for achieving the targets. The financial part is the most important segment and has been done by the company for four years. The first step in constructing the financial plan is to analyze past results and to define the targets for the coming year: investments for new machines and equipment, for technologies, and for expanding the scale of production are projected; the productivity level and ways of improving it are determined; and solutions for reducing costs are sought. The most important part is in the causality analysis, looking for the relationship among volume of production, structure, and prices. The target is set first, followed by the means to achieve it, and the required changes in the structure. This kind of analysis is done by various departments in the company, including sales, production, supply, and so forth.

The master plan is done at the company level and includes the budgeting for the administration of the firm. The financial director is responsible for this process. On the expenditure side, planning is done by departments as well. Finally, the plan concerning all expenditures is worked out by iterations to meet a target.

The methodology for setting up the plan concerning expenditures is entirely worked out by American Standard, and this is the only part that the joint venture has accepted fully. However, the calculations of all expenditures, current and short run, are evaluated by the financial director using a variety of approaches. The work is done in stages—the final, most detailed stage is the determination of the work hours: both for machines and for workers. On this basis, a reduction in expenditures is targeted by decreasing the time for a certain activity.

The whole financial management as a philosophy is directly given by American Standard Inc., but it is implemented by the company's team.

The American partner controls work in the company by receiving monthly financial reports and a lot of additional information on the company's activity is obtained by e-mail and through direct contacts every three months when the shareholder meeting takes place. At these meetings, the practice is to provide an overview of the current situation of the company in which problems are raised and results are outlined. Any initiative that improves the planned figures set up by the company, such as the increase in sales, for example, is welcome and is not coordinated by headquarters.

The first decision of the joint venture was to have a central office in Sofia and a management office in Sevlievo. Soon this idea was abandoned, and the people from Sofia moved to Sevlievo.

The only new person from the company is the financial director. All the other personnel had been employed in the firm before. However, their behavior and attitude toward work has substantially changed. There is strict discipline, and the work has changed as well.

The change in the organization is evident everywhere in the company, but the work is carried out by the same people. The level of intelligence of the employees and the managers is high enough to understand the changes and be successful. The company is working on reengineering its organizational structure. The underlying principle is that of going from functions to processes and of having an organization that supports such a principle.

## SECTOR AND MARKETS

In the 1980s, the output of the company was oriented mainly toward the domestic market. Exports were incidental and were more the exception than the rule. At the end of the 1980s, however, supplies to the Arab countries formed a substantial share in production, and due to the quality level of these markets, Bulgarian goods were easily sold there.

The structure of production at the end of 1989 was the following:
• 85–90 percent of output was for domestic sales;
• 5–10 percent was for exports.
Almost the same picture was observed through 1992.

With the establishment of the joint venture, the new company received USD 380,000 for access to the U.S. market. The American partner is responsible for obtaining export sales, which should reflect the production potential of the joint venture. However, the period through the middle of 1993 was characterized by the unchanged export performance due to investments in new machines and services, training, and so forth, for the joint venture. It was only in July–August 1993 that the company began to work seriously. Meanwhile, the process of changing the technologies continued until the end of 1994, and 1995 was, in fact, the first year of working at normal capacities.

The cash injection of the American partner of around USD 5.5 million soon increased to USD 8 million, which helped to overcome the downturn in production. The joint venture had the potential to increase production by 38 percent in six months, as indicated by the results in mid-1995 as compared to the end of 1994.

Starting with net sales of USD 9 million in 1992, the company soon increased its capacity utilization, and net sales went to USD 13 million in 1993 and USD 15 million in 1994. As of September 1995, net sales were USD 17 million. In the following year, the company expects an even bigger increase.

The company has no competition in the domestic market. Taking into account the potential of the firm, their marketing objectives are to expand the exports. European, Asian, and Arab countries are among those targeted. To realize these marketing objectives, the company needs to investigate different markets and to improve the organization of production. The competition is not global but regional, and the firm is seeking both to keep old partners and to find new importers for their products.

All output was controlled and distributed to importers through the German firm until the middle of 1995. Subsequently, export sales were carried out by the joint venture, including negotiations with clients, the signing of contracts, and direct supply to any place in the world. The company sells to many firms in New Zealand, Vietnam, South Korea, Germany, the United States, France, and Greece.

The company sells in developed markets thanks to its low prices and the good quality of its products. The company's marketing follows the trends of the consumers in these countries and identifies the segment to which sales should be targeted. German consumers are a good example, since the purchasing power of the buyers there has gone down by 10 percent recently, and, therefore, the company has aimed at developing and applying a strategy to cover this segment. The company has adopted a flexible strategy, and received many orders. It could provide greater volumes of output only by extending working hours. In October–November 1995, due to a contract with a German firm, the company increased working time to twelve hours per day and to the weekends by paying overtime to its workers.

The success of the firm in competing internationally is dependent on the ongoing process of improving its organization. Here two things are important:

1. Implementation of a DFM (demand-flow manufacturing) organization of production to ensure output with minimum inputs and high speed of turnover. In practice, all the subsidiaries of American Standard work with a DFM organization, with the few exceptions of newly established joint ventures. A project for Vidima–Ideal has been worked out since January 1, 1995, and its implementation is imminent. The project has been worked out by Bulgarian specialists who have collected experience from South Korea and Germany. Its implementation in the company will take about two years and will save at least USD 1 million. The second positive outcome of DFM is expected to be in substantially raising the productivity level.

2. Organization of management according to the principles of reengineering. The elimination of barriers between the different departments and the adoption of one level of competence within the whole managerial staff under the leadership of the director: these are the main targets for the organization of the company. This scheme will be applied in the company after 1997.

The company is a monopolist in the domestic market. It has 100 distributors organized on a regional principle and six franchises. Suppliers have changed since the start of the transition in Bulgaria. There is a variety of new components, both from the domestic and from the external market. Imports will be required if contracts for better quality are signed.

As a whole, the quality of supplied materials has improved. The main domestic suppliers of the company are the following:
• Nonferrous Metal-Processing Works Shareholding Company in Gara Iskar;
  • Brelco Trading in Sofia;
  • Corosa Engineering Shareholding Company in Sofia;
  • Kula Ring Shareholding Company in Kula;
  • Tchaika Shareholding Company in Varna;
  • Velpa Shareholding Company in Strazitza; and
  • Osam Ltd. in Lovetch.
The most important international suppliers are:
  • Bayer, Germany;
  • Atotech, the Netherlands;
  • Remeco Trading, Sweden;

- Hermes, Austria;
- Hilzinger Thum, Germany;
- VSM, Germany;
- Schamban, Denmark;
- Aielo IMR, Italy;
- Bossini, Italy; and
- Febise, Italy.

## DECISION TO INVEST

Given the regional distribution of American Standard's other subsidiaries, their desire to form a joint venture in Bulgaria reflected both the potential of the local market as well as the possibility of serving other markets from a low-cost source.

The financial director, who previously worked in a bank, was involved in establishing the joint venture. Other Western firms made offers to Vidima in 1992, but the bulk of these was for production under license. The Council of Ministers was more inclined toward attracting FDI through a joint-venture form, and therefore preference was given to the only offer of that kind, that of American Standard. American Standard visited the local firm and made its own evaluation.

The changes in the firm since it has become a joint venture are a result of the strategy of American Standard to organize its subsidiary as a highly competitive unit. Meanwhile, the transition had made it possible to form a joint venture because of the new legal environment.

### Expectations and Experience

Most of the expectations of the foreign partners have been met. The actual indicators of business performance in recent years have exceeded the planned figures.

### *General Characteristics*

The company was a leading enterprise before 1989, that is, before the economic crisis in Bulgaria. The financial situation worsened in the following years, and the firm accumulated debts and had no cash with which to operate. Domestic demand was very low, and the output that could be sold within the country shrank severely. By setting up the joint venture, the new company received access to foreign markets to increase its production, to obtain cash for working capital, and to make investments for new technologies.

### Management Structure

From the point of view of managing production, there has been a substantial change since the foreign partner's involvement in 1992. The most interesting fact here is that these changes have been brought about by the same people, the only new person in the company being the financial director, who is Bulgarian, as are all staff members. The fundamental change is based on the philosophy and methodology of reengineering: management is exercised through the chain of processes and not of functions. The functions are within different boxes (see Figure 1), but control and management follows the production processes and covers a number of departments. The walls between the departments thus disappear, and the final result becomes observable. It is the final outcome that determines wages, and people are thus explicitly motivated by the successful implementation of the entire process and not by only their part of it.

This type of organization depends to a great extent on planning and forecasting because everything is a function, above all, of the expected figure for the outcome and, second, of the success in selling the planned output. In the beginning it was difficult to understand and apply this principle in the company.

### Production

A new organization of production, DFM, was implemented in the company in October 1994. Before the experimental introduction took place, managers of all levels went through a series of courses. This philosophy of demand driving the whole production process and defining a new organization for the chain from marketing to production is quite new for Bulgarians, and Vidima–Ideal is the first to implement such a system in the country. The German subsidiary of American Standard Inc., Ideal Standard, has already been implementing DFM since 1992. The Bulgarian project was worked out and is managed by a Bulgarian, and she is well acquainted with the applications of the system in other subsidiaries of the company. The experience of Korea

Figure 1. **Organizational Structure of Vidima Ideal Ltd.**

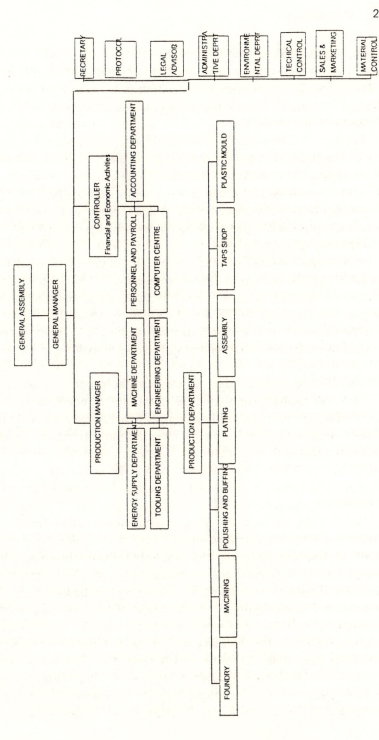

is highly applicable to the Bulgarian situation due to the nature of Korean suppliers and the small range of the output produced there.

The advantage of the new organization is in shortening the period between the receipt of a sales contract and its fulfillment to fall from one or two months at the moment to a period from two days to a maximum of one month. By constructing a set of the required components in advance, the turnover of stock is accelerated to a maximum of fifteen times, while under current conditions the most efficient management can turn over material inputs no more than ten times per year. According to the techniques of DFM, technology is focused on the processing of the material and direct inputs, which account for the bulk of expenditures.

As of the end of 1995, the first three technological lines implementing DFM will be set up and put into operation. The following year, eleven technological lines will be fully operational, and the range of the products produced by DFM will increase to seven. By completing the first stage of the new organization, productivity is expected to increase by 20 percent. The second stage was to have begun in January 1997.

A key task is to determine the steps in the production process in detail: the number of employees, the output to be produced for a specific period, and schedules for completing subassemblies. To realize DFM, a communications system is set up in the company using cards especially created for this purpose. The latter ensure that components and subassemblies are produced just in time. By means of these cards, the process is based on contracts to be fulfilled with no inventories of finished product kept in stock.

Machines are grouped according to technology and not functions to allow the most efficient production of parts and components.

DFM technology relies on a strict supply system. The company has been preparing for several years to organize its main suppliers of both primary and intermediate inputs. The company purchases 450 different materials and parts. Eighty percent of material costs are accounted for by 50 inputs. A further analysis points to the fact that for 90 types of materials the firm pays 15 percent of all expenditures, while for the remaining 300 components it pays 5 percent. On this basis, materials are classified into three groups: A, B, and C. The company could afford a longer period for supplying goods from group C without any substantial effects on financial performance. During that time, suppliers use their time to organize the supply of the more expensive materials so as to deliver them. A special program is being worked out aiming at the timely supply of necessary materials on short notice to save resources. Components and parts produced by Vidima–Ideal are also classified into the same categories A, B, and C. Following the principles of the process, goods from group C take more time between order and production to ensure the machines' capacities are used most efficiently, while the goods from group A are given priority in production. This process optimizes capacity utilization on the basis of a program for creating machine cells and technological chains. Operational control is included in the DFM system through a feedback technique.

The result of applying DFM affects the role of the production process in day-to-day operations and decisions: production is envisaged as a key element along with marketing. However, it is no longer the overriding determinant of strategy that it was in the planned economy.

Productivity has increased since the involvement of the foreign partner due to the technological and organization changes that have been introduced. The training provided by introducing new technologies is also a factor. There have been cost savings in the past two years, mainly due to technological changes. The company has an average annual cost reduction of around USD 250,000–300,000 for energy supply. Wastewater is treated in the company's water-treatment plant, and then it is drained out. The machine for washing wastewater is supplied by American Standard, and its value is around DM 700,000. It is part of the environmental policy of American Standard Inc., which has introduced its own standards and criteria for an ecologically sound environment.

### Sales and Marketing

The strategy of sales was worked out by the German subsidiary in the beginning. Step by step, the Bulgarian company is developing its own foreign trade relations and is gaining speed at working by itself in this area. Although the share of external markets in sales increased steadily, by the mid-1990s, only 5 percent of export went through the German firm.

The difference between domestic and foreign markets is mainly in prices. Before exporting to any country, the process of identifying consumer taste is always undertaken.

The following are the international clients of the firm:
- Ideal Standard, Germany;
- Issa Moh'd al Issa' Est., Saudi Arabia;
- Malas and Kutrache, Damascus, Syria;
- Bul–Pol, Poland;
- Direx, Czech Republic;
- G. Marcou Hellas, Greece;
- Bassam Trading and Commission Est., Jordan;
- Madara, Vienna, Austria.

There are no other Bulgarian producers of Vidima–Ideal's products, so the main domestic competition is from imports, and, therefore, the company is developing both the range and the quality of its products. The company does not engage in intensive advertisement, and this is done on purpose.

### Employment, Wages, and Training

The employment level has been almost constant. The company began with 1,040 workers in 1992 and has 970 at the moment. There have been no layoffs; the decrease is due to natural attrition. The level will probably be kept the same in the short run because around 150 workers cannot be used efficiently at the moment.

Following the management structure and the DFM organization, wages are not fixed but vary according to the volume of output and the volume of sales. This provides powerful economic incentives to all. The average wage in the company is above BGL 12,000, which is the highest in the region. Taking into account the activities of the workers outside the company, on their private farms, this wage is high enough to meet their requirements.

The managerial staff is provided with a 12.5 percent bonus, which is the same for all white-collar workers. The bonus becomes effective if actual results are more than 105 percent compared to the planned figures. The motivation mechanism works in both directions: if performance is less than 97 percent of expected, wages are reduced. Wages for blue-collar workers are determined on the basis of a norm and therefore depend on personal activity only.

Training is a continuous process at Vidima–Ideal. The company's employees have been trained in the United States and in other countries according to the technological requirements of the lines on which they work. Up to the middle of 1993, all the personnel went through various courses in analogous companies in the United States. At the moment, this process is not as intensive. The current practice includes business trips for visits, seminars, and workshops. The managerial staff went through courses for reengineering to develop DFM further and to implement it in the company.

Workers are well qualified, and the company thinks highly of the skills of its employees. Their technical experience was accumulated long ago, but the organizational improvements have come with the involvement of the foreign partner. That is why it was no problem to go through new courses for qualifying under different conditions: people were trained in three months instead of the planned three years. Labor productivity has substantially increased in the company since the involvement of the foreign partner. If estimated by the ratio of sales per worker, the increase is 60 percent over three years. In real terms, if quality is taken into account, the improvement in productivity is around 100 percent compared to 1992.

Industrial relations in the company are evaluated as very good by the managerial staff. The two most widespread trade unions in the country, the Independent Trade Union Confederation and the Trade Union "Podkrepa," are both represented in the firm. There have been no problems on either side, since there is more social support than before in terms of social assets, payments, health care, and so forth, which are provided as a result of the director's decision and not that of the unions. The management of personnel is flexible, and the hiring of additional part-time workers depends on the volume of orders. When work expands as a result of a new contract, for example, the company adds a third work team to the production lines.

## Finance

In the field of managing and making decisions about the current situation, the company is independent of headquarters. The joint venture is fully free to make any decision that is favorable for the company's development. As long as it is well run, the company has the freedom to make most decisions locally. The managerial staff of the joint venture works under the philosophy of first accepting everything, any new change, and next thinking over and planning how to implement it. They consider themselves to be reasonable people and their partners to be people with the same interest in practice. The three years of joint work has not provided any arguments against the strategy of the company.

Decisions concerning both organization and management are made entirely by the company, and there has been no case of pressure on the part of American Standard Inc.

In case of financial problems, however, headquarters could make the company accept their decisions. The company has experienced such situations on the technological side in the first two years. Emergency consultation by the German subsidiary was provided in due time.

There has so far been no problem on the management side and consequently no pressure on the decision-making process in the company in this sphere.

Operational control of expenditures is entirely done in the company. Every month, the managers organize meetings with the heads of production, and, with their help, they analyze deviations of actual expenses from the planned figures. Deviations are considered normal within certain percent boundaries. Estimates of indirect expenditures are filled in on a special form by the heads of production units, and in this way feedback on deviations is brought to the attention of workers, who already know the results of their work. This type of financial information is for the company only.

American Standard Inc. sold stock until 1988, when the company withdrew from the U.S. capital market. By the mid-1990s, the company was experiencing a shortage of capital and planned to raise it on the New York Stock Exchange to finance an expansion of the business. The parent company's strategy was to increase sales up to USD 5 billions from each of its divisions for 1995.

For the affiliates, investments as a rule are determined by headquarters as a result of previous discussion. However the affiliates are free to make an investment of up to USD 100,000. The Bulgarian joint venture could operate with the amount on its accounts within the annual limit generated by the profits of the company. The firm also uses interfirm credits for short-term purposes, of which 7–8 percent is for working capital.

### Ownership

The structure of the ownership since the setup of the joint venture to the present is as follows: state owned, 49 percent; American Standard Inc., 51 percent.

Following the principle of American Standard to incorporate employees as shareholders in its structure, a change in the structure of the company in the short run is quite possible; however, such a possibility has not yet been discussed with the managerial staff of the local company.

American Standard put forward an offer to buy part of the state-owned share at the beginning of 1994, but there was no response. The initial interest was to buy the company, and, since things did not develop, the company is seeking an increase in the capital proportionately to the shares.

### Dealing with the Government

The company uses regional branches of a Bulgarian bank, where a credit line has been opened. The firm also has contacts with the Bulgarian branch of ING Bank. There have been no problems with the banking system so far.

The board of directors has applied to the Council of Minister to increase the capital of the company and to the Agency for Privatization to buy additional shares, but there has been no response. The main problems for foreign investors, according to the experience of the joint venture, are a bureaucratic attitude and changes in laws and decrees. The company has had a problem with duties on imported equipment since the time of signing the initial contract for the joint venture. The machines are imported as a temporary import and are not taxed if they remain for up to three years. Meanwhile there has been a change in the tariff structure. The company has applied for a reduction in many places but has not yet received any answer. Problems of a similar nature have been observed in some other companies, and the solutions for them have been found through company-specific preferences.

### Technology

The technology used currently in the design of new products and in the tooling for production is based on using 3D CAD–CAM systems to develop NC computer software for CNC machines. This type of technology is among the leading types in the world. The quality of the products is guaranteed by strict control over the products using precise spectral-analysis equipment. The casting technology varies according to the complexity of the components from modern low-pressure die casting to conventional methods in the casting of complex components and of small series. The machining of components is done by precise and highly efficient multispindle machines and by specialized aggregate machines for processing. The process of washing out and degreasing components is environmentally friendly. The company has implemented modern technologies that give the most up-to-date chrome-nickel, aranya, golden, and epoxy-polyester wear-resistant coatings to be applied, providing the designer with many solutions to meet the different tastes of customers.

### Unbundling and Social Assets

All the social assets that existed before the establishment of the joint venture were kept. During recent years, the funds for social assets and services have increased, and employees enjoy more benefits. The vacation homes of the company have been renovated, as have been the workers' canteen and other free-time facilities. There is a health center at the company.

### Performance

#### Economic Performance

The performance of the joint venture in 1995 was crucial. For the first nine months, the company's sales totaled BGL 818 million, of which exports were 55 percent. The expected figure for overall sales was BGL 10.1 billion, which exceeds by far the planned BGL 600 million. The gross profit was USD 12,301,000, 30 percent more than the previous year. The ratio of profit to net sales was 11.6 percent; the planned figure was 12.8 percent. Inventories have decreased by 15 percent, more than BGL 21 million. Expenditures for investments amounted to BGL 26 million, with another 11 million expected by the end of the year. The financial director of the company estimates a growth in activities of around 40 percent on average for all financial indicators for the end of 1995 as compared to the previous year. The budget for the following year includes an increase of 10 percent in all financial-performance indicators, though as Table 1 shows, this target was easily met.

Table 1

**Summary of Operating Results** (million)

|  | 1992 | | 1993 | | 1994 | | 1995 | | 1996 | |
|---|---|---|---|---|---|---|---|---|---|---|
|  | BGL | USD[a] | BGL | USD | BGL | USD | BGL | USD | BGL | USD |
| Net sales | 205.0 | 9.0 | 360.0 | 13.0 | 484.0 | 15.0 | 656.0 | 20.0 | 829.0 | 25.0 |
| Operating earnings before taxes | 20.0 | 0.8 | 22.0 | 0.8 | 37.0 | 1.1 | 64.0 | 1.9 | 87.0 | 2.6 |
| Cash flow before interest and taxes | 61.7 | 2.6 | 57.0 | 1.5 | 55.1 | 1.7 | 41.4 | 1.3 | 91.3 | 2.8 |
| Inventory | 47.2 | 2.0 | 49.7 | 1.5 | 44.0 | 1.3 | 75.8 | 2.3 | 77.7 | 2.4 |
| Inventory turnover | 4.700 | | 6.800 | | 10.000 | | 10.000 | | 10.000 | |
| Capital expenditures | 30.1 | 1.3 | 85.5 | 2.6 | 31.1 | 0.9 | 32.1 | 0.9 | 25.1 | 0.8 |
| Sales (units) | 1.069 | | 1.074 | | 1.184 | | 1.301 | | 1.449 | |

[a]The exchange rate is as of the end of the years quoted by the BNB.

## *Prospects*

American Standard signed a contract with an investment group in Hong Kong for a joint venture of around USD 100 million at the end of 1994. The new investment in China will be realized with the involvement of Vidima–Ideal. The Chinese firm will benefit from the experience of the Vidima–Ideal, whose financial director is setting up the system for defining and controlling output expenditures and revenues. The systems of establishing new affiliates of American Standard worldwide do not differ. The experience in the management of Vidima–Ideal is being used to develop new business ventures in other countries as well.

## *Vidima–Ideal—The Most Successful Company in the Region*

Success has come out of reorganizing the whole process and the attitude and behavior of the employees. The main contribution of the foreign partner is considered to be in the following three fields: markets; technological change; and changes in organization.

The advantage of the FDI is evaluated to be not so much in the cash flow as in market access. The name of the company is that of American Standard Inc., and its reputation brings with it favorable conditions for selling output. The firm has the potential to produce huge volumes of output by investing only approximately USD 1 million. It could achieve production of around USD 35 million by the year 2000.

The performance of the company has exceeded the expected results, as they were estimated at the beginning and set up in the initial plan. The company has improved financial indicators and its position on the domestic and external markets, the employees are better off, and industrial relations form a friendly environment. The point where the company has failed is in getting permanent access to the Russian market. There are some sales, but relative to the potential of the market, they are meaningless. There are no traditional contacts in the field; however, the potential is great since Russian imports exceed domestic production. The company still cannot find reliable partners on Russian markets. The strategy of American Standard Inc. is to make a joint venture in Russia and develop it using the experience and the initial help of the Bulgarian subsidiary. The same approach has already been applied in the case with the German company and the Bulgarian partner Vidima–Ideal.

# 4

# Zagorka J.S. Co.

## Malinka S. Koparanova

## COMPANY PROFILE

Branch: Brewery;
Production: 100,000 tons of beer;
Core investors: Heineken and Coca-Cola.

## HISTORY OF THE COMPANY

The first Bulgarian predecessor of this firm was established in 1903 as a
joint-stock company, but it went bankrupt in only three years. A new
joint-stock company was started in 1926, yet it also ceased operating in
three years. It was only in 1956 that the idea arose for building a brewery
on the site. At present, only one of the old buildings is preserved. In 1958,
the first bottle of beer was produced at the same site yet under the trademark "Zagorka." In the first year, 12 million liters of beer were produced.
Since then, production has been growing continuously. In the period
1958–94, the brewery was a state-owned enterprise operating in conditions typical for the state sector.

## COMPETITION AND MARKETS

The beer market in Bulgaria is highly competitive. There are thirteen
local producers of beer. With the liberalization of trade in recent years,
foreign competition has gained a share of the market as well. Several
brands have been imported, even at dumping prices sometimes, which
sharpens the battle for the local market. The company holds a stable
leading position among the local producers. At present, Zagorka ac-

counts for 22 percent of the beer market in Bulgaria. Next in rank among its competitors comes Plevensko Pivo, with production of about 70 million liters in 1994, followed by Sofiisko Pivo, with about 65 million liters, and Astika, with about 40 million liters, the last of these being Zagorka's major competitor in the high-quality beer segment. The other producers, therefore, are relatively smaller compared to Zagorka. Both in the past and currently, the quality of production is the main competitive tool of Zagorka. The company has strengthened and stabilized its position due to its constant efforts at improving the quality of production.

The terms of competition have changed a great deal as well. Ten years ago, the beer market was divided by regions, and breweries were not allowed to sell their production outside their region, which coincided with their geographic location. At that time, it was only Zagorka that had the right to supply its production to some of the high-class tourist sites and some governmental residences. Except for these exclusions, however, regular sales outside the local region were forbidden. In this sense, the company was the only one with some experience in a competitive environment as compared to other breweries.

Competition is being intensified by the changes in ownership as well. The brewing industry in Bulgaria is among the leaders in the process of privatization. So far, several companies have been sold to strategic foreign investors, who aim at expanding their share of the local market. Given its relatively favorable position as a high-quality local producer, Zagorka has been the target of special competitive efforts to penetrate its market segment.

The emergence of privatized breweries produced certain changes in the terms of competition. Private brewers are trying to raise quality while covering their production costs. The state-owned breweries that work under soft budget constraints are rather indifferent to their costs of production. Low prices are their main competitive tool, even if they fall below production costs. State-owned enterprises in Bulgaria maintain unreasonably low prices because their main goal is to cover their wages. They are not interested in attaining high profits since the latter are taken by the state. As a result, both the industry and the state suffer great losses. If the pricing of state-owned firms is very close to production costs or even below them, they are the first to lose. The state itself gets nothing either. Moreover, the firms lack resources for renovation and development. In this way, they can provide for a miserable existence over the next four or five years and then totally collapse. Each of them is hoping for privatization; meanwhile, they are functioning on a "day-to-day" basis. A stable private company could never afford such behavior and, by virtue of necessity, always thinks and acts according to its strategic goals.

In the absence of strategic motivation, state firms create an environment favoring completely unfair competition. It is impossible, for example, for a bottle of beer to be cheaper than a bottle of soda water. Most state producers do not sell but simply make presents of beer for roughly 10 cents a bottle. The parallel existence of state-owned and private firms in the branch will always produce unfair competition and inefficient markets. In this sense, inefficient state enterprises, through unfair competition, can endanger and even destroy efficient private firms.

The solution is the rapid privatization of the rest of the state-owned breweries. Once the majority of them are privatized, all the main components, including raw materials, energy, wages, amortization allowances, investments, and so forth, become comparable for everybody, and quality and efficiency remain the key variables.

The company is not sufficiently competitive in international markets, and 98.5 percent of its production is directed at the domestic market. Exports, if any, are negligible and random, transactions being mainly with neighbor countries and Russia.

The strategy of the company is to address a single main requirement, that is, the quality of production. The name of the company is an absolute priority regardless of price or losses suffered. The complexity of the activity notwithstanding, there are possibilities for certain economies in the process of fermentation, for example. The moment the quality of production is endangered, however, such changes are not permitted, because small cost savings could prove to be great losses if the brand is discredited. The promotion of a new brand is a long and costly process. From the perspective of marketing strategy, because Zagorka has a considerable share of the domestic market, the introduction of new brands is not a high priority. At present, the company offers three brands, one each in the three quality ranges of beer. There are plans to improve the quality of the light beer so that it has a longer shelf life because it is difficult to sell beer with less than a one-month shelf life. The standard duration for light beer is seven to eight days, although the beer offered by the company lasts longer.

Market strategy, therefore, is based on the existing brands of beer.

Plans exist for the introduction in the next two or three years of one of the products of Heineken, the parent company. These plans are aimed at developing its local production and at import substitution, which will also help Zagorka to improve the product range and to acquire new production technology and training. These plans, of course, face some obstacles. Zagorka needs to become known for being able to produce a European type of beer, since no compromises are admitted for famous brands. Obviously, under present conditions, the parent company still feels insecure about the quality of Bulgarian beer and is quite reluctant to undertake steps that might risk the image of its own brand. Instead, it provides constant support to the local brands in spite of initial fears about the eventual liquidation of the Bulgarian brands by the foreign investor.

Zagorka has its own views about normal market condition in Bulgaria. According to its estimates, there is excess capacity in brewing because none of the breweries operates at full capacity, which suggests the advisability of closing many of them. In the future, most probably only six or seven will survive. Half of the Bulgarian breweries will be forced either to close down or to reduce production to a level meeting only local demand, similar to world practice. A company such as Zagorka, which has never suffered losses and has been profitable even in hard times, has good prospects. In 1993, the company ranked ninth among the top one hundred most profitable companies in Bulgaria, being the only brewery on the list.

## STRUCTURE OF OWNERSHIP

Bulgaria has undertaken large-scale economic reforms, although this has been accomplished at a slower pace than in some other countries. The privatization of state-owned enterprises is an important component of this process. In different cases, privatization is motivated by different goals. In the case of Zagorka, however, the motivation was to secure the vitality and development of the enterprise. According to Bulgarian standards, the brewery had modern equipment, yet it was quite worn out by European and world standards. Under the conditions of general economic recession and in a macroeconomic environment hostile to investments, large-scale technological renovation and transformation of Zagorka into a modern enterprise proved to be impossible due to the lack of resources. According to the estimates of managers, there was no chance to raise funds while Zagorka remained a state-owned company. Given all these considerations, the management of the company decided to initiate the privatization of Zagorka.

The company went through a classical privatization procedure. First, the privatization procedure was announced by the Privatization Agency. Then the applicants, including five Western companies and one Bulgarian company, submitted their offers to the Privatization Agency. These offers were submitted to the management of the company as well. In the opinion of the managers, all the applicants were highly qualified and were aware of the matter in question. The applicants had a clear-cut idea about the condition of Zagorka, its future development, and so forth. The Privatization Agency carried out preliminary negotiations with all the applicants. The managers also submitted their views about the future development of Zagorka and their expectations regarding the would-be business partner.

The Privatization Agency selected the buyer, Heineken Co., on a competitive basis from among the applying investors. The main criteria were price, future investments, preservation of jobs, and wage growth. The guarantee of the secure and successful development of Zagorka in the future was given particular significance, and it was in large part reflected in the volume of investments the various bidders were willing to make.

Heineken Co. had had no business contacts with the brewery in the past. Its interest was triggered by the opening of the privatization procedure. After visiting the enterprise and acquiring information about its condition, Heineken Co. prepared and submitted its offer to the Privatization Agency. The offers of all applicants were independent and secret. All bidders interested in Zagorka had a clear understanding of its condition and its dominant market position due to the quality of its production. In other words, little or no effort would be required for marketing and relevant activities. In the course of negotiations, good relations were established between the investor, Heineken Co., and the management of the company. As a result, Heineken Co. decided to integrate the managers of the former state-owned enterprise into the management of the newly privatized company.

Regarding the strategy of participation in the privatization, there were some plans for a manager buyout of the company. The top management, however, objected to the idea by stating that it was a question of a large enterprise demanding large investments that could be provided only by a reliable foreign partner.

In the course of privatization, there were considerable difficulties stemming from the legal analysis of the company. A number of unsettled issues arose connected with the real estate of Zagorka. It took about a year to determine its boundaries, because in the past there was not strict differentiation of state, municipal, and private sites, and construction was often carried out without proper documents and licenses. According to the contract with the Privatization Agency, the buyer was obligated to make extensive investments. Annual reports would have to be prepared on the course of investment and to show that they conform to the schedule as designed in the contract with the agency. In the first year, the planned investment amounted to about USD 10 million and was covered in full.

As of this writing, 80 percent of the stock of Zagorka is owned by Brew Invest Co. The latter was established by Heineken and Coca-Cola especially for the purchase of Zagorka in Bulgaria. About 3 percent of the stock was purchased by the employees, and 17 percent remained state-owned. Under the applicable regulation, the 17 percent stake should be offered to Brew Invest Co. first, and in the case of refusal, the state can sell it to another investor.

A number of Western firms practice offering blocks of shares to the managers as a specific form of motivation. The new buyer of Zagorka has not made such an offer. According to the Law on Privatization in Bulgaria, the employees of a privatized company are entitled to a certain share of preferred stock. Within this preference, the managers of the company have a very small share, yet it is neither connected with their professional status nor a bonus.

As is typical in Bulgaria, there were accusations that Zagorka was sold cheaply, although the transaction amounted to USD 22 million net, paid in cash. In fact, Zagorka is one of the best privatization deals in Bulgaria so far. The attitude of the new owner toward the former managers is rather typical as well. They were quickly integrated due to their professional qualities. One of the first steps by the foreign investor was the purchase of nine cars for the personal use of the members of the board of directors. In this way, the image of the "bloody exploiter" is gradually being eroded, since the state, and a poor state in particular, is always aiming at getting as much as possible.

As far as relations with the state as owner of 17 percent of the stock is concerned, the state lost its ownership interest in the company after the privatization transaction. According to the managers, they have no problems with the authorities because they pay their taxes regularly. The company is relatively independent of the branch ministry that is the formal holder of the state's stake. The ministry is in charge of making global branch decisions and has no special attitude toward Zagorka. In spite of the state's share, however, the company is subject to control and inspection. In compliance with an amendment to the law, any company is subject to financial inspection by the local municipal authorities, regardless of the state's share in the equity.

Regarding the general economic policy of the state, the company finds no serious grounds for criticism. On the contrary, its concerns have always been considered favorably by the government. At one time, for example, the government decided to ban barley exports until October in order to protect supplies for the domestic market. In 1993, there was real chaos in beer imports in Bulgaria. For instance, Czech beer was imported a month before its expiry term provided that the standard duration was one year. The declared import price was 5 cents, and, since there was no customs duty at all, the market began to collapse. To prevent this, the government introduced a minimum import price of 20 cents. The situation stabilized in 1994. Now, imports are allowed, but the price is different so that Bulgarian producers are not ruined by dumping prices. The attitude of Zagorka toward the economic policy of the state is most probably motivated by the favorable effects on the company itself.

## RELATIONS BETWEEN THE MOTHER COMPANY AND THE SUBSIDIARY

### Profile of the Mother Company

The structure of ownership relations in Zagorka is shown in Figure 1.

Heineken has twenty-six branches all over the world. One of the strongest branches is located in Greece. At present, Heineken has 80 percent of the beer market in Greece. The Heineken mother company has authorized its Greek branch to acquire, jointly with Coca-Cola, the Zagorka block of shares. Heineken has three enterprises in Greece, two

Figure 1. **Structure of Ownership Relations in Zagorka**

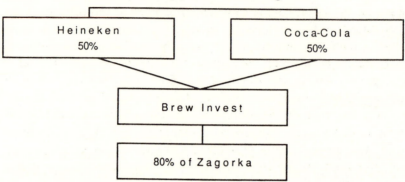

of which are governed by Dutch directors and the third by a Greek director. Heineken is an international company. Many of the Greek specialists who work in Greece now have long experience abroad. The company has no specific policy giving priority to a particular country in one or another sector of the company's activity. Everybody can occupy different hierarchical levels depending on his/her personal capabilities and qualification. The Greek branch is not authorized to develop independently of Heineken. It has to follow the strategy of the mother company.

### Personal Relations

Zagorka is governed by a board of directors. There are three executive directors and a chief executive officer. The CEO is a Bulgarian, and he is the director of the former state company.

In this case, Heineken is following a strategy according to which former employees should be given the chance to remain in the new company. Experts from the mother company have had interviews with all Bulgarian specialists and technologists so as to get acquainted with their professional and personal qualities. The new owners prefer a local managerial staff instead of sending the mother company's experts for two reasons: first, a specialist or manager from the head office will certainly get much higher remuneration than a Bulgarian specialist; second, he/she would face problems connected with the language barrier as well as obstacles stemming from the specifics of business in Bulgaria.

For the time being, local management receives the full approval and understanding of the head office. So far, any proposals related to future prospects for development or necessary investments have been approved by the mother company. In this way, people feel secure about the potential of Heineken and rely on its advice and assistance in the solution of problems.

## Responsibilities

The mother company and the branch share different responsibilities in running the different activities in the company. The branch bears full responsibility for marketing and sales. The strategy of the mother company is to win the domestic market. Both Heineken and Coca-Cola are present in Bulgaria as independent firms, which means that their investment in Zagorka is a specific form of export. Their strategy does not include the export of the Zagorka trademark due to the uncertainty in international markets. For this reason, they support a policy of nearly 100 percent sales on the domestic market, even with a considerable annual production of about 100 million liters of beer. In general, they agree with the Bulgarian managers, who propose that the Heineken trademark be produced by Zagorka as long as this production does not exceed 5 or 6 percent of total volume.

In the field of investments, decision making is much more centralized. The executive directors can make independent decisions within the approved plan of investments and up to USD 100,000. For larger amounts, decisions are made by the board of directors. The board has regular quarterly meetings at which, based on preliminary information, it makes decisions and develops the investment program. These decisions are limited within the annual investment program of the firm approved by the mother company.

The volume of production is determined by the board of directors exclusively. The latter approves the annual plan and the quarterly production volumes. In the event that the planned quantities are not produced, the reasons are reported and discussed at a meeting, and measures are outlined to be undertaken to overcome the problems.

The managers estimate that, after privatization, the decision-making chain became longer and slower in pace. In the previous years of transition, firm managers had greater freedom due to the weak position of state institutions. Now, many issues and problems must be coordinated, and, in urgent cases, confirmation is first given by telephone, which is then followed by the standard procedure of approval by the mother company. The board of directors confirms decisions orally and at its subsequent meeting gives additional written approval.

The system of reporting that has been instituted is standard for the mother company. Reports are prepared and submitted weekly. There are also monthly and quarterly reports on the results of the fulfillment of particular parts of the annual business plan. Income statements and balance sheets are prepared on a monthly basis. The statement of cash flows is the most important for the company's activity.

The mother company pursues a very strict policy with respect to quality. This is the main sphere of observation and control, and no compromises are allowed. The response to any deviation from the standard is quick. The company gets assistance from the Bulgarian Brewing Institute in Sofia and the brewing department at the Plovdiv Institute of Food Industry. If necessary, management can do a quick analysis and make quick decisions. So far, the assistance of the head office has not been requested, although a group of specialists is constantly available.

The parent company demands explanations for nonperformance and downward deviations in the fulfillment of the financial plan. There have so far been no large deviations from the annual financial plan indicators. Finances have been varying within the budget limits or have gone slightly higher. There are some other indicators, however, that show poorer development. These are analyzed at the meetings of the board of directors, at which the relevant remedial measures are outlined.

For the company, most Western-type financial management procedures are still new and in the process of implementation. The question therefore arises of whether the mother company will allow for some compromises in financial management in the period of its adoption by the new company. There is some evidence of some compromises in this respect. The head office is well aware of the level of financial management in a postcommunist state company. It is particularly emphasized, however, that this compromise is connected with the lack of experience in modern management and accounting and not with the lack of an adequate intellectual level. Many problems result from the low level of communications, and so forth. The process of management is not fully computerized, and many accounting operations are still manual. New software for general management is being introduced. Regarding the preparation of the balance sheet, the internal auditing is done by officials of the head office as a guarantee that the balance sheet meets the requirements of the parent company.

## ORGANIZATION

At present, Zagorka is governed by a board of directors consisting of nine members. Of these, three are representatives of Heineken, three represent Coca-Cola, and three are Bulgarians, including two inside directors and one outside director. The everyday operations of the company are the responsibility of three executive directors. The chief executive director is a Bulgarian, and he was director of the former state company. There are four specialists from Heineken who have come to implement Heineken's universal system of accounting and reporting. As in all transnational companies, English is the official language of Heineken. All branches of the company apply the same accounting system, so that it is easy to interpret any report or document regardless of its branch origin. There is one expert from Coca-Cola, who is in charge of developing marketing in Bulgaria.

Changes in the organizational structure are coordinated with the head office to unify it with the Heineken system. Heineken follows a policy of identical structure in similar-scale enterprises regardless of their location, be it in America or in Bulgaria. Of course, there are some peculiarities stemming from the underdevelopment of market factors in the transition period. Until recently, for example, Bulgarian firms had no tradition of developing their own distribution systems. Marketing was traditionally underdeveloped as well. The first significant organizational changes were therefore connected with the strengthening of the sales department and the creation of the marketing department. In its present condition, the organizational structure of the company is approximately identical to that of other branches.

Along with the chief executive director, there are several other directors, namely, the technical manager, the financial manager, the second executive director, and the commercial director. The positions of the commercial and the financial directors are new to the company. There is a chief technologist and an assistant to the technical manager, who was sent by the head office to introduce Heineken's organizational and management system. There are still some vacancies in management. Next in the hierarchy come the heads of production departments, the chief engineer, and the heads of shops.

The technological chain includes the following organizational units:
- malt production;
- brewing department;
- storage depot;
- bottling department;
- sales;
- general maintenance;
- ancillary activities;
- steam station;
- refrigeration compressors;
- air compressors;
- servicing department.

The organizational structure of the company is still a transitional one, since it combines the organizational interactions of both a technological and a functional character. Managers show greater interest in their units and activities than in the creation of a complete management organism.

## PRODUCTION AND PRODUCTIVITY

The company has a stable position as the largest Bulgarian beer producer. The annual production of 100 million liters of beer is close to the production capacity of the brewing facilities.

Compared to local standards, the company has a good technological level, but it lags considerably behind the well-known European brewers. The maintenance of the technological level and the volume of production is to a great extent connected to the re-equipment of a number of production units. To this end, a large-scale investment program was negotiated and stipulated by the privatization contract. At present, orders for new machinery and equipment are based on the best products available. In the opinion of managers, technological sophistication of the operation has improved.

The technological bottleneck is the bottling unit. Due to a shortage of bottling capacities, the company is forced to use outside facilities consisting of fourteen enterprises, including small workshops. The company plans to solve the problem during the current year by importing a new large-capacity bottling machine with a capacity of 5,000–6,000 bottles per hour. In this way, a great number of subcontractors will become useless, and the company will contract bottling operations with three or four well-equipped enterprises so as to achieve geographic diversification of supply.

The company did not change its suppliers after privatization. The main raw materials are purchased on the basis of preliminary offers, and a decision to buy is made on the basis of quality and price. The manager is required to choose the best offer. As a rule, the domestic production of hops is insufficient, and about 70 percent is imported from Australia, Germany, and other countries. This is done by other Bulgarian firms, who then sell the hops to breweries. The necessary volumes are delivered through intermediary firms. The company maintains stable relations with importing firms who have proved their loyalty and high quality of performance over the years.

According to management, productivity has improved in recent years. This is one of the mainstays of changes in the company's activity. The causes are both internal and external. The internal causes include changes in the market and marketing policy resulting in larger sales relative to fixed costs, as well as a change in the style of work. An external cause is the central geographic location of the company, implying low transport expenses.

Costs have not changed considerably, but reductions are expected as a result of the implementation of new, more efficient capacities with lower energy consumption and higher productivity. The company is in search of its own water sources, since water is becoming an increasingly large expenditure item. More considerable economies of expenses are therefore expected in the longer run.

## INVESTMENTS

Investments were one of the major criteria in selecting the buyer of the company. The investment program, along with the five-year schedule, is an integral part of the contract. Within this period, Heineken plans to invest about USD 40 million, or twice the initial purchase price of the company. The mother company is fully aware of the need for modernization of production and supports the ambitious investment program, although it realizes that in this way the size of the repatriated profit will be reduced. An annual investment plan is developed, including particular investment targets. Within the annual volume of investments, investment decisions of up to USD 100,000 are made by the chief executive director, and those exceeding USD 100,000 by the board of directors, that is, by a decisive vote of the head office.

The main short-term investment will be in the purchase of bottling technology amounting to about USD 5–6 million, which will take place within the current year. The main source of funds for invest-ments is retained earnings. In addition, it is possible to increase the company's capital, so that investments can be financed partially by the internal resources of Zagorka and partially by the head office.

## FINANCE

The system of financial planning and financial control was introduced following the privatization of the company in accordance with a scheme imposed by the head office. The scheme includes the elabora-tion of monthly, quarterly, and annual plans.

A medium-term financial plan is worked out at the beginning of each year, covering a period of three years, with an annual breakdown. The plan for the next year is elaborated in detail and on a monthly basis. Although detailed, the system of financial planning is only ap-proximate and often inexact, since it is quite difficult to attain a high level of precision in Bulgaria, for at least two reasons. First, due to weaknesses in the forecasts of key macroeconomic parameters, such as the foreign exchange rate, the budget of the company is worked out in two versions, in USD and in Bulgarian leva (BGL). The greater part of expenses is made in foreign currency, while incomes are only in leva. For this reason, the company's results are highly sensitive with respect to changes in the exchange rate, which makes long-term financial plan-ning difficult. Second, the uncertain pricing policy of the company's local contractors is a factor further worsening the quality of financial planning. Most prices of local raw materials are difficult to predict, thus the lower reliability of financial forecasting. In such an environ-ment, budget adjustments are inevitable. For example, if an exchange rate of 70 BGL / USD is forecast and all of a sudden it increases to 90–100 BGL / USD, the budget will be adjusted immediately. Finan-cial management would show that, "in the current year, matters are developing the way they were planned."

As a whole, the company's activity is planned to such a degree that it makes the management jokingly comment, "We are doing the same things we used to do in the past." That is, total and absolute planning.

All expenses, raw materials, funds, and so forth, are planned on a monthly basis. The new element is that all items are planned in greater detail. Once approved, the planned targets are no longer discussed. The main difference in comparison with the business plans in previous years is the availability of funds for the fulfillment of the plan. In the past, managers had a lot of ideas and will, but they were short of money. Now, money is not the factor that can block business. "Although not fundamental, all the changes are positive," states the executive director.

Regarding the concrete financial parameters of its activity, the company politely refuses submitting any information and gives rather conditional answers, which hardly allow for well-grounded summaries and conclusions. The system of financial management is a company secret. The desire for secrecy is so great that the company has broken its contacts with the statistical offices. Even the annual balance sheet and the annual income statement, which are obligatory by virtue of the Law on Statistics, are not submitted. The company intends to proceed this way even at the risk of payment of penalties. The company submits regular and on-demand information to the head office. The fieldwork data is collected by authorized officials or auditors sent by the head office.

The company maintains good relations with banks. It has no problems with the Bulgarian banks and evaluates its relations as absolutely perfect. Actually, the company is serviced by one bank only, and this is the local branch office of a bank in Sofia. The company has no intention of changing its servicing bank or of using the services of other banks. For the present, the company is operating without bank credits. It has used commercial credits in previous years and does not exclude the eventual demand for new ones in the future.

Larger financial expenses are planned in advance, that is, they are spent according to decisions made in advance. Any large financial expenditure is coordinated with the head office. According to the financial managers, in order to work efficiently, the company should plan all payments due the following year. Moreover, managers give full support to the system of detailed planning and control introduced by the head office.

## LABOR

The company's production is not labor intensive. Of total expenses, raw materials amount to about 70 percent, while the share of wages does not exceed 20 percent. In terms of wage level, Zagorka ranks first in the region. The average wage amounts to BGL 17,000, about USD 250. The company makes social security payments equal to 35 percent of payroll. The company has about 500 employees on the payroll, which slightly increases in the summer due to the employment of part-time workers. The administrative staff numbers 40 persons.

In the past, unemployment was an unknown phenomenon in Bulgaria. Being a subbranch of light industry, brewing was considered a simple and therefore low-paid job. Working conditions were very difficult, however. The low level of wages in the branch meant that skilled workers could not be attracted. In the past, it was common practice to compensate for labor shortages by employing students. Regarding personnel, therefore, the company started from a difficult initial position. As time has passed, the situation has changed a great deal. The high rate of unemployment in the region has made for increased labor supply. For its part, Zagorka began offering higher wages, thus attracting skilled labor. Employed workers and specialists have to meet certain requirements regarding their technical skills and need to have graduated from professional secondary schools. For the present, new labor is hired to replace retirees only, and it has to meet very high qualification requirements. According to management, within the next five or six to eight years, the staff will reach world standards. This is a realistic prospect given the availability of high-skilled specialists for the technical staff. Most of the former top managers and chief technologists have retained their jobs, since they are professionals with a lot of experience who have graduated from Bulgarian universities.

The parent company evaluates the local staff highly as well. This was proved by the confidence and trust shown to the former management. The head office insists on the continuation of the company's contacts with brewing institutes in Bulgaria, despite its own research units in the West. Each year, the company assigns four or five research contracts to Bulgarian researchers, thus providing funds for their existence.

Within their respective scope of activity, each of the executive directors is responsible for the motivation of the staff. Heads of departments are responsible for their staff only. Until recently, the executive director was in charge of all the activity of the company, including personnel management. This took up a lot of time and caused a lot of aggravation. At present, each vacancy is filled on a competitive basis, and the applicant, especially for certain higher positions, must have a good knowledge of English and an appropriate educational degree. All top positions, including the assistant of the commercial director, the marketing director, the technical director, and the sales director, have been occupied by new persons following competitions. To this end, a special selection commission has been formed, consisting of four members.

Regarding the size of wages, the heads of divisions or departments are given freedom to maneuver within certain limits. Let us take a department of 50 employees, for example. Each employee meets the requirements for particular qualifications and receives appropriate remuneration within predetermined limits. The head of the department gives a personal appraisal of each employee, and on this basis the individual wages are determined. In practice, wages are not equal; most are differentiated, yet nobody gets more at the expense of others.

A new system of remunerating the administrative staff was introduced as well. Initially, fixed wages were changed under the influence of two factors: production outcome and the rate of inflation. In addition, regular bonus payments were made. The size of bonuses was determined in the period following October, that is, when there was a clear idea about the annual rate of inflation. In this way, wage indexation was included in the bonus payment but only at the managers' discretion. Bonuses for the administrative staff are determined on the basis of production results.

Developments in employees' morale have marked a positive tendency as well. In the past, a great number of workers was considered unreliable, and the management tried to find ways to dismiss them. Once the situation changed, 90 percent of them turned into good and very good workers. Still, there is a group of 10 or 15 percent who have a negative work attitude, and they will never change. The rest of them, however, were obviously influenced by the former environment and were in this way predisposed to low discipline and leisure. One-hour lateness, for example, was common practice. Now, everybody comes to work fifteen minutes before their shift begins, even to the first shift, in spite of transportation difficulties. Lateness is very much the exception. In the past, the philosophy of supervision was followed, that is, there was a supervisor for every two or three workers. At present, everybody is solely responsible for his or her own work, since this is the basis for his or her appraisal.

So far, the majority of the management staff has completed one week of training at Heineken. Planned investments include a special program for technical assistance rendered by the head office. The qualification and retraining of personnel, including the top staff, is an important item on this program.

Contrary to the fears expressed about the future of social expenditures, the latter were not at all reduced but rather increased by the new owner. The increase applies to food and rest breaks. Besides, the company pays kindergarten fees, doctors' fees, dentists' fees, maintains the rest homes, and so forth. Because the greater part of social services to personnel is provided by municipal departments, the company is motivated to assist the municipality in order to maintain the level of services. To this end, support is provided to the municipal hospital, poorhouses, and so forth.

## ECOLOGY

In general, brewing is an ecology-friendly production. The company has to solve the following ecological problems:

• the steam power station using mazut—the measures include investment in filter facilities;

• some industrial wastes with higher than standard alkalinity—the company plans to build a general waste purification station to replace present palliative solutions.

As a whole, the company faces no significant problems in addressing ecological requirements.

## GENERAL VIEW

According to the present management, the greatest achievement of the company is connected with calming down and stabilizing the staff as a result of satisfied positive expectations about the privatization deal and a clear awareness of the intentions of the new owner. There was some turmoil and insecurity in the beginning, because the employees feared that a new owner could bring unemployment and therefore worsen their situation. It is quite natural that people are interested only in their own job and wages. Now employees feel secure about the future of Zagorka, and this is a very important positive change.

# Index

# About the Editors

**Saul Estrin** is Professor of Economics and head of the Economics subject area at the London Business School. He was Programme Director of the Post-Communist Reform programme at the LSE's Centre for Economic Performance until 1992, and then Research Director of London Business School's CIS-Middle Europe Centre until 1997, when he became the Centre Director. His research concentrates on the process of economic reform and transformation in Central and Eastern Europe, particularly questions of privatization, company restructuring, and different ownership forms. Recent publications include *Privatization in Central and Eastern Europe* (1994); *Foreign Direct Investment into Central Europe* (1997); and *Competition, Trade and Integration in the European Union* (1997). He has worked as consultant for the World Bank, OECD, and European Community, as well as for a variety of companies investing in the region.

**Xavier Richet** is Professor of Economics and Dean of the College of Economics and Management at University of Marne le Vallée. He received his M.A. from the University of Paris-Sorbonne and his Doctorat d'Etat from the University of Paris-Nanterre. He is Director of the University Center for Hungarian Studies at Université de la Sorbonne Nouvelle (Paris III) and former director of R.O.S.ES., the Center for the Study of the Reform and Opening Up of (former) Socialist Economies. Professor Richet is a specialist in comparative economic systems, industrial organization, and the theory of the firm. He has authored five books and more than 50 papers and chapters on these topics.

**Josef C. Brada** was born in Prague, Czechoslovakia, and educated at Tufts University and the University of Minnesota. He has served on the faculties of Ohio State University and the Graduate School of Business at New York University and has held visiting appointments at Stanford University, the Catholic University of Leuven, and the University of Michigan. Professor Brada was formerly the editor of the *Journal of Comparative Economics* and is currently the editor of *Eastern European Economics*. He has served as a consultant to the United Nations, the World Bank, the OECD, and the governments of the United States and the Czech Republic. He is currently Professor of Economics and Director of the College of Business International Programs at Arizona State University.